D0286594

A GUIDE TO CHURCH PROPERTY LAW

Theological, Constitutional and Practical Considerations

LLOYD J. LUNCEFORD
GENERAL EDITOR

CONTRIBUTORS

RAYMOND J. DAGUE
PEGGY M. HEDDEN
ROBERT L. HOWARD
LLOYD J. LUNCEFORD
THOMAS C. ODEN
R. WICKS STEPHENS II
PARKER T. WILLIAMSON

REFORMATION PRESS

A Guide to Church Property Law: Theological, Constitutional and Practical Considerations

Reformation Press books, monographs and other resources are available at special discounts in bulk purchases for educational and ministry use. For more details, contact:

Director of Publications
Reformation Press
136 Tremont Park Drive
Lenoir, North Carolina 28645

Call us at 1-800-368-0110
Or Visit Reformation Press on the Web at www.resourcecatalog.org

Cover Design: Joel McClure/HeuleGordon, Inc.; Grand Rapids, Michigan

Printed in the United States of America

ISBN: 9711919-6-4

10 9 8 7 6 5 4 3 2

TABLE OF CONTENTS

INTRODUCTION

. . . And Lot, who went with Abram, also had flocks and herds and tents, so that the land could not support both of them dwelling together; for their possessions were so great that they could not dwell together, and there was strife between the herdsmen of Abram's livestock and the herdsmen of Lot's livestock . . .

Then Abram said to Lot, 'Let there be no strife between you and me, and between your herdsmen and my herdsmen, for we are kinsmen. Is not the whole land before you? Separate yourself from me. If you take the left hand, then I will go to the right, or if you take the right hand, then I will go to the left.'[1]

Conflict over property is as old as the Bible itself. Wisdom acknowledges the problem and seeks equitable solutions. This book has been prepared in recognition of the growing conflict in Protestant hierarchical denominations – particularly Presbyterian, Methodist and Episcopal – over the use and control of local church property. It is offered in the hope that it will be of practical assistance and will contribute to a better understanding of the issues involved and the law that applies in fashioning fair solutions.

Recent court decisions in the United States have generated significant publicity and prompted many congregations to seek a review of the status of their local church property. The quickening pace of denominational strife in many segments of American mainline churches makes a thoughtful review of this important subject prudent and timely. Underlying theological disagreement has brought to the surface several earthly questions: Who is the owner, or real title-holder in interest, of local church property in a hierarchical

1 Genesis 13:5-9.

denomination? Does a trust attach to local church property in favor of the national denomination, as some denominational constitutions assert, such that the local church may not leave the denomination with its local property intact without the denomination's permission? Is any such trust valid or revocable under state law? If so, by whom can any such trust be revoked and by what means? Underlying all of these particular questions is the general question of how state courts resolve church property disputes. What methods or legal principles are followed?

This book is intended for practical use by local church ministers and church officers — elders, vestrymen and women, administrative board members and trustees — and by local or regional church legal counsel. Although characterized by sound legal scholarship and complemented by numerous citations to court decisions useful to attorneys, this book is not designed to be read solely by lawyers sitting in law libraries. It also should be read by the men and women in pulpits and pews who increasingly find themselves caught in the tension between competing loyalties, between the institutional commitment to their denomination and – in the face of a departure by some denominational entities from traditional Christian belief – the commitment "to contend for the faith that was once for all delivered to the saints."[2] Determining how to resolve that tension is a task that ultimately lies with local church leaders after considerable prayer and reflection. The material provided in this book neither advocates that local churches sever their ties with their respective denominations nor remain forever fastened to them. Rather, the purpose of this book is to provide local decision makers with accurate legal information which, in consultation with their local counsel, is required in order to make informed decisions.

The topic at hand, church property law, does not lend itself to generalization. Although there are common threads that run through the case law, the controlling constitutional law on church property ownership sometimes is nuanced, and the outcomes often are determined by the circumstances of each case. While there are definite, guiding legal principles, the relevant body of case law – particularly in states that follow the "neutral principles of law" method – is fact specific. The cases furnish a very helpful road map that points readers in the right direction, but they do not necessarily guarantee the same destination in every case. This is not to say, however, that the law is capricious. Reasonable predictions of legal outcomes are possible based on factors that courts, with regularity, have said are important. To evaluate the strengths or weaknesses of a particular church's claim of property control or ownership requires attention to the underlying facts in the cases

2 Jude 1:3.

that have shaped the law, and comparison to the specific facts presented by the particular church.

Many people on both sides of the current church property ownership and trust controversy seek an easy, bright-line rule that would apply to achieve the same result for every member church in a hierarchical denomination. At one end of the spectrum, some want denominational trust clauses, which assert a trust for the use and benefit of the national denomination over local church property, to be given binding effect over the property of every local congregation in the denomination. At the other end of the spectrum, some seek the wholesale repeal of denominational trust clauses.

What governs under current law in those states that have adopted the neutral principles method, however, is the mutual intent of the parties. And that intent may vary from particular church to particular church, according to the accumulated facts and documents of each congregation's property history. Moreover, in those states that follow the "hierarchical" method of resolving church property disputes, in which civil courts generally defer to ecclesiastical decisions on ownership and trusts, the civil courts retain limited subject matter jurisdiction to review designated aspects of those ecclesiastical decisions.

In other words, the law provides a required framework but no one-size-fits-all answer. Individual analysis is required. The assertions contained in some denominational constitutions, of the denomination's right to determine local ownership and the existence of a trust over local property in favor of the denomination, are not necessarily conclusive or self-operating. They are only the starting points of analysis. There is much more to the discussion. Therefore, it becomes imperative for church ministers and officers, and their legal counsel, to know what the courts in their states have said on this subject.

Although the body of this book focuses on the law that governs the resolution of church property disputes, it begins and ends with chapters that emphasize theological rather than legal issues. Although civil courts are precluded by the First Amendment's establishment clause from considering theology when deciding cases and, thus, are prohibited from deciding church property disputes based on which faction is most faithful to founding doctrines, it remains true that church property disputes often arise in the context of an underlying disagreement over religious belief. It is appropriate, therefore, that the body of this book be framed by beginning and ending chapters that explore theological issues that are present in many church property disputes.

The first chapter discuses the theology of loyalty – both to the oneness of the visible Church as a witness to Jesus Christ's divinity and to the

Church's faith that a denomination exists to preserve and proclaim. What happens when those two loyalties, intended to operate in tandem, become difficult to reconcile? The first chapter approaches and views these questions through the lens of stewardship. The last chapter explores the theology and ethics of property ownership and civil lawsuits. The Bible's admonition against Christians using the civil courts to resolve grievances against each other must be considered and rightly understood. How is this admonition to be reconciled with the Apostle Paul's own appeal[3] to the civil magistrate in the exercise of his rights as a Roman citizen (albeit under markedly different circumstances)? Can a Scripturally faithful distinction be made between Christians, on the one hand, inappropriately using civil courts to seek vindication against each other for personal offenses and, on the other hand, appropriately availing themselves of legal remedies when necessary to fulfill a moral, ethical, or legal obligation to act on behalf of others? Local church corporation trustees, for example, have a fiduciary obligation to the corporation. A failure in some instances to seek legal recourse may not only jeopardize the rights of the corporate entity but also expose the trustees to personal liability.

Litigation, of course, is always a last resort and is to be avoided when possible in favor of negotiation. Sometimes, however, it is unavoidable. In such cases, may civil courts sometimes provide a permissible forum within which to orderly resolve differences? The last chapter explores theological and ethical issues raised by church property ownership, corporate law and the use of court systems.

In between these two theological bookends, this book is devoted to the law that applies in resolving church property disputes. Chapter Two explains the federal constitutional principles that govern and provide the parameters within which state courts must operate. Chapter Three walks the reader through sample case law from selected state jurisdictions in order to illustrate how two constitutionally-approved methods for resolving church property disputes – the neutral principles of law method and the hierarchical method – have been applied in a variety of real-life situations.

Chapters Two and Three are of equal relevance to Presbyterian, Methodist and Episcopal churches. Chapters Four, Five and Six, however, take turns exploring considerations that are specific to the Presbyterian Church (USA), the United Methodist Church, and the Episcopal Church (USA).

Chapter Seven addresses the relevance of state trust law and state corporation law as it applies to local church property control or ownership. Chapter Eight concludes the legal discussion and, based on the case law

3 Acts 25:1-12.

discussed earlier in the book, offers practical steps for local churches interested in evaluating their prospects for "winning the property trust battle without losing the ownership war."

What instruction should be given to local churches considering whether to retain legal counsel? Where should the attorneys retained begin the process of evaluating the strength or weakness of their client's position? In addition to the guidelines and checklists offered in Chapter Eight, several appendices are included as useful models and citations to additional resources that are available.[4]

This book has been a collaborative effort. A talented and experienced team was assembled: Methodist and Presbyterian theologians; Episcopalian and Presbyterian vestrymen and women and elders; veteran reporters; and attorneys with a breadth of litigation and negotiation experience who have been retained by local churches to advise on church property matters. Their credentials are described more fully in the List of Contributors included in the appendices for the reader's review.

This book is offered in humble service. It is the hope of all who contributed that it will be oil on troubled waters to ease a turbulent situation and encourage equitable solutions.

Lloyd J. Lunceford
General Editor
Baton Rouge, Louisiana

4 This book is not intended as legal advice, nor is an attorney/client relationship created with any of its contributing authors by the purchase of the book. Readers are encouraged to seek the advice of local counsel familiar with the laws of the state in which the property of concern is located.

A GUIDE TO CHURCH PROPERTY LAW

THEOLOGICAL, CONSTITUTIONAL AND PRACTICAL CONSIDERATIONS

CHAPTER ONE

FIDUCIARIES OF THE ULTIMATE TRUST

> *I gave you a land on which you had not labored and cities that you had not built, and you dwell in them. You eat the fruit of vineyards and olive orchards that you did not plant. Now therefore fear the LORD and serve him in sincerity and in faithfulness. Put away the gods that your fathers served beyond the River and in Egypt, and serve the LORD.*[1]

The subject of this volume is church property. To whom does it belong? In disputes between a denominational hierarchy and a local congregation, who can lay claim to the sanctuary, educational facilities and other assets that have been entrusted to the congregation for the empowerment of its mission?

Subsequent chapters in this book will address the legal issues – property law, corporate law, trust law and other "neutral principles" considerations – that pertain to these questions. This chapter has a different focus. Its purpose is to consider the matter of property from a theological perspective.

Unlike the practice in the United Kingdom, theology has been deemed an improper subject for adjudication by civil courts in the United States. The First Amendment to the U.S. Constitution properly restricts the scope of judicial review to preclude secular courts from deciding matters on the basis of religious doctrine. No student of the history of American jurisprudence, however, can deny the fact that a substantial body of Judeo-Christian theology, morality and ethics has undergirded and informed much of the law.[2] Thus, while not directly applicable to the legal discussion that appears

1 Joshua 24:13-14.

2 See Williamson, Rene deVisme; *Faith as Foundation: A Christian Reorientation of Church/State Relations in America* (Lenoir, N.C.; Reformation Press; 2006).

elsewhere in this book, the following theological reflection may provide a helpful background for Christian women and men who find themselves drawn into litigious ecclesiastical disputes.

Belonging to God

To whom does church property belong? The Heidelberg Catechism offers a succinct answer to all questions of ownership, which Christians of every denomination can appreciate: "I belong – body and soul, in life and in death – not to myself, but to my faithful Savior, Jesus Christ. …" In and through the Son of God, the Gospel of John says, every created thing came into being. The Lord made it all. All that we are and all that we have belong to him.

Genesis describes human beings as caretakers, not owners. We are called to "have dominion" over God's creation. We are to tend it, care for it, feed it and prune it, cause it to bear fruit, and then, as a matter of first priority, present "first fruits" to the Lord. In making that offering at harvest time, we recognize his ownership.

As explained in the chapters that follow, the legal definitions of "ownership," "use" and "trust" are distinctly different from one another. Theologically speaking, however, these concepts are closely related. Theologically, a deed to a piece of property does not represent ownership of the property, but a permission to use the property. From the Biblical standpoint, a deed, therefore, is an aspect of a trust. Creation is the ultimate trust. "I gave you a land on which you had not labored … You eat the fruit of vineyards and olive orchards that you did not plant," the Lord said.

Indicative/Imperative

In Joshua's account, God's people are reminded of their inheritance. It was the Lord who brought them out of bondage in Egypt. The Lord guided their pathway through the sea and into the wilderness. The Lord fed them with manna from heaven and quenched their thirst with water that sprang forth from a rock. It was the Lord who sent "the hornet" before their armies, filling the Amorites and other occupants of the Promised Land with dread. "You did not do it with your own sword and bow," the Lord said.

Included in this Scriptural passage are indicatives and imperatives. As God's people lay claim to the Promised Land, they are told that this possession is the result, not of their own doing, but of God's grace. That is the indicative. An imperative follows immediately thereafter: "Now therefore, fear the Lord and serve him in sincerity and in faithfulness. Put away the gods that your fathers served beyond the River and in Egypt, and serve the Lord."

This indicative/imperative juxtaposition demonstrates that our possessions have been entrusted to us for a purpose. They are not things in themselves, but tools that enable their recipients to serve the Lord. Thus, Scripture affirmatively spells out the ultimate trust clause, a divine directive that transcends all human instruments with respect to property. It also delineates our fiduciary role. A "fiduciary" is someone whose position is analogous to that of a trustee and who has a legal obligation to manage the property of another for the other's benefit, and to exercise a prudent standard of care in such management. Everything we are – our bodies, souls and minds – and everything that we claim to possess has been placed in trust by our heavenly Father for our use according to purposes that he alone specifies.

Scripture often underscores an affirmative principle by stating its mirror image, the same principle described negatively, in order to leave no doubt as to the principle's meaning. This is the case in the passage from Joshua and in subsequent narratives that describe Israel's life while residing in the Promised Land. Those who misuse the land, squander their possessions, assume the role of creator rather than creature, pay homage to lesser gods, violate the First Commandment or otherwise enthrone themselves or claim the possessions belonging to the Lord forfeit their claim to the land.

When Adam and Eve chose to "be like God," they were driven from the garden. Occupants of the Promised Land – the Amorites, Perizzites, Canaanites, Hittites, Girgashites, Hivites and Jebusites – were defeated in battle, not by the sword and bow of the Israelites, but by the Lord's own hand. Even Israel, God's chosen people, learned from their exile, and later in the destruction of Jerusalem, that their claims to property were only as good as their faithfulness to the Lord who owns the land.

Covenant Theology

The ancient Patriarchs were part of a nomadic people who emerged from Upper Mesopotamia and traveled along the edges of settled territory. They migrated into Egypt, where they were enslaved. During this patriarchal period, there was no entity that could be called Israel. How did these disparate nomads who became slaves and then fugitives become a people called Israel? Two essential components were foundational for Israel's self-understanding. Those components were election and covenant. "Once you were not a people," Scripture says, "but now you are God's people; once you had not received mercy, but now you have received mercy."[3]

---

3 I Peter 2:10.

Historian John Bright reminds us that Israel "was made up of elements of exceedingly heterogeneous origin, and she was held together by no central government or machinery of state, yet for some two hundred years, with incredible toughness and under the most adverse of circumstances, she managed to survive and maintain her identity as a people."[4] He names election and covenant as the key factors in constituting that corporate identity.

"The covenant," Bright says, "was in no sense a bargain between equals, but a vassal's acceptance of the Overlord's terms. It therefore laid conditions on election and injected into Israel's notion of herself as a chosen people a moral note, which she would never be allowed to forget, try though she might. She was no superior people, favored because she deserved it, but a helpless people who had been the recipient of unmerited grace. Her God-King was no national genius, bound to her by ties of blood and cult, but a cosmic God who had chosen her in her dire need, and whom she in a free moral act had chosen. Her society was thus grounded not in nature but in covenant. Religious obligation being based in Yahweh's prevenient favor, the covenant provided Israel no means of placing Yahweh in debt for the future. Covenant could be maintained only so long as the divine Overlord's stipulations were met; its maintenance required obedience and continual renewal by the free moral choice of each generation."[5]

The Significance of the Land

One cannot read the Old Testament without being moved by the importance it places on "the land." Israel's faith was an earthy faith. Its God was not a mystical deity to be accessed by Gnostic séance and earth-denying rituals. To the contrary, the Lord visited his people beside a brook, under an oak or on a mountain top. He identified himself, not as the Lord above history, but as the Lord who intervenes in history: "the God of Abraham, Isaac and Jacob," and as "the Lord who brought you out of the land of Egypt," and as "the Lord who gave you the land, flowing with milk and honey." His intervention continued as he appointed judges and kings, and as he called them to account through his prophets. Finally, he intervened – ultimately and permanently – in the flesh and blood person of Jesus Christ. This is a God who was directly and concretely involved with the day-to-day affairs of his people, a reality that the patriarchs symbolized by creating piles of stones ("here I raise my Ebenezer"), memorials built on particular places where he

4 Bright, John; *A History of Israel, Second Edition* (Philadelphia; Westminster Press; 1972) p. 145.

5 Ibid; p. 150.

confronted his people. This significant connection between the land and the faithfulness of God's people can be seen throughout the Biblical narrative.

THE PATRIARCHS

When the Lord extended his call to Abram, he picked a nomadic wanderer, one for whom land meant nothing more than a temporary resting place as he and his flocks moved from one patch of grass to another. The Lord told Abram to break the ties with his past and travel "to a land that I will show you."[6] In this earliest covenant, before there was a people called Israel, land became a part of the equation. Abram (who made a few detours along the way) was instructed to obey the call of God, being assured that God would make of him and his progeny "a people." That covenant was sealed in the changing of Abram's name to Abraham and in Abraham's receipt of "place," the land that the Lord revealed to him.

In the next generation, property became a bone of contention as Jacob struggled with Esau to obtain Isaac's blessing.[7] Jacob's desire to obtain that blessing is *prima facie* evidence that even at this early stage of Israel's life – before it was "Israel" – one's covenant relationship with God and one's access to property went hand-in-hand. Jacob needed his father's "blessing" in order to obtain property.

In the patriarchal tradition, the son who received the father's blessing was awarded a double portion of the inheritance. This favor came with strings attached, for the person who received the blessing also inherited a burden of responsibility. He would become head of the clan. If a member of the family was in debt, the son who had the blessing would redeem that debt rather than allow the family's property to be alienated from the trust. If a son died, the son who had been blessed would care for his wife and children. If a family member were assaulted, the son who had the blessing would be the blood avenger. Thus, even at this early pre-nation stage, the Jews understood that one's possessions (blessings) come from the Lord, and that those possessions imposed covenant obligations.

THE PROPHETS

Israel's faith/land connection comes powerfully to the fore in the story of Namaan's healing of leprosy through Elisha's prophetic ministry.[8] Naaman,

6 Genesis 12:1.

7 Genesis 27:18-29.

8 II Kings 5:1-19.

right-hand man to the king of Syria and the army's commander in chief, was deemed incurable by the physicians and diviners of his pagan land. Having heard that Israel's prophet had miraculous healing powers, he called on Elisha for help. Elisha ordered him to take a bath in the Jordan River – which initially was an affront to Naaman, whose native rivers were far more beautiful to him. But the desperate leper did as he was told, traveling into Israel for a bath in the Jordan, where he was healed.

This miracle placed Naaman in debt, not only to Elisha, but also, and more importantly, to the Lord whom Elisha served. From this moment on, he would worship Israel's Lord. But how could Naaman offer prayers of thanks to the Lord, while living and working in a territory that was dedicated to a different deity? Naaman knew that, once he returned to his homeland, he would be required to bow down beside his king in the temple of Rimmon. The Syrian commander sought to extricate himself from the horns of that dilemma by requesting that he be allowed to load two of his mules with Israel's soil. With that soil, he would create a tiny piece of Israel, a spiritual oasis in Syria, where Naaman could pray to Israel's God.

In his commentary on Naaman's request, Gerhard Von Rad says: "The request has more than once led commentators to express a poor opinion of Naaman's faith. But they are wrong, and their mistake is due to their tacit philosophic assumption that, like ourselves, Israel made a clear division of the world into material and spiritual spheres. Admittedly, even an Israelite reading the story must have felt that there was something odd in the request for a load of earth, but he would not have been taken aback in the slightest at Naaman's inability to rise to the level of the spiritual. He would have been touched by the way in which a man who had encountered the God of Israel here expressed his eager desire to be able to continue to worship him on heathen soil. Indeed, since he believed that the land which Jahweh granted was the saving gift *par excellence*, he would have felt that, in the difficult situation in which Naaman was placed, the latter was perfectly in order in seeking to give his faith what might be called a point of sacramental attachment, even if he took an unusual way of doing this."[9]

This "point of sacramental attachment" frequently is experienced by many church members today. Church members rarely look upon the sanctuaries in which they worship as incidental pieces of real estate whose value is determined by county appraisers but, rather, as symbols that are intimately tied to the faith in which they have been nurtured. Surrounded by memorial plaques, inscriptions on windows, chancel furniture and other testimonies

9 Von Rad, Gerhard; *The Theology of The Old Testament*; Vol. II (New York; Harper & Row; 1965) p. 31.

to their faith heritage, the congregation is reminded that divine-human encounters have occurred in this particular place. It is here that they have gathered to baptize their children, celebrate the covenant of marriage, and claim the resurrection for their loved ones who have died. It is within these walls that they have heard the Word of God and sung the songs of faith while struggling with the vicissitudes of daily living. Thus, this piece of property is more than simply an entry on the ledger of congregational assets. It is a point of sacramental attachment.

This is not to suggest that congregations have made an idol of their church property. They understand that, in the final analysis, they are dealing with sticks and stones, just as did Israel's patriarchs when they raised their Ebenezers throughout Palestine. Church members find themselves drawn to their sanctuary because of its association with sacred moments in their life together. They are simply honoring the particular place where they have met the Lord.

For this very reason, however, a congregation that proclaims "the faith that was once for all delivered to the saints"[10] and has shared that faith for many generations in a particular sanctuary is likely to be hostile toward claims of ownership or control from an outside entity or third party, especially if that entity or third party does not appear to share the faith that is associated with this sanctuary. Such claims of ownership or control would be deemed a sacrilege, for those who are perceived to have departed from the faith would have desecrated a sacred place.

AMOS

The prophet Amos made a direct connection between one's right to possess property and one's faithfulness in observing covenant obligations. Von Rad comments: "Amos shows us a society whose social life is cleft in two – a property-owning and therefore economically self-sufficient upper class lived at the expense of the 'little people,' and the wrongs done were particularly apparent in the administration of justice, since only full citizens could sit and speak in the law court. …"[11] The courts, therefore, were slanted heavily in favor of the very persons who committed unjust acts. As property owners, the judges were interested parties, and slaves, widows and orphans had no standing to argue their case.

Amos scornfully noted that the very property owners who used their possessions to oppress the poor comprised the group that was most zealous in

10 Jude 3.

11 Von Rad; op. cit.; p. 135.

observing religious rituals. Declaring that covenant blessings are inextricably tied to covenant obligations, Amos conveyed the Lord's scathing criticisms of the Israelites' empty ceremonies: "I hate, I despise your feasts, and I take no delight in your solemn assemblies. Even though you offer me your burnt offerings and grain offerings, I will not accept them; and the peace offerings of your fatted animals, I will not look upon them. Take away from me the noise of your songs; to the melody of your harps I will not listen. But let justice roll down like waters, and righteousness like an ever flowing stream."[12]

Not only did Amos' prophecy reject Israel's worship, but also, concomitantly, it rejected Israel's claim to the land. "I will send you into exile beyond Damascus, says the Lord, whose name is the God of hosts."[13]

Amos' words of condemnation concluded with words of grace. Israel would be cleansed of its sin through a punishing exile, and the Lord would not forget his people. Not only would they be restored to the covenant relationship, but also, as a consequence of this restoration, they would regain possession of the land. "'I will restore the fortunes of my people Israel, and they shall rebuild the ruined cities and inhabit them; they shall plant vineyards and drink their wine, and they shall make gardens and eat their fruit. I will plant them upon their land and they shall never again be uprooted out of the land that I have given them,' says the Lord your God."[14]

Hosea

The prophet Hosea also includes the promise of restoration in his message to Israel. Although Hosea's use of the parallel between marital and covenant unfaithfulness is most often seen as his distinctive prophetic contribution, another element of his prophecy is worthy of note. Hosea ties Israel's loss of the land to the Lord's gracious act of redemption. He says the Lord will "speak tenderly" to his people as he takes them back into the wilderness.[15]

Bringing Israel back into the wilderness, of course, means that the Lord is removing his people from the Promised Land, but this is seen as a "tender" act since, in depriving the Jews of their possessions, he is placing them in a state of complete dependence upon him. He is taking them back to a point of intimacy with the one who brought them out of Egypt and into the wilderness, where he gave them covenant law and constituted them as a people.

12 Amos 5: 21-24.

13 Amos 5: 27.

14 Amos 9: 14-15.

15 Hosea 2: 14.

The message here suggests that while the land was a blessed gift to those who had experienced intimacy with their Lord in the wilderness, it was only a gift insofar as that intimacy remained intact. When the people allowed their passion for possessions to separate them from the Lord, violating their covenant with the very source of their life as a people, the Lord graciously removed the land impediment from them in order to restore the primary covenant relationship.

Von Rad comments on Hosea's vision: "There, in the wilderness, no gods of fertility can come between Jahweh and his people; there Israel will be thrown back completely upon Jahweh; Jahweh will have her all to himself, in order that from the desert he can once more grant her the land."[16] For Hosea, as was true for all the prophets, possession of the land is an expression of the covenant relationship.

JEREMIAH

Jeremiah drew a powerful connection between obedience to the covenant and possession of the land. Believing that Israel's covenant violations were so thorough that she never could redeem herself, Jeremiah predicted the fall of the kingdom. His prophecy was explicitly harsh: "Thus the Lord said to me: 'Make yourself straps and yoke-bars, and put them on your neck. … It is I who by my great power and my outstretched arm have made the earth, with the men and animals that are on the earth, and I give it to whomever it seems right to me. Now, I have given all these lands into the hand of Nebuchadnezzar, the King of Babylon, my servant. …'"[17]

Viewed as a traitor for having predicted the kingdom's fall, Jeremiah was imprisoned. Meanwhile, beyond the walls of Jerusalem, it became increasingly clear that the unhappy prophet's words were accurate. Babylonian forces surrounded the city, their armies stretched across the plain as far as the eye could see. They had only to wait until the city's food supplies dwindled and the wells went dry.

It was then, while still confined by prison walls, that the prophet of doom did a strange thing. He purchased his cousin Hanamel's land located outside Jerusalem, in the very territory that had already been conquered and occupied by Nebuchadnezzar's forces. As the deed to that property was signed, Jeremiah repeated these words from the Lord: "Take these deeds, both this sealed deed of purchase and this open deed, and put them in an earthenware vessel, that they may last for a long time. For thus says the Lord of hosts, the God of

16 Von Rad; op. cit.; p. 146.

17 Jeremiah 27:2, 4-6.

Israel: Houses and fields and vineyards shall again be bought in this land."[18]

Why would Jeremiah purchase land to which he had no access? He did so because he understood the relationship between property and covenant. The Jews originally received the land from the Lord, its ultimate owner, as a part of their covenant relationship with the Lord. Violating that covenant, they forfeited their right to possess the land. But Jeremiah knew what Israel's leaders, in their shortsightedness, could not envision. Trusting the Lord's promises to his chosen people, Jeremiah knew that the Lord would once again visit his people, offering them a new covenant that would be written, not on stone, but in their hearts.[19] And because covenant and possessions go hand-in-hand, he believed that the land again would be entrusted to Israel.

This scan of Old Testament passages referring to property leads to a conclusion that Job stated succinctly: "Naked I came from my mother's womb, and naked shall I return; the Lord gave, and the Lord has taken away; blessed be the name of the Lord."[20]

New Testament Considerations

Consistent with the divine character that he revealed to Israel, the Lord made his ultimate investment in humanity through the Incarnation of Jesus Christ. God was in Christ, reconciling the world to himself.

Jesus had a great deal to say about possessions and property, reaffirming the Old Testament theme that one's right to use property is a contingent privilege that is conferred upon those who honor the Lord and obey his commands. In the parable of the talents, the Lord rewarded those servants who made appropriate use of their possessions, and he took property away from an unproductive and unfaithful servant who did not acknowledge his master when making use of his master's property.[21]

The servant's offense was not simply the fact that he failed to produce a return on investment, but that he did not publicly acknowledge the master's ownership. Had he placed the money in the bank or in any other investment instrument, he would have had to acknowledge the master's title to the property. By burying the money, he avoided acknowledging title, making an implicit wager that the master would die while traveling to or from the far country, leaving the servant free to claim ownership for himself. The important element in this parable is not profit *per se*, but the servant's

18 Jeremiah 32:14-15.

19 Jeremiah 31:31-34.

20 Job 1:21.

21 Matthew 25:14-30.

obligation to use the master's property in a manner that identified the master's ownership and benefited the master.

Jesus tells his disciples not to be consumed with anxiety about material things. Why should we not have any anxiety? Because all these things belong, not to us, but to the Lord – and it is the Lord who created us and nourishes us, caring for all of our earthly needs. Our security is not based upon what we possess. It is based on the fact that the Lord owns everything that he has made. Since the owner loves us and knows our needs, therefore, we should be like the birds of the air and the lilies of the field, trusting our heavenly Father.[22]

This counsel does not encourage a slothful lifestyle, for we are trustees of the Lord's property and faithful trustees are very busy people. But it does mean that we have been liberated from the anxieties of ownership.

The Nature of God and God's Image

God is love, an eternal communion of three persons, Father, Son and Holy Spirit. The character of this communal relationship is love, a dynamic giving of self that is expressed in God's Word. In Genesis, God's speaking brings forth creation. God's Word pours itself out, invests itself into the beloved, thereby engendering new life.[23]

Scripture tells us that human beings were created in the image of God. As such, we were commissioned to "have dominion" over the rest of creation,[24] not in the sense that we grasp it, consume it, or dominate it for our own interests, but in the sense that we are to care for it lovingly, investing ourselves in actions that nurture and engender new life. When we who are made in the image of God reflect his presence by honoring our call to be caretakers, creation flourishes and reveals the glory of God.

But in our sin, we have fractured that image. Not content to be made in God's image, we claim to be God. Insisting on our autonomy, we assume the place of owner and become self-serving, rejecting our roles as stewards and fiduciaries of God's good gifts.

Having declared ourselves to be God, we then presume to have the power of God and address creation, not as the cosmic giver, but as the cosmic consumer. We seek to exercise God's power, but not God's love. We stake claims – engendering enmity, fear and loneliness. We hoard. We consume. We spend principal. We waste, spoil and squander. We deplete rather than build

22 Matthew 6:25-34.

23 Genesis 1 and John 1.

24 Genesis 1:26.

up. We turn God's garden into a jungle of competing interests and claims.

This is the judgment that humanity brings upon itself because we presume ownership rather than stewardship. We exercise power rather than investing ourselves in the creating, up-building, engendering, multiplying, dynamic of love – a love that is the nature of God, the nature of the image of God, and the first principle of creation.

But the good news is that the Lord does not leave his wayward people forever to wallow in the consequences of their sin. The Word of God, that same Word that brought forth creation, engendered a new creation. He entered the world as the Word made flesh, dwelling among us, full of grace and truth. Jesus Christ, the Word of God incarnate, took on sinful humanity and suffered the consequences of its sin. In so doing, he cleaned up our act, offering redeemed humanity as his gift to the Father in a restored communion of love.

"Have this mind among yourselves, which is yours in Christ Jesus," Scripture says, "who though he was in the form of God, did not count equality with God a thing to be grasped, but made himself nothing, taking the form of a servant. …"[25] He who had every right to grasp, claim, possess, control, dominate, and hoard creation redeemed, restored and returned it to its owner. Thus, in Jesus Christ, the new Adam, the divinely intended relationship between creator and creature has been restored, the ultimate trust clause has been reaffirmed, and we are welcomed into fellowship with him as servant/trustees, managing the things of this world for the glory of him who made them.

This stewardship role is the call of Christ not only to individual disciples, but also to the congregations within which those disciples bear witness to that call. The congregation has a fiduciary responsibility for all real and personal property with which it has been entrusted. It is obliged to lovingly care for that property and to ensure that its use glorifies its ultimate owner. This property is not to be "grasped," any more than the Son of God grasped his equality with God. Rather, it is to be held in trust – not for the benefit of a wayward third party but, instead, for the faithful purposes specified by its ultimate owner.

The Rise and Fall of Denominations

In the United States, congregations historically have chosen to join hands with other congregations, creating institutional forms of governance that help them accomplish together tasks that would be difficult for them to do

25 Philippians 2:6-7.

individually. It remains to ask to what extent these denominations share their member-congregations' fiduciary responsibility with respect to properties entrusted to the congregations.

Historically, denominational structures were created to be instruments of congregations, organizational arrangements that would facilitate the collective mission activity of the congregations. Working together through a variety of denominational configurations, congregations have founded hospitals, children's homes, educational institutions, and missionary-sending agencies that have dispatched evangelists throughout the world. To the extent that they have been instrumental in providing expanded opportunities for congregations to proclaim the Gospel, denominations have served a useful and laudable purpose. But denominations have never warranted the claim that they have any standing in themselves. Congregations are the front line of mission. Denominations have value insofar as they serve those congregations and help advance the mission of their member churches.

Some denominational advocates may wish to argue that their institutions are grounded in a theological tradition, not merely a practical one. There is some truth to that assertion if one considers the foundational documents of Reformed, Wesleyan, Anglican and other communions. But those doctrinal distinctions among denominations were more viable 100 years ago than they are today, since several decades of church leadership have de-emphasized doctrinal differences. People join congregations today without paying much attention to theological distinctions among denominational documents. The primary interest of those joining is in the characteristics of the local church, not in its secondary affiliations.

Tracking the Trend

The growth of denominationalism in the United States during the 19th and early 20th centuries was less a matter of theology than that of cultural accommodation. The organization of congregations into denominational structures in large measure reflects the industrial development that was prevalent during this period. Business and industry trended toward mergers and centralized headquarters. Directives from headquarters moved in disciplined fashion through a pecking order of well-defined administrators. Everyone knew where he or she stood on the organizational chart. Borrowing from these developments in the secular world, church leaders often crafted parallel structures for their ecclesiastical institutions. This is not to say that those leaders could not have learned beneficial lessons from the business world. It is to say, however, that, over time, they carried some of those lessons – especially the trend toward centralization – too far. Ecclesiastical headquarters expanded into bureaucracies, and administrators were reduced to functionaries.

As this trend took hold in denominational circles, a major reversal occurred in the relationship that existed between denominations and their congregations. Originally, denominations were created for no other purpose than to efficiently facilitate the mission of congregations. Now, congregations began finding themselves in the service of the denominations that they created. Increasingly, power shifted from local to regional and national bureaucracies. Ministers came to understand that their upward mobility depended on favorable reviews from higher up the administrative chain of command. Headquarters began calling for dues and assessments. Higher governing bodies began to flex their newfound muscle, squeezing congregations into nationally defined molds. The bishop, whose shepherd's crook was designed to represent a servant-pastoral leadership, increasingly functioned as a corporate manager.

It was during this period of increasingly centralized bureaucracies that the Presbyterian Church (US) and the United Presbyterian Church in the USA amended their constitutions in the early 1980s to include a clause asserting that all property, real and personal, is held by their member congregations in trust "for the use and benefit of" those denominations. When the two denominations merged in 1983 to form the Presbyterian Church (USA), a version of this trust clause was included in its new constitution. Likewise, during this same period, the Episcopal Church (USA) amended its constitution to add its own version of a trust clause.

The result of these clauses, if given legal effect, would be to shift ultimate control of local church property from the local congregation-titleholder, whose financial gifts acquired and built the property, to the national entity.

The trust clause in the governing documents of American Methodism date to the late 18th century, but its text suggests that it is intended for the benefit only of those who are faithful to God's purposes traditionally understood and specified by the sermons and writings of John Wesley.

While a 1979 decision by the U.S. Supreme Court, discussed in the next chapter, may have been the presenting cause for the adoption of the trust clauses in the Episcopal and Presbyterian denominations, it remains true that these changes occurred during a period when the denominations were claiming increasingly centralized power over their member congregations.

Those who were successful in convincing the denominations to enact the trust clause argued that they were simply making explicit what always had been the case. This argument was erroneous on its face. Presbyterian congregations existed and held deeds to property for almost 100 years before the first General Assembly (the national denominational structure) was organized. Likewise, The Falls Church, home to 2,200 Episcopalians near Washington, D.C., was founded in 1732, and its charter predates by several decades the existence of the Diocese of Virginia.

FROM INDUSTRIAL TO INFORMATION AGE

Just as an accommodation to industrial America encouraged the development of centralized denominations, the advent of a post-industrial, decentralized, information economy is leading churches into a period described by some observers as a post-denominational age. In the global economy, businesses are diversifying and moving from location-bound corporate offices to collaborative and widely disbursed centers of activity. The advent of digital communications has liberated individuals from their former dependence on centralized information sources, freeing them to "surf" the Internet to obtain the information they want and need.

These developments in the corporate world have encouraged the growth of an anti-institutional mind-set that significantly has destabilized the authority that all centralized structures, including denominations, once claimed. Two decades ago, congregations that purchased church school material other than the curriculum published by the denomination or that chose to restrict the use of their mission offerings for purposes other than funding the national church budget were considered "disloyal." Today, less than 10 percent of Presbyterian Church (USA) congregations use the denominational curriculum and more than 80 percent place restrictions on their mission giving. Annual income to the denomination's mission budget has fallen dramatically, from $144 million in 2001 to an estimated $96 million in 2006.

United Methodist church school literature hit a low ebb in 1968, when Good News, a renewal ministry within the denomination, published a stinging criticism of the curriculum's departure from Biblical faith. By 1975, Good News and its publishing unit, Bristol House, were producing their own independent curricula. Today, this evangelical alternative has drawn a large market share away from the denomination's official publications.

Later, when it became obvious to evangelicals that leaders of the United Methodist Church had lost their enthusiasm for missions, they established their own independent Mission Society For United Methodists. With headquarters in Decatur, Ga., the Society has placed more than 114 persons in service in more than 20 foreign mission fields.

The Episcopal Church (USA) has experienced significantly diminished income from its congregations since the 2003 consecration of Bishop V. Gene Robinson, a man who divorced his wife and entered a homosexual partnership. Denominational officials tried to dispute the fact of their losses, claiming that the national denomination's income has been only marginally affected, but what their disclaimer failed to acknowledge was the fact that liberal bishops in several of the denomination's dioceses (regional bodies) were using their reserve funds to make up for lost income from congregations.

These bishops hoped that the furor over Robinson's consecration would be temporary and that they could ride out the storm by drawing down on reserves. But pressure from the Worldwide Anglican Communion, the intervention of bishops from Africa and the Southern Cone,[26] and regional reactions to heavy-handed tactics by bishops in New England, Florida, Alabama and California have exacerbated the tumult, resulting in the loss of millions of dollars to the national denomination.

The Anglican Communion Network in the United States has grown to include more than 1,000 congregations that represent more than 250,000 communicants. More than 70 congregations are now under the jurisdiction of dioceses in Uganda, the Southern Cone, Kenya and Central Africa. These rapidly increasing developments indicate that the day of centralized authority within the Episcopal Church (USA) may be coming to an end.

These sociological factors, together with a host of demographic data, have led observers like George Barna,[27] Loren Mead,[28] Ellison Research,[29] Wade Clark Roof,[30] Coalter, Mulder and Weeks, [31]and many others to suggest that denominations are on the fast track toward extinction. When the centralized, industrial model was in vogue, denominations flourished, but that model no longer has traction on the American scene.

To be clear, these observations are not intended as an argument against denominations *per se*. Denominations have the potential capacity to do great good, if rightly organized and if they remain true to their founding principles as servants of their congregations. Rather, these observations are merely descriptive, a portrait of historical influences and the current state of affairs.

---

26 Southern Cone. The term refers to a geographic region composed of the southernmost areas of South America. Typically, it includes Argentina, Paraguay, Uruguay, Chile and the southernmost part of Brazil.

27 The George Barna Group – a market research firm that specializes in studying non-profit and Christian organizations.

28 Mead, Loren; *The Once and Future Church* (Herndon, Va.; The Alban Institute; 1991).

29 Ellison Research, a market research firm based in Phoenix, Ariz.

30 Roof, Wade Clark; *American Mainline Religion: Its Changing Shape and Future* (Rutgers, N.J.; The State University; 1987).

31 Coulter, Mulder, Weeks; *The Organizational Revolution* (Louisville, Ky.; Westminster John Knox Press; 1992).

The Theological Divide

Sociological factors are not the only reason why denominational control over individual congregations is declining. An inquiry into the stated motives of congregations that over the past decade have distanced themselves from their denominational structures reveals their contention that the cause of their estrangement is theological. Many of the separating congregations have concluded that the boards and agencies of the denomination with which they have been affiliated are no longer faithful to the essential tenets of the Christian faith.

While mainline denominations were founded on constitutional documents that affirm orthodox Christian teaching, many of the policies and programs of their current infrastructures often reveal a different faith that is alien to those documents, a faith that is rooted in post-modern assumptions about the nature of truth and morality. By elevating the autonomous individual as the ultimate arbiter of truth, many leaders of these denominations have violated Scripture's First Commandment, and they have undermined the very basis of their own constitutions.

Increasingly, executive presbyters, bishops and governing council leaders are publicly denying the singular saving Lordship of Jesus Christ, denying his bodily resurrection and declaring the Trinity a functional rather than ontological reality (a resurgence of Sabellius's third-century heresy called "Modalism," in which the persons of the Trinity are replaced by functions – e.g., "creator, redeemer, sustainer" – and the Godhead becomes an amorphous whole). With increasing frequency, many mainline church leaders articulate a view that regards Scripture as a product of culture rather than a God-breathed expression of divine presence and purpose, and that aligns their ethical codes with cultural rather than Scriptural mores.

Marks of the True Church

Congregations that are committed to orthodox Christian faith are struggling to find their place within these denominational structures. Many question whether they can continue to call their denominations "churches" when they assess these institutions in light of the classical "marks of the true church." In the Reformed tradition, those identifying marks are: (1) where the Word of God is faithfully preached; (2) where the sacraments are faithfully celebrated; and (3) where Biblical discipline is faithfully exercised.

Many congregations are asking if they can continue to be the true church while living and working within broader institutional structures that no longer reliably exhibit its marks. Increasingly, congregational leaders are publicly acknowledging that their denominations are merely humanly connected institutions, and they are unwilling to describe them as the church.

Separating Within

Some congregations have taken the position that as long as local congregations and their pastors are not required by the institutional hierarchy to affirm or support apostasy, they can continue, albeit uncomfortably, to live within such denominations as members of a loyal opposition. These churches are associating with like-minded congregations in growing evangelical networks, and they are re-directing their offerings to trustworthy ministries that are demonstrably faithful to Jesus Christ. For them, the denomination is functionally irrelevant to their daily life and work.

In the United Methodist and Presbyterian denominations, many of these congregations are linked to one another under the name "Confessing Church Movement." More than 1,300 Presbyterian congregations, representing nearly 435,000 members, have named themselves confessing churches. The Methodist movement, which provides opportunities for individuals as well as congregations to join, now numbers more than 650,000 members.

Three affirmations characterize the confessing churches: (1) the singular saving Lordship of Jesus Christ; (2) the authority of Scripture as the Word of God written; and (3) the Lord's requirement that his disciples live a holy life that includes lifting up the sanctity of marriage as defined by Scripture.

Confessing churches understand that there are additional essential doctrines within the Christian corpus, but they lift up these three because they have been subjected to particular contemporary challenges and often are rejected by the policies and programs of their denominational agencies.

The Language of Barmen

The name "confessing church" has historical significance. This was the name given to a faithful band of Christians who dared to confront leaders of Germany's Third Reich. Distressed that the established church had accommodated its theology to a culture that, in fact, was hostile to Christian faith, these Christians gathered in the town of Barmen and publicly confessed their faith: "Jesus Christ, as he is attested for us in Holy Scripture, is the one Word of God which we have to hear and which we have to trust and obey in life and in death," they said. "We reject the false doctrine, as though the

Church could and would have to acknowledge as a source of its proclamation, apart from and besides this one Word of God, still other events and powers, figures and truths, as God's revelation."[32]

Using words that would invite martyrdom for many, confessing Christians at Barmen excoriated leaders of the established German Evangelical Church. They said the faith that holds the church together – namely, its Biblical faith – was being "grievously imperiled, and with it the unity of the German Evangelical Church."[33] They said that policies and programs of the ruling church party threatened the very existence of the German Evangelical Church. "This threat consists in the fact that the theological basis, in which the German Evangelical Church is united, has been continually and systematically thwarted and rendered ineffective by alien principles. ... When these principles are held to be valid, according to all the Confessions in force among us, the Church ceases to be the Church and the German Evangelical Church, as a federation of Confessional Churches, becomes intrinsically impossible."[34]

The language of Barmen is being spoken today by evangelical Presbyterians, United Methodists and Episcopalians. While orthodox Episcopal groups – the American Anglican Communion and the American Anglican Council, for example – do not employ the confessing church label *per se*, their work is similar to those of the Presbyterian and United Methodist confessing church movements, and the denominational offenses that they have challenged are virtually identical.

Orthodox groups within the three denominations have concentrated on networking with their supporting congregations and developing lines of communication and fellowship. They have stopped just shy of organizing alternative denominations, although the Episcopalians appear to be on the cusp of that reality. Oversight by overseas Anglican bishops and a bid by the American Anglican Communion to gain recognition from the Archbishop of Canterbury are realities that could form the substance of an alternative Anglican denomination in the United States.

For the most part, the present state of affairs for orthodox Christians in these three denominations in the United States appears to be an uneasy and dissenting relationship, an attempt to "be the Church within the church," minimizing their public identification with the denomination, cutting off all unrestricted giving beyond the parish, and otherwise conducting their ministries as if the denomination did not exist, but without launching a nationally organized move toward formal separation (schism).

32 The Theological Declaration of Barmen, 8.11, 8.12 (1934).

33 Ibid; 8.07.

34 Ibid.

The Coercion Factor

Recent developments have made this separating-within, live-and-let-live stance increasingly difficult to maintain. As congregational contributions to national church structures decrease and denominational reserves are being exhausted, the bureaucracies are beginning to fight for the survival of their institutions. Coercive measures, once unheard of, are being used against those who in conscience cannot support denominational policies and programs, and this is the place where the issue of church property often surfaces. A primary target is any minister whose evangelical convictions have led her or him to be openly critical of denominational leadership or to cut off financial support for its programs. These ministers are suffering threats to their ecclesiastical careers and are being warned that their pension accounts also might be in jeopardy.

The preferred method for coercing ministers often is administrative, rather than judicial. By working administratively, bureaucracies believe they can bypass fundamental fairness and due process requirements that would otherwise be imposed on them if they filed judicial charges against troublesome ministers. This assumption is flawed – administrative discipline is subject to due process requirements in all three of the cited denominations, especially the right of the accused to face his or her accusers and certain evidentiary requirements – but ministers who seek judicial relief from violations of due process must undergo lengthy and often expensive litigation that few can afford. Thus, the threat that they face at the hands of a hostile executive or bishop is palpable, resulting in widespread clergy intimidation.

Institutional action toward self-preservation also is aimed at dissenting congregations in the form of denominational takeover attempts. (In Presbyterian parlance, the vehicle used is called an administrative commission. In Episcopalian and United Methodist circles, it is an act of the bishop.) Denominational officials only have to ferret out a minority of denominationally inclined members in a congregation whose leaders are resisting denominational policies, and then name this minority "the true church." In so doing, denominational leaders would, if unchallenged, effectively disenfranchise the majority of the congregation and its leadership, asserting control through a surrogate minority.

Recent Cases

• On March 25, 2006, the Rev. Dr. Alan J. Meenan, former senior minister of the 2,700-member First Presbyterian Church in Hollywood,

Calif., renounced the jurisdiction of the Presbyterian Church (USA) and removed himself from ordained office. This action by a highly esteemed minister serving one of the denomination's strongest evangelical voices sent shock waves across the country.

Meenan had been forced out of his position by a presbytery administrative commission whose leader, Mr. Tony de La Rosa, is an outspoken homosexual activist who has served as legal counsel to denominational headquarters. Meenan's career with the denomination was effectively ended without his having had the opportunity to face his accusers or even know the specifics of their accusations. Ministers throughout the denomination shivered, some of them saying, "If it could happen to Hollywood First, it can happen to any of us."

• On July 13, 2005, Bishop Andrew Smith, joined by diocesan staff, locksmiths, computer experts, and security guards, seized control of the St. John Episcopal Church in Bristol, Conn. He issued an inhibition (a formal action that limits the scope of a priest's activities) against the congregation's priest, Father Mark Hansen, and forced a revisionist priest-in-charge upon the orthodox congregation.

Four days later, flanked by his attorneys, the bishop stood before the congregation in a meeting that he said was designed to "rebuild trust." Under intense questioning, he admitted that the grounds for his actions against the pastor and parish were based on the pastor's having signed a letter earlier in the year that had called on the bishop to recant his un-Biblical theology, and for his participation in an unprecedented vote to elevate Bishop V. Gene Robinson, a man who had divorced his wife and entered a homosexual partnership.

• In 2005, Bishop Jon Bruno filed suit against three congregations in the Diocese of Los Angeles after they renounced his leadership and placed themselves under the Diocese of Luwerro in the Province of Uganda. Bishop Bruno's suit claimed the congregations' real and personal property (even the hymn books) for the Episcopal Church (USA). He lost all three cases at the trial level and was required to pay damages to the three congregations. The denomination has appealed.

• On December 22, 2005, The Church of the Resurrection, an Anglican start-up church that had been meeting in the sanctuary of a Presbyterian congregation in Baltimore, was given an eviction notice. The conservative congregation, a member of the worldwide Anglican Communion, had been organized under the authority of the Anglican Diocese of Bolivia, placing it outside the jurisdiction of the Rev. John Rabb, the liberal Suffragan Bishop of the Diocese of Maryland. The Rev. Rabb complained to the Rev. Peter Nord,

Baltimore's presbytery executive, who pressured the Presbyterian congregation under his jurisdiction to evict its Anglican tenant.

"This new roadblock will only make Church of the Resurrection stronger," the rapidly growing congregation's newsletter said. "As long as we remain faithful to our Lord, he will never desert us, and we will continue to grow through his grace."

• On March 26, 2002, representatives of Maumee Valley Presbytery made an unannounced early morning visit to Norcrest Presbyterian Church in Findley, Ohio, where they removed the pastor's possessions, changed the locks and took over the congregation's property.

On April 4, the first Sunday after the presbytery's raid, the minister, most of the church's officers and about 90 percent of its members banded together for a worship service hastily arranged at the city's dog pound. Since then, the exiled congregation has mushroomed to 700 members, holds three worship services each Sunday in the auditorium of a school, and has started construction on a $3.5-million complex located on 20 acres of land.

The remainder of the original congregation, some 60 members whom the presbytery labeled "the true church," occupies an almost empty building and struggles to meet an $800,000 mortgage obligation.

• On January 26, 2005, United Methodist Pastor Ed Johnson decided that a man who was openly engaged in a homosexual relationship could not be received into the membership of his congregation unless the man terminated the relationship. Bishop Charlene Kammer intervened, ruling that the pastor must accept the applicant. The Rev. Johnson stood by his conscience and his understanding of the United Methodist *Book of Discipline*. Nevertheless, charges were filed that led to the pastor being dismissed from his pulpit June 13, 2005.

His dismissal was appealed to the denomination's Judicial Council, which issued Ruling 1032, reinstating the Rev. Johnson. That decision upset the United Methodist hierarchy. The Council of Bishops met and issued an open letter criticizing the ruling and arguing that there can be no barriers, no required belief or behavioral expectations or standards, for anyone who wishes to join a United Methodist church. In an appeal for reconsideration to the denomination's Judicial Council, the bishops argued that they have the authority to trump and overturn any pastor's decision on membership within his congregation.

The Confessing Church Movement of the United Methodist Church responded to the Council of Bishops' request for reconsideration, declaring: "(a) The Judicial Council ruling was correct and should stand; (b) If changes are to be made in our system to mandate inclusiveness, this should be done legislatively (at General Conference) and not by bishops' decree or political pressure on the Judicial Council; (c) We have a denominational-wide conversation about whether the church upholds its traditional position about conversion and holy living as a basis for membership."

On April 28, 2006, the United Methodist Church Judicial Council, by a 5-4 vote, denied the Council of Bishops' request for reconsideration.

The Property Trust Clause

Underlying the coercive pressure that increasingly is being applied to Biblically faithful ministers and congregations is the property trust clause that appears in the constitutions of the Presbyterian, United Methodist and Episcopal denominations. From a theological perspective, any humanly devised trust that has the effect of undermining the Lord's ultimate trust cannot be valid. Scripture is clear that the Lord will not bless any possessor of property who denies his truth, no matter what secular instrument he or she may claim. Denominations whose leaders deny or compromise the faith may not take property away from Biblically faithful congregations without offending the Word of God. They may or may not be able to legally seize property from a believing congregation – that justiciable issue is addressed elsewhere in this book – but such actions cannot escape the moral judgment of heaven's highest court.

Fiduciary Obligation

Not only are Christian believers permitted within the bounds of the law to resist the confiscation of property that belongs to the Lord, the Bible imposes on believers *a fiduciary obligation* to resist it. Scripture is replete with references to this obligation. Paul counseled Timothy in trust-specific language: "O Timothy, guard the deposit entrusted to you. Avoid the irreverent babble and contradictions of what is falsely called knowledge, for by professing it, some have swerved from the faith."[35]

Similar counsel is found in Jude: "I have found it necessary to write, appealing to you to contend for the faith that was once for all delivered to the saints. For certain people have crept in unnoticed who long ago were designated for this condemnation, ungodly people who pervert the grace of our God into sensuality and deny our only Master and Lord, Jesus Christ."[36]

Scripture teaches that it is not only Biblical faith that believers are called

35 I Timothy 6:20-21.

36 Jude 3-4.

to preserve and protect, *but also those properties that were entrusted for the propagation of that faith.* When the sons of Eli, whom Scripture describes as "worthless men,"[37] misused offerings that the people had dedicated to the Lord, the words of Scripture were harsh in their condemnation: "Thus the sin of the young men was very great in the sight of the Lord, for the men treated the offering of the Lord with contempt."[38] Eli and his sons clearly had a responsibility to ensure that property dedicated to the Lord was used for its intended purposes.

Thus, when church officers collect the congregation's offerings and dedicate them to the Lord Jesus Christ, their task is not complete. Having dedicated this property, they now have a fiduciary responsibility to monitor the church's faithfulness regarding the manner in which this property is being used.

Honoring our Inheritance

The trustees' sacred obligation to preserve and protect church property for its Biblically intended use relates not only to current gifts by a living congregation, but also to gifts that were given by the congregation's forebears now deceased. Consider the inscriptions on stained glass and memorial plaques that enhance most congregational structures. These inscriptions remind the living congregation – as did Joshua among those who were about to inherit the Promised Land – that they "eat the fruit of vineyards and olive yards that they did not plant."

Summary Conclusion

A review of Scripture leads us to the following affirmations:

(1) The earth and all that dwells within it belongs to the Lord.

(2) The Lord has entrusted to human beings the use of his creation. This is the ultimate trust clause, whose moral claim subordinates all human property arrangements.

(3) The use of the Lord's property must be in accordance with his will, always recognizing and giving glory to him as its owner.

(4) The Lord has given and the Lord can take away. Violating our fiduciary responsibility may result in his revoking our right to use the property that has been entrusted to us.

(5) The church exists wherever the Word of God is faithfully preached; the sacraments are faithfully administered; and Biblical discipline is faithfully

37 I Samuel 2:12.

38 I Samuel 2:17.

exercised.

(6) The church has a sacred obligation to guard the faith that has been entrusted to it, and to protect all property that serves as a "point of sacramental attachment," property that has been dedicated to the proclamation of the Gospel.

(7) A denomination is not a church. It is an institutional structure, created by one or more churches to facilitate their missionary calling.

(8) Theologically speaking, the Biblical witness leads us to conclude that any dispute between a denomination and a congregation over the right to use the Lord's property – regardless of whose name appears on deeds and other instruments of human origin – shall be morally resolved in favor of the body that exhibits the true marks of the church. Possession of any property only can be validated by the tenant's faithfulness to him who placed his whole creation in the ultimate trust.

This, then, is the theological and sociological backdrop against which current courtroom dramas are being played. With increasing frequency, civil courts, which are prohibited from using theological considerations, nevertheless are themselves tasked with the responsibility to sort out competing claims to church property. The legal principles that guide those courts and the factors often relied on are explained in the chapters that follow.

CHAPTER TWO

FEDERAL CONSTITUTIONAL PRINCIPLES

The discussion of church property law begins with the controlling principles established by the U.S. Supreme Court. The law of church property rights largely is a matter of state statutory law and state case law, but decisions by the Supreme Court interpreting the religion clauses of the First Amendment to the U.S. Constitution set the guidelines within which state courts must operate. The First Amendment provides in part that, "Congress shall make no law respecting an establishment of religion, nor prohibiting the free exercise thereof. …" These restrictions on the federal government found in the First Amendment were made applicable to the states through the due process clause of the Fourteenth Amendment by the use of two judicial devices, "substantive due process" and "incorporation."

In *Everson v. Board of Education* 330 U.S. 1 (1947), the U.S. Supreme Court held that when Congress passed the Fourteenth Amendment in 1868 requiring states to guarantee "due process" to individuals, this meant more than requiring that fair procedures be used when implementing laws. "Due process" meant "substantive due process," a guarantee that had substantive content. This content included the protection for religious liberty. *Everson* held that the due process clause of the Fourteenth Amendment included or incorporated the guarantee of the establishment clause of the First Amendment. As a result, the establishment clause no longer restricted just the federal government. It applied with equal force to the states. In *Cantwell v. Connecticut* 310 U.S. 396 (1940), the Supreme Court had earlier held that the free exercise clause of the First Amendment likewise applied to the states through incorporation into the due process clause of the Fourteenth Amendment.

Multiple Methods

The courts at different times in history have used different methods to resolve questions of church property use and ownership, initially using an "implied trust/departure-from-doctrine" method (now deemed unconstitutional), later following the "hierarchical/deference"[1] method and, more recently, also following the "neutral principles of law" method.

The first method, sometimes referred to as "the English rule," harkens back to pre-Colonial days and the once-prevailing view in England and Scotland. Under this method, any dispute between a denomination and a congregation, or between factions within a congregation, concerning the ownership or use of church property was resolved by awarding the property to the party deemed by the court to most closely adhere to the founding religious doctrines. See *Craigdallie v. Aikman*, 1 Dow. 1, 3 Eng. Rep. 601 H. L. 1813 (Scot). This approach eventually was held incompatible with the establishment clause of the First Amendment to the U.S. Constitution. Civil courts opining on what

1 The word "hierarchical" is used in this book in two distinct ways, with reference to hierarchical churches and to the hierarchical method (or the hierarchical/deference method) for resolving church property disputes. The reader should not infer, though, that hierarchical churches must follow the hierarchical method. The hierarchical method or the neutral principles of law method may apply in hierarchical churches to resolve property disputes. Which method is used is a matter of the law of the state in which property at issue is located.

The term "hierarchical churches" refers to a form of church government. Forms of church government fall on a continuum. At one end of the spectrum are congregational churches, each of which is governed autonomously. At the other end of the spectrum lies the Roman Catholic Church, in which individual churches or parishes have comparatively little autonomy and are subject to the ascending authority of bishop, cardinal and pontiff. In between these two ends of the spectrum lie intermediate forms of government that mark Presbyterian, Methodist and Episcopalian denominations, wherein individual churches enjoy comparatively greater autonomy than Catholic parishes but are not wholly autonomous like congregational churches. In Presbyterian, Methodist and Episcopal denominations, individual congregations are subject in varying degrees to the supervisory jurisdiction of regional or national bodies – presbyteries, dioceses, conferences, synods, General Conferences and General Assemblies. [But see Chapter Six, which suggests that Episcopal parishes are congregational with respect to property issues.]

Although there are several gradations on the spectrum, the U.S. Supreme Court, for purposes of legal analysis, has adopted a two-fold classification – congregational churches and hierarchical churches. This book only addresses church property law in the context of hierarchical or quasi-hierarchical churches and does not address the resolution of church property disputes in congregational churches, which are determined in civil courts by ordinary principles governing voluntary associations, without regard to religious doctrine. This book also does not address those exceptional circumstances where, by express language in a deed, ownership and control are made contingent on some specific form of religious doctrine or belief, or where ownership and control are governed by a specific state statute.

does or does not conform to correct doctrine is an unacceptable intrusion by civil authority into ecclesiastical affairs and would constitute an impermissible state establishment of religion. Although the problems with the departure-from-doctrine rule increasingly were recognized during the 19th and 20th centuries, it was not expressly declared unconstitutional until *Presbyterian Church v. Mary Elizabeth Blue Hull Memorial Church*, 393 U.S. 440 (1969).

In *Watson v. Jones* 13 Wall 679, 20 L.Ed 666 (1872), the U.S. Supreme Court stated that, in the absence of express trust language in a deed or charter, the "hierarchical theory" could be applied to resolve church property disputes. This method is constitutionally permissible and remains operative in many states today. Under the hierarchical theory, civil courts are to defer to the decision of the highest ecclesiastical tribunal to which the matter may have been appealed. Not surprisingly, this deference in practice tends to favor the parent body to the disfavor of local congregations. Such deference was thought required in order to avoid undue governmental involvement in church affairs that had resulted from applying the implied trust/departure-from-doctrine rule. That rule was later held unconstitutional in *Presbyterian Church*, a case in which the Court emphasized that civil courts have jurisdiction to resolve church property disputes but have to exercise that jurisdiction using a constitutionally acceptable method. In *Presbyterian Church*, the hierarchical/deference method survived constitutional muster and, as noted, continues to be used in many states.[2] However, *Presbyterian Church* went on to say that the "neutral principles of law" method also was a constitutionally permissible, alternative approach to resolve church property disputes.

Ten years after *Presbyterian Church*, in *Jones v. Wolf* 443 U.S. 595 (1979), the U.S. Supreme Court elaborated on the meaning of the "neutral principles of law" method. In elaborating on its meaning, the Court articulated several benefits of using this method and encouraged its adoption by the states. The application of neutral principles of law does not prohibit the consideration of denominational rules on property ownership, nor the consideration of the text of certain religious documents such as denominational constitutions. It does, however, preclude the consideration of denominational rules or constitutions to the effective exclusion of other relevant evidence. An analysis that too readily defers to denominational documents would be akin to a *compulsory* deference rule, which was deemed unconstitutional by *Wolf*. Under the federal constitution, states are free to adopt the hierarchical/deference method, but the establishment clause of the First Amendment prohibits any federal mandate that would *require* states to follow that method. In other words, both

2 For examples of the continued use of the hierarchical/deference method, see the discussion of Texas case law in Chapter Three.

the hierarchical method and the neutral-principles method are constitutionally permissible and states are free to decide which method to adopt.

Thus, according to *Wolf*, states that choose to follow the neutral principles of law method for resolving church property disputes are to look not only to the denominational constitution and other governing rules of the general church (including any express trusts clauses), but *also* are to look to the text of local property deeds, articles of incorporation of the local church, relevant state statutes or code provisions affecting property matters, and other actions of the parties that may reflect intent. Although *Wolf* did not overturn *Watson*, the nation's highest court strongly commended the neutral principles method for consideration by the states.

Key Language

Subsequent to the U.S. Supreme Court's decision in *Wolf*, many state supreme courts adopted the "neutral principles of law" approach to resolving church property disputes. Thus, any potential judicial determination of a church property dispute in any state that has adopted, or will adopt, the neutral principles of law approach would be governed by *Wolf*. It is, therefore, instructive to excerpt *Wolf's* key, explanatory passages:

> [T]he First Amendment prohibits civil courts from resolving church property disputes on the basis of religious doctrine and practice. … As a corollary to this commandment, the Amendment requires that civil courts defer to the resolution of issues of religious doctrine or polity by the highest court of a hierarchical church organization. … Subject to these limitations, however, the First Amendment does not dictate that a State must follow a particular method of resolving church property disputes. Indeed, "a State may adopt any one of various approaches for settling church property disputes as long as it involves no consideration of doctrinal matters, whether the ritual and liturgy of worship or the tenets of faith."
>
> At least in general outline, we think the "neutral principles of law" approach is consistent with the foregoing constitutional principles. …
>
> The primary advantages of the neutral-principles

> approach are that it is completely secular in operation, and yet flexible enough to accommodate all forms of religious organization and polity. The method relies exclusively on objective, well-established concepts of trust and property law familiar to lawyers and judges. It thereby promises to free civil courts completely from entanglement in questions of religious doctrine, polity, and practice. Furthermore, the neutral-principles analysis shares the peculiar genius of private-law systems in general – flexibility in ordering private rights and obligations to reflect the intentions of the parties. Through appropriate reversionary clauses and trust provisions, religious societies can specify what is to happen to church property in the event of a particular contingency, or what religious body will determine the ownership in the event of a schism or doctrinal controversy. In this manner, a religious organization can ensure the dispute over the ownership of church property will be resolved in accord with the desires of the members.
>
> This is not to say that the application of the neutral-principles approach is wholly free of difficulty. The neutral-principles method … requires a civil court to examine certain religious documents, such as a church constitution, for language of trust in favor of the general church. In undertaking such an examination, a civil court must take special care to scrutinize the document in purely secular terms, and not to rely on religious precepts in determining whether the document indicates that the parties have intended to create a trust. In addition, there may be cases where the deed, the corporate charter, or the constitution of the general church incorporates religious concepts in the provisions related to the ownership of property. If in such a case the interpretation of the instruments of ownership would require the civil court to resolve a religious controversy, the court must defer to the resolution of the doctrinal issue by the authoritative ecclesiastical body.

Jones v. Wolf at 602-604 (citations omitted), holding that states may constitutionally adopt the neutral principles of law method to resolve church property disputes.

Wolf explained the circumstances under which the hierarchical method still might be followed, authorized use of "neutral principles," and discussed when, in applying neutral principles, a denominational trust proviso should be given effect. It is a fundamentally important case, and so it is essential to have a clear understanding of what it did and did not say. Some denominational statements seem to suggest that *Wolf* held that, if a denomination adopted express trust language, then civil courts necessarily must follow the hierarchical method to resolve questions of church property and defer to the denomination. That may be wishful thinking. It is not what the Court said in *Wolf.*

In *Wolf,* the U.S. Supreme Court reiterated that the First Amendment prohibits civil courts from resolving church property issues on the basis of religious doctrine and practice and, as a corollary, that the First Amendment requires civil courts to defer to the resolution of issues of *religious* doctrine or polity to the highest ecclesiastical court in a hierarchical church organization. The *Wolf* court went on, though, to say that the First Amendment does *not* require "the States to adopt a rule of compulsory deference to religious authority in resolving church property disputes, even where no issue of doctrinal controversy is involved." *Wolf* at 605. Rather, states also are constitutionally entitled "to adopt neutral principles of law as a means of adjudicating a church property dispute." Id. at 604. In other words, while the hierarchical method is permitted under the federal constitution, it is not mandated by it. *Wolf* explained the many benefits of using a different method, the "neutral principles of law" approach, and commended it to the states.

In subsequently adopting the neutral principles of law approach, some states have gone further than *Wolf* required (states, after all, are free under their own state constitutions to grant more protection to individual liberties than the minimum federal guarantees). In *Wolf,* the U.S. Supreme Court said that the First Amendment did not require compulsory deference by the states to the hierarchical approach, and encouraged the states to consider adopting the neutral principles of law method as a constitutionally permissible, alternative approach. *Wolf* stopped short of declaring the hierarchical approach itself to be inconsistent with either the establishment clause or the free exercise clause of the First Amendment, and only held that a federal rule compelling its use by the states would be unconstitutional.

The Louisiana Supreme Court went further. In its view, the adoption of the neutral principles of law approach was "necessitated" by both the free exercise clause of the First Amendment and by provisions in the Constitution of Louisiana:

> Indeed, we think the safeguards against laws establishing religion and prohibiting the free exercise thereof contained in the First Amendment and Article I, Section 8 of our state constitution *necessitate* our adoption of the "neutral principles" approach. Whatever authority a hierarchical organization may have over associated local churches is derived solely from the local church's consent. Refusal to adjudicate its feud over property rights or contractual obligations, even when no interpretation or evaluation of ecclesiastical doctrine or practice is called for, but simply because the litigants are religious organizations, may deny a local church recourse to an impartial body to resolve a just claim, thereby violating its members' rights under the free exercise provision, and also constituting a judicial establishment of the hierarchy's religion.

Fluker v. Hitchens, 419 So.2d 445 at 447 (La. 1982) (emphasis added), citing A. Adams & W. Hanlon, *Jones v. Wolf*: Church Autonomy and the Religion Clauses of the First Amendment, 128 U. Penn. L. Rev. 1291 (1980). C.f. Hargrave, Louisiana Constitutional Law, 42 La. L. Rev. 596 (1982).

In applying the neutral principles approach, *Wolf* noted that there may be cases where a property deed, corporate charter, or denominational constitution "incorporates religious concepts in the provisions relating to the ownership of property." Id at 604. As a practical matter, incorporating religious doctrine into the text of property provisions would be unusual, but conceivable.[3] On such exceptional occasions, in the event that interpreting the instruments of ownership require civil courts to delve into religious doctrine, the courts are to fall back on the hierarchical method and "defer to the resolution of the doctrinal issue by the authoritative ecclesiastical body." Id.

Wolf also discussed the application of the neutral principles approach in those circumstances where religious documents, such as church constitutions, contain trust language in favor of the denomination. Under such circumstances, civil courts "must take special care to scrutinize that document in purely secular terms, and not to rely on religious precepts in determining whether the document indicates that the parties have intended to create a trust." Id. At 604. At the time *Wolf* was decided, the constitutions

3 Methodist theologian Thomas Oden argues that religious doctrine is incorporated into the text of the United Methodist Church's trust clause. See discussion in Chapter Five.

of the Episcopal Church in America, the United Methodist Church and the Presbyterian Church US and the United Presbyterian Church USA, the two predecessors to the Presbyterian Church (USA), did not contain express trust provisos. *Wolf* said that a subsequent denominational adoption of an express trust proviso would be one way "to ensure ... that the faction loyal to the hierarchical church will retain the church property. ... And the civil courts will be bound to give effect to the result *indicated by the parties, provided it is embodied in some legally cognizable form.*" *Wolf* at 606 (emphasis added).

Some who advocate a binding property trust in all cases have seized on this language or, more accurately, a portion of it. First, they argue that the hierarchical method should apply but, in the event that neutral principles apply, they cite the quoted language in *Wolf* to argue that the courts are bound to give effect to the denomination's trust clause. However, and here is the point that sometimes is glossed over, the quoted language in *Wolf* does *not* say that the denominational adoption of an express trust proviso always would be conclusive.

Mutual Intent

The quoted language from *Wolf* does not end with the word "result." *Wolf* left unaddressed the question of whether, if adopted at the national level, an express trust proviso always would be given local effect regardless of whether a local congregation accepted or rejected the denomination's asserted trust, and regardless of the property facts of a particular church or the laws of the state in which a particular church's property is located. In other words, the issue is the mutual intention of the parties as indicated in some form recognized as legally enforceable.

The *Wolf* court's emphasis on mutual intent first can be seen by its instruction that civil courts should give effect to the result "indicated by the *parties.*" Id. at 606 (emphasis added). The emphasis on mutual intent also can be seen by *Wolf's* suggested alternative to amending denominational constitutions to include an express trust clause: "They (local churches) can modify the deeds or the corporate charter to include a right of reversion or trust in favor of the general church." Id (parenthesis added). Obviously, if the local church voluntarily chooses to amend its property deeds or articles of incorporation to specify a trust in favor of the denomination, it has given its consent to such a trust.

As for the U.S. Supreme Court's other suggested means of obtaining clarification of church property status (amending the denominational constitution to add express trust language), the *Wolf* court apparently presumed that national adoption of any proposed amendments would be contingent on relevant, local ratification. In the Presbyterian Church (USA), however, to cite one example, the adoption of amendments to the denomination's constitution occurs by vote of a requisite number of regional presbyteries, rather than by a vote of local churches. And it is often stated within the denomination that the individuals who participate in a presbytery vote do not act in a representative capacity on behalf of a local church.

In any event, recent state court decisions make it clear that the amendment of denominational constitutions to include express trust language is not, by itself, determinative. Courts following the neutral principles of law method consider many factors in seeking to determine the mutual intent of the parties, which intent must be reflected in some form that is acknowledged in the law as binding.[4]

FREE SPEECH PROTECTIONS

In addition to the First Amendment "separation" and "free exercise" issues addressed by the U.S. Supreme Court in developing the neutral principles of law approach for resolving church property disputes, another First Amendment issue ought not to be overlooked.

A trial court in Orange County, California, has ruled in favor of a local Episcopal parish and against all claims of the diocese concerning the parish property. The court also ruled that the parish established that it had been sued by the diocese claiming trust rights on its property after the parish publicly had disagreed with the national church's views on homosexuality and other issues of public significance. In its final order, the trial court stated:

> Such acts arise out of and are in furtherance of the exercise of the right to speak out on a matter of public interest. The views expressed by the defendants concern matters of public interest. How churches in America are reacting to the different viewpoints of homosexuality is currently a topic of much public significance.

That case, *Los Angeles Diocese, The Episcopal Church (USA) v. St. James Church*, now is on appeal to California's 4th Circuit Court of Appeals and should be decided sometime in 2007.

Many evangelicals have strong disagreements with their national

4 For a broader survey of U.S. Supreme Court treatment of this topic, see "Church Property Disputes: A Constitutional Perspective" by Kenneth E. North in the Appendices.

denominations over faithful Biblical responses on many matters of current public interest. Local church officers should not be reluctant to give voice to their consciences.

As discussed in Chapter Nine, *infra*, a local church may determine its highest duty is to protect its local property from denominational misuse. Whether or not they determine to withdraw from their denominations with their local property, the congregation's officers should clearly articulate and document their conscientious views of what Scripture teaches pertaining to matters of public interest.

In the event of a denominational attempt to invoke a trust on local church property, civil courts may extend free speech protections to the local church for expressing such views, and may well conclude that the protected speech was a precipitating cause of denominational retaliation, tainting its claim to an enforceable trust.

CHAPTER THREE

SAMPLE CASE LAW FROM SELECTED STATE COURTS

The U.S. Supreme Court's interpretation of the religion clauses of the First Amendment set the permissible parameters within which courts may operate when considering church property disputes. Those disputes most often present questions of state law and are thus heard in state court, guided by the federal, constitutional principles discussed in the previous chapter. This chapter discusses illustrative cases in selected state jurisdictions, including both "neutral principles" states and "hierarchical" states. The cases selected involve Methodist, Episcopal, African Methodist Episcopal, AME Zion, Nazarene, and Presbyterian congregations.[1]

Readers are reminded to pay careful attention to the facts of each case. Previously reported judicial opinions have controlling or persuasive value as precedents to the degree that they are "on point" with the facts of the case that may be at hand. It is therefore important to not only know *what* a court held, but also *why*. The facts in the cases below should thus be compared and contrasted with the facts of the local church of interest to the reader.

CALIFORNIA

On December 1, 2004, the California Supreme Court declined to review a decision of the California 5th District Court of Appeal, letting stand that

1 For a fuller compendium of case law, see 52 A.L.R. 3d 324 (Determination of Property Rights Between Local Church and Parent Church Body: Modern View). Though updated with cumulative supplements that list additional case citations, the main annotation originally was published in 1973, prior to the U.S. Supreme Court decision in *Jones v. Wolf*, 443 U.S. 595 (1979). Thus, the "modern view" articulated no longer is current. Nevertheless, this American Law Reports citation is of value to practitioners. Although the cumulative case law citations are not listed by hierarchical states versus neutral principles states, the state-by-state listing of cases, though not exhaustive, will expedite state-specific research.

lower court's ruling allowing a local Methodist church to revoke the trust language contained in the United Methodist Church *Book of Discipline*. This permitted the local congregation to leave the denomination with its property. *California-Nevada Annual Conference of United Methodist Church, et al v. St. Luke's United Methodist Church, et al*, 121 Cal. App. 4th 754, 17 CAL. RPTR. 3rd 442 (decided August 13, 2004; review denied December 1, 2004).[2]

The facts in *St. Luke's* are important to note. St. Luke's United Methodist Church was first incorporated as a member of the Methodist Church in 1948. Among its authorized purposes, as stated in its articles of incorporation, was "to acquire, manage and hold in trust for the benefit of said St. Luke's Methodist Church, property of every kind and nature, both real and personal. …" In 1968, the Methodist Church united with the Evangelical United Brethren Church to form the United Methodist Church, governed by the denomination's *Book of Discipline*.[3] The denomination is governed by a General Conference, but the primary, regional administrative unit is termed "Annual Conference." Annual Conferences have supervisory responsibility over the local churches within their respective geographic bounds. Subsequent to incorporation, St. Luke's acquired title to nine parcels of property, six prior to the formation of the United Methodist Church and three after its formation. Some of the deeds contained trust language and some did not, with testimony at trial indicating that it had been the intention of the local trustees that trust language be included in all deeds.

---

2 Although decisions by state supreme courts are only controlling over lower courts within that state's jurisdiction, state court decisions (especially those in California and New York) sometimes have wide influence and serve as bellwethers for national legal trends. State court decisions, however, often are predicated on unique or particular provisions of that state's statutes, as well as on the specific language in relevant property documents, thus potentially limiting a decision's persuasive authority in other jurisdictions whose statutes may be different. Careful attention to the facts of each case is therefore necessary.

3 Paragraph 2501 of the United Methodist Church *Book of Discipline* provides in part that "titles to all properties held … by a local church … shall be held in trust for the United Methodist Church and subject to the provisions of its Discipline." Paragraph 2503 sets forth specific trust language to be used in instruments of conveyance and adds that "the absence of a trust clause … in deeds and conveyances previously executed shall in no way exclude a local church or church agency from or relieve it of its connectional responsibilities to the United Methodist Church." The *Book of Discipline* also states that although title to all properties held by a local church shall be held in trust for the United Methodist Church, the United Methodist Church is not a legal entity and does not nor can it hold title to property. Rather, various conferences, councils, boards, agencies and local churches and other units bearing the name United Methodist are the entities that have legal capacity.

Switching The Locks

In doctrinal disputes that first arose in 1999, St. Luke's pastor was on one side of the dispute and the regional bishop was on the other. The bishop replaced the pastor. When the succeeding pastor newly named by the bishop arrived on his second day to work at St. Luke's, however, he found that the locks had been changed. The former pastor (and church members who supported his doctrinal position) chose not to record corrected deeds containing trust language but, instead, recorded deeds without the trust language in order to secure a line of credit from a bank. The Annual Conference of which St. Luke's had been a part, the bishop, and the district superintendent for the Fresno district within the Annual Conference where St. Luke's was located then filed suit against St. Luke's, the former pastor and the president of St. Luke's board of trustees. The suit alleged breach of a charitable trust and sought injunctive relief and damages.

St. Luke's filed a cross-complaint seeking a declaration that the plaintiffs had no interest in the property and that St. Luke's had the authority to revoke the trust by which the local church property was said to be held in trust for the benefit of the denomination. While the litigation was pending, St. Luke's amended its articles of incorporation and formally disassociated itself from the United Methodist Church, explicitly declaring that all property was held in trust only for the sole benefit of the local church corporation.

The trial court held in favor of the denomination, concluding that a trust existed in favor of the United Methodist Church and that St. Luke's was without authority to unilaterally revoke that trust. On appeal, however, this decision was reversed. The California appeals court first reviewed the law that governs the extent to which civil courts have jurisdiction to decide ecclesiastical disputes over church property. It correctly cited U.S. Supreme Court decisions and California precedents for the proposition that civil courts are without authority to decide questions whose answers are religious in nature but could, without violating First Amendment prohibitions, resolve church property disputes based on "neutral principles of law."

After reviewing the mixed and inconclusive provisions of the property deeds, articles of incorporation, and rules of the general church, the California appellate court ultimately rested its decision on provisions in the California Corporations Code, which held in part that, "[u]nless a trust is expressed and made irrevocable by the trust instrument, the trust is revocable by the settlor. This section applies only where the settlor is domiciled in the state when the trust is created, or the trust instrument is executed in this state, or where the trust instrument provides that the law of this state governs the trust."

Self-dealing Not Allowed

The trial court had read the California Corporations Code to mean that the settlor (the person who creates a trust) was the United Methodist Church, and that it had created a trust in favor of itself and had taken no action to amend its own *Book of Discipline* to revoke the trust. The appellate court reversed the trial court's ruling, however, holding that such apparent "self-dealing" was at odds with the basic principles of trust law, which did not include the creation of a trust by the declaration of a non-owner that the owner holds the property merely as trustee for the non-owner. Rather, the appeals court held that the *Book of Discipline* did not, by itself, create the trust, but that the trust had, in fact, been created by St. Luke's own articles of incorporation, language in several of St. Luke's property deeds, and by St. Luke's demonstrated intent to hold its property in trust for the benefit of the United Methodist Church *and* for its own benefit. Having created the trust, St. Luke's had specific authority under the California Corporations Code to revoke the trust.[4]

The relevant provisions of the California Corporations Code cited by the court stated that "no assets of a religious corporation are or shall be deemed to be impressed with any trust, express or implied, ... unless, and only to the extent that, the articles or bylaws of the corporation, or the governing instruments of a superior religious body or general church of which the corporation is a member, so expressly provide." The California Corporations Code went on to state that a trust so created "may be amended or dissolved by amendment from time to time to the articles, bylaws or governing instruments creating the trust." The appellate court ruled that St. Luke's, as settlor, initially had created the trust for the mutual benefit of the local and general church, but subsequently had so amended its articles of incorporation to expressly state that it no longer would be affiliated with or subject to the United Methodist Church and that St. Luke's would thereafter hold its property in trust for the sole benefit of the local church corporation.

---

4 Before reaching its decision, the appellate court in *St. Luke's* said in "dicta" that, "California's rule that a trust is presumed to be revocable differs from the rule in many other states where trusts are presumed to be irrevocable unless the settlor reserves the right to revoke." "Dicta" is a legal term used to distinguish between, on the one hand, the actual holding of a court and its supporting rationale from, on the other hand, dicta – verbiage and opinion that go beyond the facts before the court and, therefore, constitute the individual views of the author of the decision and are not binding on other courts in subsequent cases. In *St. Luke's*, the court rested its decision on specific provisions of the California Corporations Code, rather than reliance on a general presumption of revocability.

Significantly, the court in *St. Luke's* acknowledged that its decision was at odds with another recent decision by a California appellate court in another district of equal authority. In *Guardian Angel Polish National Catholic Church of Los Angeles, Inc. v. Grotnik*, 118 Cal. App. 4th 919, 13 Ca. Rptr. 3rd 552 (2004), the trial court had found that church property belonged to the local church, but the California 2nd District Court of Appeals reversed that ruling in favor of the general church.

Although the facts in *Grotnik* were quite different from those in *St. Luke's*, the 5th District Court in *St. Luke's* still found fault with the rationale used by its sister court. In *Grotnik*, the general church constitution required that the election of local church boards be subject to diocesan approval, a provision mirrored in the local church's bylaws. Although the local church board had repealed those provisions in its bylaws, the 2nd District Court of Appeals held that because the diocese had not approved the election of the new board, the action taken by it to sever ties with the general church was null and void.

In critiquing this decision by its sister court, the *St. Luke's* court said, "We respectfully disagree with the view that acts of a board of directors of a lawfully formed corporation may be viewed by a civil court to be a nullity simply because those acts are deemed unauthorized not by any recognized rule of state law, but rather only by the general church's own rules." In the opinion of the 5th District Court in *St. Luke's*, the 2nd District Court's decision in *Grotnik* essentially subordinated civil control of church property disputes to ecclesiastical control by following the hierarchical theory that gave undue deference to the higher ecclesiastical body, in apparent derogation from *Jones v. Wolf, supra.*[5]

LOUISIANA[6]

Fluker Community Church v. Hitchens, 419 So.2d 445 (La. 1982), is a

5 As of the date of this writing, there is pending in a California trial court the matter of Serone Church, a Korean Presbyterian Church (USA) congregation in Artesia, Calif., within the Presbytery of Hamni. The congregation renounced the jurisdiction of the PCUSA and, relying upon the California appellate decision in *St. Luke's, supra*, is contending that it is not subject to the denomination's held-in-trust property clause. Preliminary rulings have favored the local church, but the matter awaits trial and appeal.

6 A survey of Louisiana case law involving church property disputes discloses more than a score of reported decisions, most of which do not address questions of trusts, revocability or disaffiliation; or which predate *Wolf* and the 1982 Louisiana Supreme Court decision in *Fluker v. Hitchens*, 419 So.2d 445 (La. 1982), which adopted the *Wolf*-authorized neutral principles approach. Only discussed in this section, then, are the benchmark decision in *Fluker* and, with the exception of one instructive Third Circuit Court of Appeal decision, the pre- and post-*Fluker* decisions by the Louisiana First Circuit Court of Appeal.

Louisiana Supreme Court decision noteworthy for its reliance on *Wolf* and the adoption of neutral principles of contract and property law to resolve church property disputes in Louisiana. At issue was an unincorporated association that had functioned for many years as a freestanding religious congregation (society) and which eventually had affiliated with the African Methodist Episcopal Church, but subsequently chose by majority vote to disaffiliate. In a brief opinion, the Louisiana Supreme Court concluded that, under the circumstances presented, the text of the A.M.E. *Discipline* and the property deed overcame the Louisiana presumption of majority rule (for unincorporated associations), such that the minority faction loyal to the A.M.E. Church had the right to control the actions of the titleholder to the tract of land at issue and, hence, the use of the tract.

The actual ownership of the property involved was not at issue; both sides concurred in the validity of the deed that placed title in the local congregation represented by the majority. Because ownership of the property was deemed not to be contested, there was no occasion by the court to address the comparative rights of a local congregation versus a parent denomination. Thus, the validity of any trust under the Louisiana Trust Code was not an issue. [The court did incidentally note, however, that under the A.M.E. *Discipline*, title was vested with the local congregation but, in the event the local congregation dissolved and abandoned the property, title then would vest in the A.M.E. Annual Conference in which the local church was located.]

Denominational Designation Determinative

In examining the deed of acquisition, the Louisiana Supreme Court ruled that the local Fluker church had acted exclusively in its capacity as an A.M.E. church when it acquired the land (i.e., the property deeds included express mention of the denomination with which the local Fluker church was affiliated). The specific provisions of the A.M.E. *Discipline* concerning disaffiliation or abandonment, therefore, reflected the intention of the parties and therefore determined the outcome, allowing the minority faction of the local congregation to control the actions of the majority faction titleholder with respect to the use of the tract.[7]

Turning to appellate court decisions, the only post-*Fluker* decision reported in Louisiana is *Thomas v. Craig*, 424 So.2d 1090 (La. App. 1st Cir.

7 *LeBlanc v. Davis*, 432 So.2d 239 (La. 1983), is the only other Louisiana Supreme Court case found that cites *Fluker* to apply neutral principles to resolve a church dispute. At issue in that case, however, was the dismissal of a pastor rather than a dispute over contested property.

1982). The First Circuit Court of Appeal acknowledged the jurisdictional distinction between ecclesiastical matters and neutral principles of law, citing *Katz v. Singerman*, 241 La. 103, 127 So.2d 515 (1961); *Wilkerson v. Battiste*, 393 So.2d 195 (La. App. 1st Cir. 1980); and *Bourgeois v. Landrum* 396 So.2d 1275 (La. 1981). At issue in *Thomas v. Craig* was a dispute in governance between the pastor and the board of deacons. The reported decision does not address a specific controversy over property.

In *First Methodist Protestant Church of Baton Rouge v. First Congregational Methodist Church of Baton Rouge*, 184 So.2d 265 (La. App. 1st Cir. 1966), rehearing denied 4/4/66; writ refused 6/7/66, which pre-dates *Wolf* by 13 years and *Fluker* by 16 years), the First Circuit addressed a dispute over legal title between two Methodist factions. The court used "neutral principles" (without referring to them as such) to examine the denominational *Book of Discipline* and local articles of incorporation.

The facts in the case are distinct. Prior to the purported sale of the local church property by a dissonant local congregation, the Mississippi Conference had declared the petitioner/seller church to be extinct, with the property thus reverting for an interim to the mother church pursuant to the *Book of Discipline*. Subsequently, however, the petitioner church was "reactivated" and full title was again vested in the First Methodist congregation. The dissonant faction, the First Circuit Court ruled, thus did not have the authority to sell it.

The legal dispute over property ownership, then, actually was between two separate, local Methodist congregations, and the Mississippi Conference was not a party to the suit. In affirming the trial court's dismissal of one faction's exception of failure to join an indispensable party, the court ruled that at the time the suit was filed the Mississippi Conference "had no claim or interest in the property in question" *First Methodist* at 268. Thus, the validity of any trust under state trust law was not an issue.

Louisiana District, Church of the Nazarene v. Church of the Nazarene, 132 So.2d 667, (La. App. 1st Cir. 1961), was an action by a parent church corporation, the Louisiana District, Church of the Nazarene, to be declared the owner of real property recorded or titled in the name of its local or subordinate corporate member, the Bible Holiness Church of Ponchatoula (formerly Church of the Nazarene, Ponchatoula, Louisiana). The parent corporation's claim to ownership rested on the alleged subordinate corporation's withdrawal from the parent church without the parent's consent, in purported violation of the parent church's governing constitution, the *Manual of the Church of the Nazarene*. The First Circuit Court of Appeal relied on the provisions of the *Manual of the Church of the Nazarene* and decided in favor of the parent church, following the "hierarchical theory" set forth in *Watson v. Jones*, 13 Wall. 679, 80 U.S. 674, 20 L.Ed. 666 (1871). This theory has since fallen into disuse in Louisiana, however, in favor of the "neutral principles of law" theory subsequently approved by the U.S. Supreme Court in *Presbyterian Church* and *Wolf, supra*,[8] and adopted by the Louisiana Supreme Court in *Fluker, supra.*

In *Annual Mississippi Conference of the Methodist Protestant Church, et al v. First Methodist Protestant Church, et al* 121 So.2d 256 (La. App. 1st Cir. 1960), the trial court ruled that the plaintiff lacked procedural capacity. This decision was affirmed on appeal.[9]

Ascertaining the Intent of the Parties

The only germane post-*Wolf* and post-*Fluker* opinion found outside the Louisiana First Circuit Court of Appeal is the Louisiana Third Circuit Court of Appeal opinion in *Bethany Independent Church v. Stewart*, 645 So.2d 715, 93-1252 (La. App. 3rd Cir. 10/5/94), writ denied, 649 So.2d 421, 94-2967 La. 2/9/95. At issue was a local congregation's disaffiliation from its

---

8 *Church of the Nazarene* is of doubtful validity after *Fluker*. Its heavy, if not exclusive, reliance on the *Manual of the Church of the Nazarene* probably constitutes an unconstitutional application of the hierarchical theory. In addition to relying on *Watson*, the Louisiana First Circuit Court of Appeal quoted Pennsylvania state court decisions whose analysis likewise followed the hierarchical theory, and cited an earlier Louisiana Fourth Circuit Court of Appeal decision, *Brooks v. Chinn*, La. App., 52 So.2d 583 (1951), which similarly had followed the hierarchical theory to rule in favor of the parent body.

The First Circuit in *Church of the Nazarene* differentiated or distinguished an earlier Louisiana Supreme Court decision, *Katz v. Singerman*, 241 La. 103, 127 So.2d 515 (La. 1961), in which the court declined to interfere with the action of the local governing body of a congregation with respect to property. The First Circuit noted that, in *Katz*, the synagogue at issue was an autonomous congregational entity (and thus, under the hierarchical theory, the captain of its own ship). More fundamentally, the First Circuit noted that the issue in *Katz* did not involve civil or property rights but, instead, the determination of whether a proposed course of action was in conformity with religious ceremonies and prescribed rituals and was, therefore, beyond the scope of a civil court's subject matter jurisdiction.

9 The denomination's Annual Conference sued a local Methodist church for buying and selling property without declaring that it was to be held in trust for the use and benefit of the denomination. The Annual Conference alleged in its petition that, under the denomination's constitution and *Book of Discipline*, the property was to revert to the denomination upon the extinction of the local congregation. The petition also alleged, though, that under the *Book of Discipline*, no church should be deemed extinct until so declared by the Annual Conference. The petition, however, failed to allege that the Annual Conference had so acted in this instance. Accordingly, the petition by the Annual Conference was dismissed for lack of procedural capacity.

denomination, the Cumberland Presbyterian Church. Following disaffiliation, the local church renamed itself Bethany Independent Church.

The court ruled that the property of the local, unincorporated Presbyterian church belonged to the national denomination. The court based its decision in part on the proposition that the text of a denominational constitution and church regulations should be considered in determining property disputes, citing *Wolf, Fluker* and *Louisiana Church of the Nazarene, supra.* Like *Fluker*, the court sought to ascertain the intent of the parties agreed upon before the dispute arose. Applying neutral principles, it found that the presumption of rule-by-majority, normally applicable to non-profit, unincorporated associations under La. R.S. 9:1051, had been overcome by the text of the property regulations in the denomination's 1984 *Confession of Faith* (the denomination's constitution).

According to § 3.32 of the 1984 *Confession of Faith*, all property was to be held in trust for the use and benefit of the parent denomination as an expression of the connectional nature of the general Presbyterian church. The *Confession of Faith* also expressly provided that in the event of the dissolution or departure of a local congregation, all property held in trust was to revert, or be transferred, to the parent church's designated presbytery. The 1984 *Confession of Faith* further required the permission of the designated presbytery before a particular church could lease or sell its real property. The local congregation argued, however, that La. R.S. 9:1051.A permitted a non-profit, unincorporated association (the original local congregation) to transfer property to a separate entity (Bethany Independent Church).

The Louisiana Third Circuit Court of Appeal ruled that all of the provisions of the Louisiana statute had not been properly followed and, therefore, the local church could not rely on the statute. Thus, the denominational provisions controlled. The court concluded that, "it was the intention of the parties, agreed upon before the dispute arose, to be bound by the provisions of the *Confession of Faith*, 1984, including those provisions relative to property." *Bethany* at 722. The validity of "held in trust" language under state trust law apparently was not raised by the parties and, thus, not addressed by the court.

MARYLAND

A case that has received considerable national publicity, and which is very instructive, arises from the state of Maryland. In *From the Heart Church Ministries, Inc., et al v. African Methodist Episcopal Zion Church, et al*, 370 Md. 152, 803 A.2nd 548 (2002), the supreme court for the state of Maryland (called in Maryland the "Court of Appeals") was asked to address the issue of whether, when a local church withdraws from a religious denomination, the property belongs to the local church or to the denomination. The Maryland court followed neutral principles to consider the competing texts of local church property documents and denominational documents.

The facts in *From the Heart*, as in most church property cases, are key. In 1981, a new local congregation was organized as an affiliate of the African Methodist Episcopal Zion Church (AME Zion denomination) and was incorporated under the Maryland Religious Corporations Law in 1983 as "Full Gospel AME Zion Church, Inc." The articles of incorporation for this local church stated that its purpose was to engage in any lawful activity in accordance with the *Book of Discipline* of the African Methodist Episcopal Zion Church and anything permitted by the Maryland Religious Corporations Law.

Full Gospel subsequently purchased real property on several occasions between 1983 and 1999, with the owner in each instance listed as Full Gospel AME Zion Church, Inc. None of the deeds to any of the property contained a clause creating a trust in favor of the AME Zion denomination, nor contained a provision providing for local church property to revert to the AME Zion denomination upon the dissolution of the local church or upon its disaffiliation with the denomination.

In 1991, Full Gospel amended its articles to delete all references to the AME Zion denomination and added a dissolution provision stating that, in the event the local congregation dissolves or in the event of a final liquidation of the local church corporation, all remaining assets of the local church would be distributed to such religious, charitable, or educational organizations as the local church board of trustees may determine (i.e., the property would not revert to the control of the AME Zion denomination).

In 1998, Full Gospel amended its articles again, to adopt a new name, From the Heart Ministries, Inc. Those 1998 amendments, like the 1991 amendments, stated that upon the dissolution or final liquidation, the local board of trustees could determine the distribution of all assets to such charitable organizations as it may determine. The 1998 amendments also gave the local board of trustees full power to act on behalf of the local church, to conduct any business matters of the local church, to adopt bylaws, and to amend or promulgate new articles of incorporation.

Turning to the competing rules and regulations of the AME Zion denomination, its documents not surprisingly conflicted with the local church documents. The denominational provisions are contained in the AME Zion *Book of Discipline*, which includes a requirement that property held or thereafter acquired by a local church for the purpose of worship or parsonage be held in trust for the denomination. The *Book of Discipline* provision stated that the trust was "solely for the benefit of the grantee, and the grantor reserve[s] no right or interest in said premises."

The AME Zion *Book of Discipline* imposed a duty upon the pastor and presiding elder of each local congregation to see that "… [O]ur Church Property is deeded according to our *Book of Discipline.* …" In the event that the appropriate trust clause was for whatever reason omitted, the *Book of Discipline* provided that "the absence of the trust clause … in deeds and conveyances previously executed shall in no way exclude a local church from, or relieve it of, its African Methodist Episcopal Zion Church Connectional responsibilities nor shall it absolve a local congregation or board of trustees of its responsibility to the African Methodist Episcopal Zion Church."

CONTINGENT CONNECTIONALISM

This connectional responsibility, even in the absence of specific trust language in property deeds, was made contingent on certain conditions. The *Book of Discipline* provided that the intent and desire of the founders and/or the later congregations and boards of trustees to create a trust must be shown by any or all of the following indications: (a) the conveyance of the property to the trustees of the local African Methodist Episcopal Zion Church or any of its predecessors; (b) the use of the name, customs and policy of the African Methodist Episcopal Zion Church in such a way as to be thus known to the community as a part of the denomination; (c) the acceptance of the pastors or ministers appointed by a bishop of the African Methodist Episcopal Zion Church, or employed by the Presiding Elder of the district in which it is located.

Finally, the AME Zion *Book of Discipline* stated that the trustees of a local congregation shall not mortgage, sell or dispose of any property of the AME Zion Church without confirmation by denominational authorities. In the event of the dissolution of a local congregation, the *Book of Discipline* stated that the local AME Zion Conference, with the approval of the bishop, could order the sale of the property, with the proceeds to be delivered to the Annual Conference.

In due course, From the Heart Church Ministries notified the AME Zion denomination that it intended to withdraw from the denomination. Upon such notification, the denomination requested From the Heart to turn over and transfer ownership of the local church property. From the Heart declined to do so, and filed suit in local district court seeking a declaratory judgment that it was the sole and rightful owner. The denomination filed a counter claim seeking its own declaratory judgment. Both the regional Annual Conference and a newly incorporated Full Gospel AME Zion Church (presumably populated by a denominationally-loyal faction of From the Heart) filed separate actions seeking to intervene. The suits were consolidated and the matter went to the court on various pre-trial cross motions for summary judgment.

The trial court ruled in favor of the denomination, its regional Annual Conference, and the newly incorporated Full Gospel AME Zion Church, and against From the Heart Church Ministries. The trial court concluded that "under neutral principles of property law," all of the property that From the Heart had acquired, including all property acquired under the name Full Gospel AME Zion Church prior to July 8, 1999,[10] was subject to a trust in favor of the denomination, as expressed in the *Book of Discipline*. The effect of the trial court's ruling would have been to require that the property stay within the denomination, preventing the local congregation from retaining the property following its decision to end its affiliation with the denomination. The Maryland high court, however, accepted the case for review and reversed the trial court's ruling.

'It is not enough ...'

In reversing and holding for the local congregation, the Maryland Court of Appeals (the state supreme court) referred to its prior decision in *Mt. Olive A.M.E. Church v. Board of Incorporators*, 348 Maryland 299, 703 A. 2nd 194 (1997) as setting out the appropriate analytical framework:

> ... [R]esolution of church property disputes demand an analysis that involves the review of all relevant documents and circumstances. *Unless the deed to the property clearly provides for the holding of the property in trust for the parent church, it is not enough to consider simply the form of the church government, the constitution or other authoritative sources pertinent to the parent church's claim to the property, consideration must also be given to the Religious Corporations Law, the relations between the parties, and the local church charter*. The latter at the very least provides insight into the relations between the parties and may evidence the local

10 The court opinion does not explain the significance of this date, but it may be when From the Heart notified the denomination of its intent to disaffiliate.

> church's consent to the form of government and to be bound by provisions in the parent church's constitution or other authoritative sources pertaining to the ownership and control of its property.

Id. at 320, 703 A. 2nd at 204 (emphasis added).

The court also pointed to the U.S. Supreme Court decisions in *Watson v. Jones* and *Presbyterian Church, supra*, requiring civil courts to refrain from reliance on religious doctrine, polity and practice and commending for adoption neutral principles of law and well-established concepts of trust and property law familiar to lawyers and judges.

The Maryland high court noted the aforementioned property provisions in both the local congregation's articles of incorporation and property deeds and the provisions contained in the AME Zion *Book of Discipline.* In discussing the denominational provisions, the court noted that the *Book of Discipline* stated that property is held in trust for the denomination whether or not the deeds so provided – as long as certain conditions were present. The court even noted that, in this case, such conditions had been fulfilled: the property had been conveyed to the trustees of the local AME Zion Church (the trustees for From the Heart); From the Heart, operating previously under the name of Full Gospel, had used the name, customs and polity of the AME Zion denomination and was known in the community as a congregation of that denomination; and From the Heart, previously operating as Full Gospel, had accepted pastoral appointments by a bishop of the denomination.

Undue Deference

Nevertheless, the high court's analysis did not end there. In reversing the trial court's ruling, the Maryland Court of Appeals went on to say that the trial court had incorrectly based its decision only on factors enumerated in the *Book of Discipline* that had indicated congregational acceptance of the denomination's polity. But in relying exclusively on provisions in the denomination's constitution, the trial court had failed to comply with the directive in *Mt. Olive* (and *Jones*) to consider all relevant documents and circumstances. Furthermore, the Maryland Court of Appeals ruled that the trial court failed to consider From the Heart's intentional deeding of the church property in its name only, not in trust, and the national denomination's apparent acknowledgement of and acquiescence for a time in this deeding irregularity.

The trial court also failed to consider the amendments to From the Heart's charter and bylaws to remove references to the AME Zion denomination. The Maryland Court of Appeals noted that the initial charter of Full Gospel stated its affiliation with AME Zion and that its purpose was to engage in lawful activity under the *Book of Discipline* and also as permitted by the Maryland Religious Corporations Law – and that, pursuant to that state law, Full Gospel had amended its charter to delete references to AME Zion from both its articles and bylaws. In considering only denominational polity, then, the Maryland Court of Appeals found that the trial court "inappropriately has deferred to the church doctrine; it has relied on religious precepts to enforce From the Heart's Connectional responsibilities." *From the Heart* at 187, 569.

The high court in *From the Heart* reiterated that which it had previously instructed in its decision in *Mt. Olive* – that where there is no clear provision in the deed to local church property calling for the holding of the property in trust for the parent church, "it is not enough to consider simply the form of the church government, constitution or other authoritative sources pertinent to the parent church's claim to the property, consideration must also be given to the Religious Corporations Law, the relations between the parties, and the local church charter." *From the Heart* at 187, 569, citing *Mt. Olive* at 320, 204 and quoting *Jones v. Wolf*:

> In undertaking an examination of religious documents, such as a church constitution, a civil court must take special care to scrutinize the document in purely secular terms, and not to rely on religious precepts in determining whether the document indicates that the parties have intended to create a trust.

Id. at 604.

The AME Zion denomination unsuccessfully argued that when the *Book of Discipline* contains trust language and provides for the circumstance when a local church fails to deed local church property in trust to the national denomination, the court only should have to resort to the *Book of Discipline* to resolve property disputes. This position was rejected in *From the Heart*, as it had been rejected in *Mt. Olive*, with the Maryland high court stating, "Only when there is a clear trust/reverter language in the deed to the property … or a statute enacted by the Legislature … is there no need to consider other documentation." *From the Heart* at 189, 570 citing *Maryland and Virginia Eldership of Churches of God v. Church of God at Sharpsburg*, 249 Maryland

650, 663, 241 A. 2nd 691, 699 (1968).

Finally, the highest court in Maryland noted that as a matter of general principle under Maryland case law, unless otherwise specifically provided, a trust is revocable. A settlor that creates a trust may designate it to be either revocable or irrevocable but, if no designation is made, the trust is revocable by any act sufficient to manifest the settlor's intention to revoke.

Consent Once may not be Consent Always

The court then examined the trust language in the *Book of Discipline* and said that while it extended to apply to the situation when a local church is affiliated with a denomination, it gave no indication that the trust created is irrevocable nor addressed the situation where a local church terminates its affiliation. The court thus concluded:

> Consent to holding property in trust during the course of affiliation does not automatically constitute consent to relinquishing that property once the affiliation terminates. This is particularly the case where the trust is revocable and is, therefore, another reason that there must be a more expanded review of documents and circumstances, as required by *Mt. Olive*, rather than merely the review of the Church *Book of Discipline*.

From the Heart at 189, 190, 571

Pennsylvania

Although not decided recently, *The Presbytery of Beaver-Butler of the United Presbyterian Church in the United States of America, et al v. Middlesex Presbyterian Church, et al*, 507 Pa. 255, 489 A.2d 1317 is noteworthy. In this 1985 decision, the Pennsylvania Supreme Court reversed the appellate court and reinstated the trial court's decision allowing the local congregation to leave the denomination with its property.

The case is noteworthy in part because of its thoughtful review of U.S. Supreme Court case law (the hierarchical theory of *Watson v. Jones*, termed the "deference rule," the implied trust/departure-from-doctrine rule, and the neutral principles of law approach approved in *Jones v. Wolf*). It also is noteworthy because of an antecedent connection to the Presbyterian Church

(USA). In *Beaver-Butler*, the Pennsylvania Supreme Court adopted the neutral principles approach to hold that the Pennsylvania appellate court had given undue deference to the United Presbyterian Church in the United States of America.

Middlesex Presbyterian Church had been incorporated in 1907 and had been a participating church in the Presbyterian Church in the United States of America (PCUSA). In 1958, the PCUSA merged with the United Presbyterian Church in North America (UPCNA) to form the United Presbyterian Church in the United States of America (UPCUSA). The UPCUSA was the "northern church" that in 1983 merged with the "southern church," the Presbyterian Church in the United States (PCUS), to form the present Presbyterian Church (USA).

Middlesex Presbyterian Church had been affiliated with the UPCUSA and its predecessors since the Presbyterian Church's inception in America in 1799. On April 6, 1981, Middlesex duly amended its local charter to disaffiliate from the UPCUSA, effective April 18, 1981. In 1979, an amendment was proposed to modify the UPCUSA *Book of Order* to insert language expressly creating a trust in favor of the UPCUSA with respect to property owned by affiliated churches. That proposed amendment, however, did not become part of the UPCUSA Constitution until May 23, 1981, a little more than a month *after* the effective date of the disaffiliation by Middlesex.

The Pennsylvania Supreme Court found that, prior to the creation of express trust language in the UPCUSA constitution, the constitution of the UPCUSA did not contain any trust, explicit or implicit, in the property of member congregations in favor of the UPCUSA. In determining that a trust did not exist during the relevant time period, the state's high court applied neutral principles of Pennsylvania law, which provided that no particular form of words or conduct was required to manifest the intention to create a trust. An intention may be by written or spoken words or conduct indicating that the settlor intended to create a trust. Despite the lack of formal requirement, however, the appearance of all elements of a completed trust must be present:

> A trust must be created by clear and unambiguous language or conduct, it cannot arise from elusive statements admitting possible inferences consistent with other relationships.

Id. at 269, quoting *Bair v. Snyder County State Bank*, 314 Pa. 85, 89, 171 A. 274, 275 (1934).

Settling Who the Settlor Is

As in other cases, the focus of the Pennsylvania court's inquiry was the intent of the parties at the time of the alleged creation of the trust by the settlor, Middlesex. In support of its conclusion that Middlesex was the settlor (the entity that has authority to create a trust) and that it had not intended to create a trust, the Pennsylvania court found the following facts determinative:

> The putative settlor in this case was clearly Middlesex. In support of this conclusion we note that the Middlesex church was not a creation or offshoot of the central denomination. Rather, the record establishes that the Middlesex church was created and incorporated on the local level by members of the parish; and that all property was retained in the corporate name of the local church. Subsequently, when the local body voluntarily affiliated with UPCUSA's predecessor, there was no express trust language in the denomination's constitution. Also, it was undisputed that there was never any express trust language in the constitution during the entire period Middlesex remained affiliated with the denomination. In fact, a prior attempt by the predecessor denomination, circa 1929, to include express trust language in the constitution was defeated by the member churches.
>
> The denomination here has cited no evidence that Middlesex ever intended to convey their property interests to them. To the contrary, throughout their entire affiliation Middlesex retained all property in their own corporate name. The commonwealth court's reliance on selected passages from the *Book of Order* was misplaced in that the court ignored the overall intent of that book as a means of overseeing the *spiritual* development of member churches. In addition, these selected provisions, which at most evidence the putative trustee's desired interpretation, are far from constituting the clear unequivocal evidence necessary to support a conclusion that a trust existed.

Beaver-Butler at 269, 270 (emphasis in original).

Neutral Principles Cut Both Ways

In the recent case of *In Re: Church of St. James the Less* [J-18-2005] (decided December 29, 2005), the Pennsylvania Supreme Court (Eastern District) again had an occasion to address the validity of an asserted denominational property trust over local church property. The asserted trust operated in favor of the Diocese of Pennsylvania of the National Episcopal Church. The Pennsylvania Supreme Court cited its earlier decision in *Beaver-Butler, supra,* to apply the neutral principles of law method but, in so doing, reached a conclusion different from that in *Beaver-Butler* – based on the specific facts presented.

The denomination's intent was made plain by its constitution – specifically, the enactment of a new canon in 1979 (referred to as the "Dennis Canon)," which added to the National Episcopal Church constitution the following: "All real and personal property held by or for the benefit of any Parish, Mission or Congregation is held in trust for this [National Episcopal Church] and the Diocese thereof in which such Parish, Mission or Congregation is located."

In assessing the local intent of St. James the Less, the court reviewed, among other things, the congregation's original 1846 charter and actions surrounding its initial adoption, and amendments thereto in 1919 and 1967. After reviewing all pertinent documentation, the Pennsylvania Supreme Court concluded:

> [W]e find that St. James clearly intended to place its property in trust for the Diocese prior to the enactment of the Dennis Canon and consequently, the Dennis Canon does not deprive St. James of its vested property rights. Rather, the Dennis Canon "merely codified in explicit terms a trust relationship" that was implicit in St. James' charter.

In Re: St. James the Less [J-18-2005]–23.

As the court noted in the excerpted passage, the determining issue was language in St. James' own articles of incorporation. According to the text of St. James' articles of incorporation, the local church had expressly prohibited itself from ever disaffiliating from the diocese and the National Episcopal Church, and it further required that St. James always accede to the authority of the National Episcopal Church and the diocese. St. James the Less also declared in its charter that if it ever dissolved, its property would be placed in trust for the diocese.

The court distinguished *Beaver-Butler* by noting that these provisions in St. James' charter were not present in the articles of incorporation of the Middlesex Presbyterian Church and that the Middlesex church had disaffiliated from the national church prior to the effective date of the express trust proviso, which had been added to the denominational constitution then at issue.

Finally, although the Pennsylvania Supreme Court held that a property trust attached to the local church property, it rejected claims by the diocese that it was therefore the legal titleholder to the property. The trustees of St. James retained legal title, but were required to use the property for the benefit of the diocese in keeping with the existence of a trust. Significantly, though, the composition of the local board of trustees, the vestry, was to be determined by the diocese. *In Re: St. James the Less* [J-18-2005] – 24 at n.30.

Texas

Subsequent to the 1979 decision by the U.S. Supreme Court in *Wolf*, not all states have had an occasion to decide whether to adopt the neutral principles of law method in church property cases. Courts only issue opinions and establish governing precedents in response to cases or controversies brought before them, and the decision whether to exercise jurisdiction to accept a civil case for review is a matter usually within the discretion of state supreme courts. Therefore, some states that had adopted the hierarchical/ deference method prior to *Wolf* have not had an occasion since then to revisit the subject.

The Texas Supreme Court generally has been regarded by lower courts in Texas to have adopted the hierarchical method, in *Brown v. Clark*, 102 Tex. 323, 116 S.W. 360 (1909). A careful reading of this seminal decision suggests, however, that the state's lower courts have confused the Texas Supreme Court's treatment of threshold subject matter jurisdiction (absent in matters inherently religious in nature) with its treatment of the method civil courts are to apply when subject matter jurisdiction is exercised. The Texas Supreme Court has not granted writs since 1909 to revisit or clarify the matter, even though lower courts in Texas at times have expressed confusion about the controlling law.

The Hierarchical Method: The Scope of Judicial Review

The Schismatic and Purported Casa Linda Presbyterian Church in America, et al v. The Grace Union Presbytery, Inc., et al, 710 S.W.2nd 700 (Court of Appeals of Texas, Dallas) (decided April 18, 1986) is the most recent Texas appellate decision[11] citing the controlling Texas Supreme Court case, *Brown v. Clark*, *supra*, to properly require deference to the church hierarchy as an expression of the court's lack of threshold subject matter jurisdiction on issues deemed religious or ecclesiastical. Anticipating the U.S. Supreme Court's decision in *Jones v. Wolf*, 443 U.S. 595 (1979) by 70 years, *Brown* did exercise jurisdiction on other designated issues and applied the neutral principles method (without calling it such by name) to the property trust issue (characterized as a "non-ecclesiastical" issue by the court in *Grace Union* at 706). *Brown*, using the same factors that other courts use when applying the neutral principles method, concluded that no trust, express or implied, existed over the local church property then at issue. On the separate issue of ownership, the body to be correctly identified as the one to whom the property originally had been deeded, the court in *Grace Union* interpreted *Brown* to deem ownership an ecclesiastical issue to be decided by deference to the hierarchical church.[12] There is reason, though, to dispute *Grace Union's* interpretation of *Brown* on this point.

Brown involved the reunion between two Presbyterian denominations, the Cumberland Presbyterian Church and the Presbyterian Church of the United States of America (for convenience referred to as the "Presbyterian Church" and the "Cumberland Church"). The two denominations merged after the general assemblies of each found no impediment. Thereafter,

---

11 Writs were denied in *Grace Union*, and no other appellate decisions on this issue have yet been accepted for review by the Texas Supreme Court. Thus, *Grace Union* is the most recent word from the Texas courts.

12 Texas law, however, does not give a presbytery *cart blanche* on ownership determinations. A presbytery's discretion seemingly may be unfettered under G-8.0601 of the *Book of Order* of the Presbyterian Church (USA), but not under Texas case law. Under limited circumstances, civil courts have subject matter jurisdiction to review ownership determinations made by hierarchical religious organizations. "The civil courts can grant relief from such decisions only if, by the narrowest kind of review, they are found to have resulted from fraud, collusion or arbitrariness." *Presbytery of the Covenant v. Presbyterian Church of Paris*, 552 S.W.2d 865 (Tex. Civ. App. – Texarkana 1977, ____ writ), citing *Gonzalez v. Roman Catholic Archbishop*, 280 U.S. 1, 50 S.Ct. 5, 74 L.Ed. 131; *Presbyterian Church v. Blue Hull Church*, 390 U.S. 440, 89 S.Ct. 601, 21 L.Ed.2d 658. But see *Serbian Eastern Orthodox Diocese for the United States of America v. Milivojevich*, 426 U.S. 696 (1976), decided prior to *Presbytery of the Covenant*, but subsequent to *Blue Hill Church*. In *Milivojevich*, the U.S. Supreme Court eliminated "arbitrariness" as a basis for civil court review of ecclesiastical decisions. If civil courts inquired into whether an ecclesiastical body complied with its own regulations, it would encroach upon religious matters of internal organization and ecclesiastical rule, custom or law. Nevertheless, civil courts in hierarchical states retain subject matter jurisdiction to determine whether an ecclesiastical body acted "in bad faith for secular purposes." *Milivojevich* at 712-713.

dissenting members of the Cumberland Church's General Assembly who opposed the reunion filed suit to contest its validity and to contest the claim that the reunion had the effect of transferring possession of the local church property to a new session said to represent the Presbyterian Church. Those who opposed the reunion and who were seeking to have the property restored to their possession complained that no merger could properly have been made because of alleged doctrinal differences between the two denominations.

Brown held that the civil courts were without subject matter jurisdiction to decide the questions of alleged doctrinal differences, so the civil court was without authority to decide whether the reunion was legitimate. Deference on this issue must be given to the denomination. Similarly, the court in *Brown* held that civil courts lacked subject matter over another issue – whether the General Assembly of the Cumberland Church had the authority under its denominational constitution to consummate the reunion between it and the Presbyterian Church. In holding that the Cumberland Church's General Assembly had the authority to consummate the union, such that it was binding on its member churches, *Brown* said that "whenever the questions of discipline or of faith or ecclesiastical rule, custom, or law have been decided by the highest of these church judicatories to which the matter has been carried, the legal tribunals must accept such decisions as final, and as binding on them, in their application to the case before them." *Brown* at 332 citing *Watson v. Jones* 80 U.S. 679 (1871).

Brown concluded from the provisions of the Cumberland constitution that the General Assembly of the Cumberland Church had the authority to determine whether it had the power to enter into union with the Presbyterian Church and, having so decided that it had such authority and having so acted upon that authority, "the civil courts have no power to review that action." *Brown* at 333, citing *Watson*. The General Assembly of the Cumberland Church had "exclusive jurisdiction of the question, and, having decided it, there is no ground for action by this court." *Brown* at 334.

Left for decision, however, was the effect the merger had on local church property – was that a matter of a religious or ecclesiastical nature, concerning which civil courts have no subject matter jurisdiction? If, on the other hand, it was a matter concerning which civil courts had jurisdiction, what rule or method should the courts follow in reaching a decision? The court in *Brown* held that it had jurisdiction to address property issues. This topic apparently was carved out of the class of topics, ecclesiastical and religious, that require deference to hierarchical church authority for lack of threshold subject matter jurisdiction by civil courts. "This is perhaps the only question in the case of which this court has jurisdiction." *Brown* at 334.

As for the *method* to be used by the civil court in reaching a decision on the question of a property trust, the court in *Brown*, without calling the method it used "neutral principles" by name, nevertheless considered the kind of factors that courts consider under a neutral principles approach. The court in *Brown* examined the language in the property deeds to see to whom the property had been titled. It also examined the property deeds to determine whether there was any trust or limitation placed upon the title. It examined who paid for the property. It then concluded that no trust attached to the property and that the titleholder to whom the property originally had been deeded still owned the property.

The question then became which competing session was to be identified with the local church to which the property originally had been deeded and, thus, was still the owner? By what method were state courts, in the proper exercise of their subject matter jurisdiction, to follow in deciding this separate issue of ownership?

The court in *Brown* did not clearly say. The *Brown* court merely noted that because the General Assembly of the Cumberland Church had the authority to authorize reunion with the Presbyterian Church, this had the legal effect of incorporating the former into the latter. As a result, the session representing the latter became the rightful successor-in-title for property that originally had been deeded to trustees of the former. *Brown* at 334, 335. This rationale seems to follow neutral principles, but happened to result in concurrence with (deference to?) the ownership determination made by the Presbyterian Church hierarchy.

Confusion at the Court

Turning again to the 1986 Texas appellate court decision in *Grace Union*, the court in *Grace Union* relied on *Brown* and correctly characterized the issue of property ownership or title in *Brown* as a "non-ecclesiastical issue" (i.e., an issue concerning which civil court had subject matter jurisdiction). *Grace Union* at 706. The court in *Grace Union* then interpreted *Brown*, however, as having adopted the hierarchical approach ("the deference rule") for all matters, including the identity of the title owner. "Our state law requires deference to the Presbytery's identity of appellees, the loyal group." *Grace Union* at 707.

In this aspect of its ruling, it is respectfully suggested that the court in *Grace Union* confused two separate issues. *Brown* properly held that civil courts do not have subject matter jurisdiction to address questions whose answers are religious. In such circumstances, deference must be given to religious organizations to decide matters that are inherently and uniquely religious in nature. But the court's recognition that at times it should defer to a hierarchical religious organization because the court lacks subject matter jurisdiction does not automatically lead to or compel the conclusion that, when that court does have subject matter jurisdiction, it should adopt the hierarchical method/deference rule. There is a very strong argument to be made that the Texas Supreme Court did not do this in *Brown*, notwithstanding the assertion to the contrary in *Grace Union*.

Some of the other Texas appellate court decisions on church property issues decided since 1909 also exhibit confusion (as acknowledged by at least one Texas court) or rely on pre-*Wolf* case law from other states. In *Presbytery of the Covenant v. First Presbyterian Church of Paris*, 552 S.W.2d 865 (Tex. Civ.App.-Texarkana 1977, no writ), "the court purported to apply neutral principles of law in the mistaken belief that the *Hull* decision required their application (but) in fact applied the deference rule in reaching its decision." *Grace Union* at 705, commenting on *Presbytery of the Covenant* (parentheses added).

ALL IN THE NAME

Presbytery of the Covenant involved a split between two factions of a Presbyterian Church in the United States' congregation in Paris, Texas. Significantly, the Paris congregation's articles of incorporation referred to it by denominational affiliation – "The First Presbyterian Church U.S. of Paris, Inc." – and all of the property deeds referred to a denominational affiliation, naming the property owner either as the "First Presbyterian Church of Paris U.S." or the corporation "First Presbyterian Church U.S. of Paris, Inc."

The court exercised subject matter jurisdiction to decide the question of ownership and applied the hierarchical method, deferring to the presbytery's decision to award ownership to the loyalist faction – even though the vote to disaffiliate from the PCUS was *unanimous* and taken at a properly noticed meeting. As the primary authority for applying the hierarchical method to determine questions of church property ownership, the court in *Presbytery of the Covenant* cited the Texas appellate case of *Norton v. Green* (discussed below) which, in turn, relied on the suggested misreading of *Brown*.

The court in *Presbytery of the Covenant* noted that while the vote to disaffiliate was unanimous as to those in attendance at the meeting, it was not unanimous as to those on the active membership roll of the church. Oddly, the court brushed aside the denomination's own internal rules to reach a result favorable to the denomination. The court further noted that even if it was conceded that the local church owned its property and was free to dispose of it as it wished, the loyalist faction rather than the 100 percent that voted to disaffiliate constituted the local church when: a) the titleholder of record in the property deeds was the "First Presbyterian Church of Paris U.S." or the "First Presbyterian Church U.S. of Paris, Inc." and; b) the PCUS hierarchy recognized and identified the loyalist faction as being that church. *Presbytery of the Covenant* at 871, 872.

Presbytery of the Covenant also is striking because of how the court disposed of representations that had been made by the presbytery to the congregation. Prior to the split, the presbytery apparently had told the Paris church that the local church "owned its property and could make such disposition thereof as it desired." The disaffiliating members argued in court that the presbytery was therefore precluded or estopped from contesting disaffiliation-with-property. The court rejected that argument, however, and held that the presbytery's representations were made to "The First Presbyterian Church of Paris, U.S." and, thus, only could benefit that church recognized by the PCUS hierarchy as constituting that particular church – i.e., the loyalist faction. *Presbytery of the Covenant* at 872.

Identity Determines Ownership

In *Norton v. Green*, 304 S.W.2d 420 (Tex.Civ.App.-Waco 1957, writ ref'd n.r.e.), the court was not presented with the issue of whether a valid and enforceable trust existed but, rather, the separate matter of ownership. The controversy involved two factions of the North Ridge Presbyterian Church of Dallas, then a member of the Presbyterian Church in the United States (PCUS). No express trust language was added to the PCUS constitution until 1982. By a vote of 159 to 83, the North Ridge congregation voted to disaffiliate from the PCUS and took possession of the local church property. The minority who remained loyal to the PCUS brought suit against the disaffiliating group, seeking to be adjudicated as the lawful congregation of "North Ridge Presbyterian Church, PCUS" and to be adjudicated the church building and other property owned by "North Ridge Presbyterian Church, PCUS" as of the date the defendants withdrew from the denomination.

The court in *Norton* exercised subject matter jurisdiction to decide the question of identity – which of the factions was the representative and successor to the local church as it existed prior to the division or schism. In answering this question, the court followed the hierarchical method, deferring to the decision by the hierarchical religious body. This question of identity "is determined by which of the two factions adhere to or is sanctioned by the appropriate governing body of the denomination. It is a question of identity."

Norton at 425, citing a 1956 South Carolina decision; *Bramlett v. Young*, 229 S.C. 519, 93 S.E.2d 873, 883; and the 1909 Texas Supreme Court decision in *Brown*.[13] As previously noted, though, the Texas Supreme Court in *Brown* effectively followed neutral principles of law to resolve the property trust issue, and the property ownership in *Brown* seemingly was decided by following a neutral principles rationale whose result coincided with the denomination's property ownership decision.

Ten Percent Falls Short

In *Browning v. Burton,* 273 S.W.2d 131 (Tex.Civ.App.-Austin 1954, writ ref'd n.r.e.), a dispute arose between two factions of a local African Methodist Episcopal Church in which 40 members of a 390-member congregation withdrew from the AME church and purported to transfer title to the church property. The court rejected the minority claim on a two-fold basis: first, that the trustees were not authorized to transfer the church property because the transfer had not been approved by a quarterly conference and by conference trustees as set forth in the AME *Book of Discipline;* and, second, the 40 members "by their withdrawal could not destroy the identity of the local church and could not take the properties of that church with them into an independent organization."

It is difficult to determine in *Browning* whether the court followed neutral principles or the hierarchical method. The court rested its decision in part on the provisions of the denominational constitution, but also discussed at length various factors considered by the courts when following neutral principles of law. Whatever method can be said to have been followed, though, the facts in *Browning* are unique: a minority faction of little more than 10 percent seeking to remove itself from the majority and take the church property with them.[14]

---

13 The pre-*Wolf* cases from other states on which Texas appellate courts have relied in part are: *Bramlett v. Young*, 229 S.C. 519, 93 S.E.2d 873 (1956); *Adickes v. Adkins*, 264 S.C. 394, 215 S.E.2d 442 (1975); *St. John's Presbytery v. Central Presbyterian Church*, Fla. 1958, 102 So.2d 714; *Cumberland Presbyterian Church v. North Red Bank Cumberland Presbyterian Church*, 58 Tenn. App. 424, 430 S.W.2d 879 (1968); and *Fairmount Presbyterian Church v. Presbytery of Holston*, 531 S.W.2d 301 (Tenn. App. 1975).

14 The only other post-*Brown* appellate decision on church property in Texas is *Cussen v. Lynch*, 245 S.W. 932 (Tex.Civ.App.-Amarillo 1922, no writ). The plaintiff was the bishop of the Roman Catholic Church for the Diocese of Dallas, to which title to the local parish property was vested. The defendant was the local parish priest, whom the bishop had suspended from pastoral ministry and ordered to enter a monastery. The defendant refused to go and refused to deliver possession of the parish property, whereupon the bishop

Notwithstanding the indicated misreading of *Brown* by Texas appellate courts, the weight of Texas intermediate appellate authority is that Texas courts are to follow the hierarchical method. Any clarification or reconsideration of the hierarchical method or broader adoption of neutral principles must be made, if at all, by the Texas Supreme Court. Until that court does, it is axiomatic that the lower courts in Texas are bound to follow the ruling of the Texas Supreme Court. This begs the question, though, of whether the Texas Supreme Court in *Brown* did, in fact, adopt the hierarchical method/deference rule for all purposes.[15]

---

brought suit in trespass. The issue presented in *Cussen* was simply whether the bishop had the right under Catholic Canon Law to suspend the priest and whether the proceedings leading to such a suspension were regular. The court answered "yes" to both questions.

15 Just as there appears to be confusion about what *Brown* actually held, there also are differing views about what *Watson v. Jones* (the case on which *Brown* relied) held. *Watson* usually is cited for the proposition that the hierarchical approach/deference rule is permissible for adoption by states and applicable in adopting states to all matters that might arise in a hierarchical church. The U.S. Supreme Court, however, subsequently characterized *Watson* with greater nuance: "Indeed, even in *Watson v. Jones*, a common-law decision heavily relied upon by the dissent, Mr. Justice Miller, speaking for the Court, stated that, regardless of the form of church government, it would be the "obvious duty" of the civil tribunal to enforce the "express terms" of the deed, will, or other instrument of church property ownership." *Jones v. Wolf* at 603, n.3., citing *Watson*, 13 Wall, at 722-723, 20 L.Ed. 666.

EDITOR'S NOTE

The next three chapters take turns examining matters of particular interest to Presbyterians, Methodists and Episcopalians.

Each chapter, however, contains information not only specific to the particular denomination being discussed, but also contains analysis and examples whose value crosses denominational lines.

Therefore, regardless of denominational affiliation, readers will benefit from all of the chapters.

CHAPTER FOUR

CONSIDERATIONS SPECIFIC TO PRESBYTERIANS

The preceding discussion of case law provides a necessary lens through which denominational trust and ownership clauses, and property-related documents and actions of particular churches, can be viewed with understanding.

This chapter focuses on the provisions of the Presbyterian Church (USA) *Book of Order* and the constitutions of its predecessor denominations. For illustrative purposes, neutral principles of law are applied to the documents and actions of a hypothetical, local Presbyterian church. The question of whether a property trust is essential to "Presbyterian connectionalism" also is examined.

The Denominational Provisions

Fictional "Maple Street Presbyterian Church of Memphis, Tennessee," previously affiliated with the Presbyterian Church in the United States (PCUS), became a member of the Presbyterian Church (USA) in 1983 upon the creation of that body when the PCUS (the "southern church") merged with the United Presbyterian Church in the United States of America (UPCUSA) (the "northern church"). The constitution of the newly-merged PC (USA) consists of two parts, a *Book of Confessions* and a *Book of Order*. The *Book of Order* itself divides into three main sections: the Form of Government, the Directory of Worship, and the Rules of Discipline. Provisions relating to property are found in Chapter VIII of the Form of Government, G-8.000 – G-8.0700.[1]

1 Numbered subparts in each main section are preceded by the letter G, W or D that correspond to the main section in which they are found.

The PC(USA) *Book of Order*

G-8.0201 contains a much-discussed express trust clause:

> All property held by or for a particular church, presbytery, a synod, the General Assembly, or the Presbyterian Church (U.S.A.), whether legal title is lodged in a corporation, a trustee or trustees, or an unincorporated association, and whether the property is used in programs of a particular church or of a more inclusive governing body or retained for the production of income, is held in trust nevertheless for the use and benefit of the Presbyterian Church U.S.A.

This provision, and similar provisions in other denominational constitutions, *if legally enforceable against a particular church*, would require permission from the regional ecclesiastical body (presbytery, conference or diocese) before a local congregation could disaffiliate with its property intact.

G-8.0202 goes on to say that, whenever permitted by civil law, the denomination shall cause a corporation to be formed and maintained. Significantly, this provision does not specify any required language to be included in local church articles of incorporation or property deeds, such as provisos mirroring the trust language in G-8.0201.

G-8.0301 pertains to disaffiliation. It provides that when a local church ceases to be a particular church of the PC (USA), its property shall be "held, used, applied, transferred, or sold as provided by the Presbytery."

G-8.0400 pertains to dissolution or extinction. It provides that when a particular church is formally dissolved by the presbytery or for other reasons ceases to exist, the disposition of its property is to be determined by the presbytery.

G-8.0501 states that written permission by the presbytery is required before a particular church can sell, mortgage or otherwise encumber any of its real property or acquire real property subject to any encumbrance or condition.

G-8.0600 contains the denomination's ecclesiastical mechanism for determining ownership of property, although elsewhere the *Book of Order* requires local churches to incorporate – and the civil laws of the state of incorporation may stipulate a different method for determining ownership. G-8.0600 states that in the event of a split ("schism") within a particular church, the presbytery shall determine which faction is the true church within the PC (USA) and, thus, entitled to the property. In making this determination, the presbytery is not bound by whichever faction receives the majority vote within the particular church at the time of a split.

G-8.0700 provides that no particular church of the PC (USA) shall be bound by any of the foregoing provisions if it was not previously subject to a similar provision in the denomination of which it was a part before the creation of the PC (USA) – so long as that congregation, within a period of eight years following the establishment of the PC (USA), votes to exempt itself from such a provision following a prescribed procedure. In the event a particular church follows the prescribed manner and votes in a timely manner to exempt itself, it will be subject to the property ownership provisions "of the Constitution to which it was subject immediately prior to the establishment of the Presbyterian Church (USA)." [In the hypothetical case to be discussed below, Maple Street Presbyterian Church voted in a timely manner to fall back on the dissimilar property provisions in the constitution of the denomination with which it formerly had been affiliated.]

The Articles of Agreement

Before turning to the provisions of the constitution under which Maple Street Presbyterian Church was subject prior to the establishment of the PC (USA), a brief review of the Articles of Agreement is appropriate. These are the transitional provisions governing the merger of the PCUS and UPCUSA into the PC (USA) (reproduced in the PC (USA) *Book of Order*). The provisions pertaining to property ownership are found in Article 13.

Article 13.2 states that for a period of 18 months following the "consummation of union" (the effective date of the creation of the PC (USA)), the permission of the General Assembly is required before a congregation can be dismissed from the denomination. Article 13.3 states that after a year has passed from the consummation of union, a congregation formerly part of the PCUS (the southern church) may be dismissed without the permission of the General Assembly provided that certain procedural requirements are satisfied, including a two-thirds vote of those congregation members present and voting. Neither Article 13.2 nor 13.3 specifically refers to property, but Article 13.1 says that the provisions of Article 13 are not intended to alter or abridge any property ownership principles in either the PCUS, UPCUSA or PC (USA) as established by ecclesiastical or civil law. Finally, Article 13.4 states that after eight years from the consummation of union, "any petition for dismissal with property" shall be handled "under the appropriate provisions for such a request in the Form of Government." (See generally, G-11.0103i and G-11.0103y of the PC (USA) *Book of Order*.)

Life Before the PC(USA)

Turning now to the provisions of the 1982/1983 PCUS *Book of Church Order* (the constitution to which Maple Street was subject immediately prior to the consummation of union), it contains several new provisions – adopted in the wake of *Wolf* – not found in the 1980-1981 edition, or earlier editions, of the PCUS *Book of Church Order*.[2] Unlike the 1982/1983 edition, the 1980-81 edition does *not* contain any express language that says the property of the local church is held in trust for the denomination. Although the denominational provisions that apply under the facts presented by fictional Maple Street Presbyterian Church are those that existed in 1982, it nevertheless is worth examining predecessor editions of the PCUS *Book of Church Order*. Under neutral principles, courts are to look at everything relevant in determining the intent and expectations of the parties. The longstanding assumptions and legal understandings of generations of Presbyterians prior to 1982, therefore, may be relevant.

The PC (USA), newly formed in 1983, contains an express trust clause in its constitution (G-8.0201). In their long histories, however, the two denominations that merged to form the PC (USA) never had an express trust clause in their constitutions – until they were amended on the eve of the 1983 merger (after the U.S. Supreme Court's 1979 decision in *Wolf*). At the time of the merger, rank and file Presbyterians for generations had been accustomed to denominational life *without* the assertion by the denomination of an express trust over local property in favor of the denomination. When the new 1983 PC (USA) constitution granted to congregations the option of voting to fall back on dissimilar property provisions of their former constitutions, therefore, it is reasonable to assume that there was a belief by many that, by so voting, their congregation would avoid the express assertion of a trust. Many likely were unaware that the constitutions of the denominations to which they were subject immediately prior to merger had, on the cusp of the merger, been amended to include trust language. Ignorance of the newly confected

2 Because our hypothetical case study involves a local church in Tennessee, this analysis focuses on the provisions of the constitution of the Presbyterian Church in the United States. An informative textual analysis of the constitution of the United Presbyterian Church in the United States of America could be performed for churches that formerly were affiliated with it. For the purposes of this case study, it is assumed that Tennessee is a neutral principles state. Whether the text of the PCUS constitution, the UPCUSA constitution or the PC (USA) constitution is relevant, none automatically are deferred to by civil courts applying neutral principles of law. However, determining which constitution is relevant to a particular church may have a bearing on issues of intent and validity.

trust clauses was compounded by uncertainty over their meaning due to the ambiguous language in some portions of the new clauses.

Section 6-2 of Chapter 6 of the PCUS *Book of Church Order,* as it existed in 1980-81, only provides that the local charter and bylaws may give to the officers of the local church corporation responsibility for "the buying, selling, and mortgaging of the property for the church, the acquiring and conveying title to such property, the holding and defending title to the same … provided that such duties do not infringe upon the powers and duties of the session or of the board of deacons. In buying, selling and mortgaging real property such officers shall act solely under the authority of the corporation, granted in a duly constituted meeting of the corporation." This much is clear: No trust language is present.

The next section, 6-3, in that same edition also appears consistent with the absence of a trust. It states that only in the event that a local church ceases to exist, such as when dissolved by the presbytery, "and no disposition has been made of its property, those who hold the title to the property shall deliver it, convey and transfer to the Presbytery … all property of the church. …" In sum, *prior* to the 1982-83 amendments, the PCUS *Book of Church Order* did not contain an express trust clause in favor of the denomination.

The 1982/1983 edition of the PCUS constitution, the last edition prior to the merger, is markedly different, and confusing. Section 6.2 of that edition newly provided that the officers of the local corporation may be given responsibility for "holding title to church property for the benefit of the corporation *and the Presbyterian Church in the United States. …*" The former Section 6.3 was rewritten and designated 6-4, and a new Section 6.3 containing express trust language was added to the that edition. That language states, "All property held by or for a particular church … is held in trust nevertheless for the use and benefit of the Presbyterian Church in the United States." The rewritten Section 6-4 states that in the event that a local church ceases to exist or is dissolved by the presbytery – or attempts to withdraw from the PCUS – any local church property shall be under the control of the presbytery and sold or disposed of at the discretion of the presbytery.[3] The new Section 6.7 in the 1982/83 edition provides that, notwithstanding the new trust language, a presbytery may exercise its discretion to dismiss a local church with its property, subject to the request being made in proper order.

3 This latter provision parallels G-8.0401 of the PC (USA) *Book of Order*, just as the newly added Section 6-3 in the 82/83 PCUS *Book of Church Order* finds a parallel in G-8.0201 in the PC (USA) *Book of Order*. The new Section 6-5 (pertaining to a local church split) was added to the 1982/83 edition and finds a parallel with the text of G-8.0601 in the PC (USA) *Book of Order*.

Interestingly, in addition to the other new sections, the new Section 6-8 in the 1982/83 edition provides that a particular church can buy, sell or mortgage its property, acting in its capacity as a member of the PCUS, *without* the permission of the presbytery or any other church court. The new section 6-8, however, is to be construed together with whatever uncertain effect might be given to the newly added trust language. If a trust is asserted under these provisions, the new Section 6-8 may only mean that there is an obligation by the local congregation/seller, acting as trustee, to give an account of the proceeds to the trust beneficiary.

The 1982/83 amendments to the PCUS *Book of Church Order* are not a model of clarity. Its trust provisions are substantially different from those found in G-8.0201 of the PC (USA) *Book of Order*, which is not surprising. If there were no significant differences, the option given in the PC (USA) *Book of Order* to opt out and fall back on Chapter 6 of the PCUS *Book of Church Order* would be meaningless. Unlike Chapter VIII of the PC (USA) *Book of Order*, Chapter 6 of the PCUS *Book of Church Order* has not one but three trust provisos: 6-1, 6-2 and 6-3. And unlike 6-3, which asserts a trust only in favor of the denomination, 6-1 and 6-2 both state that the particular church holds title to its property in trust both for the benefit of the particular church ("the corporation" in 6-2) *and* the denomination. While asserting the creation of a trust simultaneously in favor of both the local church and the denomination may have been politically palatable or expedient as a legislative compromise, it makes no logical or legal sense. A trust in favor of the local church and a trust in favor of the denomination, over the same property, are mutually exclusive propositions.

Sections 6-1, 6-2 and 6-3 were all enacted at the same time. Using ordinary rules of statutory and grammatical construction, each must be construed in some manner that gives meaning to all. Inasmuch as 6-1 and 6-2 collectively cover both unincorporated and incorporated local churches, 6-3 seems redundant – except that in addition to covering property held not only *by* a particular church (as does 6-1 and 6-2), it also covers property held *for* a particular church. Put another way, for property for which title is held *by* a particular church, 6-1 and 6-2 assert a trust in favor of both the local church *and* the denomination (whatever that means). However, 6-3 asserts a trust only for the benefit of the denomination, applicable to property held by or for a particular church. Thus, if one were to lay 6-3 on top of 6-1 and 6-2 in an overlapping grid, the only thing that 6-3 appears to add is a trust in favor of the denomination *only*, for property held *for* a particular church. While 6-3 also includes property held by a particular church, 6-1 and 6-2 already provide for a trust for such property – but one that runs in favor of the local church just as much as in favor of the denomination.

It bears reminding that irrespective of how Chapter 6 of the PCUS *Book of Church Order* is interpreted – or which denominational constitution is relevant to a particular church – the application of neutral principles of law makes clear that the text of the denominational constitution does not alone determine the question of local church property control. All relevant documents, including local articles of incorporation, property deeds, various session, vestry, or administrative board minutes and resolutions, and congregational minutes and resolutions, must be examined to determine the mutual intent of the parties.

Express Versus Implied

The foregoing discussion has focused on the presence or absence of *express* trust language in Presbyterian constitutions. A separate question is whether, in the absence of express trust language, an *implied* trust in favor of the denomination nevertheless is to be read between the lines.

The potential presence of an implied trust was the subject of national debate when the 1982/1983 amendments to the PCUS *Book of Church Order* were being considered. Denominational officials invoked theological arguments to support the view that the proposed new trust language only expressed that which already was implied. Others argued that the addition of express trust language constituted a radical departure from traditional understanding. During the debate, advocates for the existence of a pre-existing, implied trust relied on theological doctrines concerning church unity, the organic nature of the church and the consequent, connectional nature of Presbyterian governance. Those opposed, in favor of historic local church autonomy on local church property matters, cited longstanding language in deeds and articles of incorporation, the acquisition of property or construction with local funds only, and that presbyteries were first formed by individual congregations.

The historical record of pre-1983 General Assembly actions seems to include support for both sides of this implied trust issue, leaving the matter uncertain insofar as a nationally uniform rule. In effect, a legislative truce was tacitly declared, and this potentially volatile matter was left to varying outcomes determined by the differing laws of the several states and the facts of individual cases.

The question of whether an implied trust existed under the pre-1982 PCUS *Book of Church Order* in favor of the denomination arose tangentially in two U.S. Supreme Court decisions, *Presbyterian Church v. Mary Elizabeth*

Blue Hull Memorial Church and *Jones v. Wolf, supra*, and the question in both cases ultimately was decided by the state law of Georgia. In *Hull*, decided in 1969, two local churches in Savannah, Georgia, both members of the PCUS, sought to disaffiliate from the national church. The Georgia trial court ruled in favor of the local church, holding that an implied trust of the local church property existed for the benefit of the national church, as provided by a Georgia statute, but that, in accordance with that statute, the trust terminated upon the jury's finding that the national church had departed from original doctrine.

This decision was affirmed by the Georgia Supreme Court, whereupon the PCUS appealed to the U.S. Supreme Court. The nation's highest court reversed the Georgia court's ruling on the basis that the First Amendment's establishment clause did not permit civil courts to award church property on the basis of the interpretation or significance the civil court assigned to church doctrines. The matter then was remanded back to the Georgia Supreme Court for further proceedings consistent with the U.S. Supreme Court's ruling.

Before proceeding to discuss what happened when the case was returned to the Georgia Supreme Court, it is significant to note that the existence of an implied trust, as initially determined by the Georgia trial court, did *not* rest on any provision of the PCUS Constitution. Rather, it rested on the text of Georgia Code Ann § 22-408 (subsequently found by the U.S. Supreme Court to be unconstitutional), which provided that, "A trust [in favor of the general church] is conditioned upon the general church's adherence to its tenets of faith and practice existing when the local church affiliated with it. …" *Hull* at 445 n. 3.

What then happened in *Hull*, on remand from the U.S. Supreme Court back to the Georgia Supreme Court, is explained in the U.S. Supreme Court's subsequent decision in 1979 in *Jones v. Wolf*. *Wolf* involved a local church in Macon, Georgia, that had decided to disaffiliate from the PCUS. In the process of announcing that the neutral principles of law method was a constitutionally permissible means of adjudicating church property disputes, the U.S. Supreme Court in *Wolf* reviewed the prior case law and noted that, on remand in *Hull*, the Georgia Supreme Court had concluded that without the departure-from-doctrine element, the implied trust theory would have to be abandoned in its entirety. *Wolf* at 600, citing *Presbyterian Church v. Eastern Heights Church*, 225 Ga. 259, 167 SE 2d 658 (1969) (Presbyterian Church II).

The Georgia Supreme Court on remand applied the neutral principles of law method and examined the deeds to the disputed property, Georgia state statutes of the time dealing with implied trusts, and the PCUS *Book of*

Church Order. After this review, the Georgia Supreme Court found "nothing that would give rise to a trust in any of these documents. …" *Jones v. Wolf*, 443 U.S. 595, at 600, quoting *Hull* on remand, *Presbyterian Church v. Eastern Heights Church*, 225 Ga. 259, 167 SE 2d 658 (1969) (Presbyterian Church II).

Thus, the Georgia Supreme Court eventually awarded the property on the basis of legal title to the local church. The PCUS again sought further review by the U.S. Supreme Court, but this time was denied and so the matter in *Hull* concluded. 396 U.S. 1041 (1970).[4]

PRESBYTERIAN CONNECTIONALISM

Before turning to the application of neutral principles to the fictional case study of Maple Street Presbyterian Church, it is worth pausing to examine the contention that a denominational trust clause is "essential to Presbyterian connectionalism." As the Biblical authority for this contention, some have cited Acts 2:44: "All the believers were together and had everything in common, and sold their possessions and goods and divided them among all, as anyone had need." This contention omits from its analysis, however, that this sharing in Acts of worldly goods was voluntary. It was by consent, a voluntary by-product of spiritual unity, not unilaterally asserted and enforced by law. In fact, there never has been any historical consensus on whether denominational control over local church property is essential to Presbyterian connectionalism.

Some clarity can be achieved by pausing to consider what "Presbyterian connectionalism" means. It is a phrase more invoked than defined. It is a concept and, like most concepts, its meaning in specific application can become nebulous and misunderstood. Loosely described, it refers to the common life local Presbyterian churches are to experience together as part of a broader, general church under a Presbyterian form of church governance. Put another way, it refers to a general principle of reciprocal moral obligations. Local Presbyterian churches do not govern themselves autonomously, as congregational churches do. For Presbyterians, church governance is

4 In *Wolf*, the Georgia trial court, following neutral principles, rendered judgment in favor of the local church, a decision that was affirmed by the Georgia Supreme Court. On further review, however, the U.S. Supreme Court vacated that judgment and remanded the case back down to the Georgia Supreme Court. Even though the state court had followed the correct approach (neutral principles), the U.S. Supreme Court said the state court had failed to articulate the grounds for its decision when it determined who represented the local church that was divided into two factions.

characterized by a certain degree of mutual accountability, interconnectedness and covenantal community with other Presbyterian churches in a hierarchical form of government.

Historic Principles

As described in Chapter Two, Presbyterian church government exists somewhere in the middle of the continuum, in between congregationalism at one end of the spectrum and a more authoritarian expression of hierarchical governance represented by the Roman Catholic Church at the other end of the spectrum. This idea of mutual relationship and interconnectedness in Presbyterian polity is embodied in the Historic Principles of Church Government found at G-1.0400 in the PC (USA) *Book of Order*:

> That the several different congregations of believers, taken collectively, constitute one Church of Christ, called emphatically the Church; that a larger part of the Church, or a representation of it, should govern a smaller, or determine matters of controversy which arise therein; that, in like manner, a representation of the whole should govern and determine in regard to every part, and to all the parts united: that is, that a majority shall govern; and consequently that appeals may be carried from lower to higher governing bodies, till they be finally decided by the collected wisdom and the united voice of the whole Church. For these principles and this procedure, the example of the apostles and the practice of the primitive church are considered as authority.

These "Historic Principles" are to govern the *religious* life of the community. The "one Church of Christ" is a spiritual, organic union, not a human organization. Therefore, readers may ask, "What do these 'Historic Principles' have to do with the control of tangible, real property?" The answer, it would appear, is very little. Local congregations – indeed presbyteries, synods and General Assemblies – can exist without ownership of real property. Local churches can and often do meet in homes (like the primitive church); presbyteries can and often do operate from leased office space; General Assemblies convene in rented convention centers. There is no *necessary* connection between the Historic Principles of Church Government and the ownership, and the rights of use incidental to ownership, of real property.

Existing separate from these "Historic Principles" are the civil laws of the state concerning corporations, trusts and real estate.

Historic Facts

The Historic Principles of Church Government date to 1797, when they were adopted by the General Assembly of the Presbyterian Church of the United States of America. That they bear no necessary relationship to issues of local property ownership and use is evidenced in the history of Presbyterian property dispute resolution.

In the Old World and pre-colonial era, Presbyterian property disputes often were resolved by the application of "the English rule;" i.e., the implied trust/departure-from-doctrine rule discussed in Chapter Two. In Scotland, property disputes among Presbyterians concerning the ownership or use of local church property were resolved by awarding the property to the party that the civil authorities determined to be most faithful to the founding doctrines of the Church. See *Craigdallie v. Aikman*, 1 Dow. 1,3 Eng. Rep. 601 H.L. 1813 (Scot), discussed in *Watson v. Jones*, 13 Wall 679, 20 L.Ed. 666 (1872). In the absence of any express trust language, the only implied trust was a trust not in favor of the denomination or the parent church, but in favor of the doctrinally faithful. The ties that were binding were theological – fidelity to a commonly understood faith – and not legal strictures said to arise from an asserted property trust. As previously noted in Chapter Two, however, there was a growing recognition in America that the approach formerly used in the Old World would not transport well to the New World. "The English rule" was difficult to reconcile with the establishment clause of the First Amendment of the United States Constitution and eventually was held to be unconstitutional.

As for the Colonial and Federalist eras, the 1983 Report of the Ad Interim Committee on the Study of the (PCUS) *Book of Church Order* noted that, "... congregational beginnings were diverse, ranging from worship in homes and church buildings owned by individuals to services and structures provided by colonial governments. With the arrival of American independence, Presbyterian church leaders discovered differences among themselves in many matters, including control of property. ... Gradually Presbyterian patterns of ownership evolved, diverse and varied in various states. Confessionally, however, Presbyterians recognized the Church of Christ as 'one body.'" This confession, of course, referred to a house not built of bricks and mortar. Organic union and organizational structure are not the same thing.

It was not until 1925 that the PCUS *Book of Church Order* made any reference to property at all. An attempt to add express trust language to the UPCUSA constitution was rejected by the member churches in 1929. It was not until the early 1980s that both the UPCUSA and the PCUS constitutions were amended to include express trust language.

As for the assertion that an implied trust in favor of the denomination historically characterized Presbyterianism, a review of 19th and 20th century denominational archives discloses intermittent support for both sides of the debate, with no national or uniform resolution. It is significant to note, though, that on both occasions when the assertion of an implied trust in favor of the denomination was civilly adjudicated, state supreme courts in both the North and the South rejected it. As noted in Chapter Three, the Pennsylvania Supreme Court ruled in *Beaver-Butler v. Middlesex Presbyterian Church*, 507 Pa.255, 489 A2nd 1317 (1985) that no trust, express or implied, existed in the UPCUSA or its predecessors prior to May 23, 1981. And, as noted earlier in this chapter, the Georgia Supreme Court, in examining the PCUS Constitution as it existed prior to 1982, reached the same result.

It is certainly possible that, given the facts presented by a particular church, applying neutral principles of law may result in finding that a trust attaches in favor of the denomination. The assertion that in all cases such a trust is essential to Presbyterian connectionalism, however, is supported by scant historical evidence. When some argue, therefore, that a trust clause is "essential to Presbyterian connectionalism," they are clouding the issue rather than clarifying it. Knowingly or unknowingly, they are employing a linguistic device in an effort to persuade. Threatening coercive legal action to enforce an asserted trust over all local property is not a tactic likely to win the hearts of the people. The phrase "Presbyterian connectionalism," however, resonates with a positive connotation. By enlisting this phrase in support of their viewpoint, proponents of a binding, universal property trust would make something that is potentially onerous appear palatable.

Perhaps it is true that the only glue that is keeping some local congregations bound to the PC (USA) is a concern about losing control or use of their local property through confiscatory legal action. If this is the point that proponents of the trust clause wish to make, it should be openly articulated as such and debated on those terms. To instead identify and align this argument with "Presbyterian connectionalism," however, is a misuse of language that devalues the Historic Principles of Church Government.

If a binding trust asserted by the national church in favor of itself over all local church property is essential to Presbyterian connectionalism, it is curious that John Knox, John Calvin and the *Book of Confessions* are silent on the subject. The proposition that such a property trust is essential to what it means to be Presbyterian is belied by the fact that trust language was not added to any Presbyterian constitution for more than 200 years of denominational history in America.

LOCAL CHURCH PROPERTY DOCUMENTS AND ACTIONS

The application by courts of neutral principles of law requires that due consideration be given to all relevant factors, including but not limited to denominational constitutions. Accordingly, as an instructive, hypothetical case study, this section examines documents and actions specific to the fictional "Maple Street Presbyterian Church of Memphis, Tennessee;" e.g., its articles of incorporation, property deeds, the minutes of congregational or session meetings and related resolutions, and any other records that may reflect the intent of the Maple Street congregation. To reiterate, for the sake of this hypothetical case, it is assumed that Tennessee is a "neutral principles" state.

AN INFORMATIVE ILLUSTRATION

Maple Street Presbyterian Church was first formed in 1848 as the first Protestant church in Shelby County, and was incorporated as early as 1880. The terms of that incorporation eventually expired and new articles of incorporation were executed and filed in 1925 (to continue thereafter for 99 years unless dissolved by a two-thirds vote of the congregation). Under the 1925 Maple Street articles of incorporation, it was stated that the corporation was formed because of the "desire to avail themselves of the provisions of the laws of the State relative to the formation of corporations for religious, scientific, literary and charitable purposes and to acquire and enjoy the rights, privileges and powers of a body corporate and politic in law."

Article 2 of the 1925 articles of incorporation states that the object and purpose of the local church corporation is "the worship of Almighty God according to the principles and polity of 'the Presbyterian Church in the United States,' and of the 'Presbytery of Memphis,' of which this church is in connection" (language also found in the 1880 articles). Article 3 goes on to state that the local church corporation shall have the power "… to take, have, and hold all manner of lands, tenements, rents, and hereditaments,[5] and any sum of money, and any manner and portion of goods and chattel given, devised or bequeathed unto it or acquired by it in any manner whatsoever." Article 4 of the charter further provides that "all corporate powers of the Church are vested in the Board of Trustees without the necessity of any

5 Hereditaments. To inherit, from the Latin *hered-, heres;* heritable property.

authorization or ratification of their actions by the congregation." There are, however, certain actions which, by law, require members' (i.e., congregational) approval, such as the sale or transfer of substantially all assets, the amendment of articles, etc.

It is significant that there are no specific provisions expressing or implying that the board of trustees' authority is limited by or subject to any national or regional denominational rules. Article 5 provides that, in the event that the local church corporation ceases to exist and dissolves, then the local congregation shall elect three liquidators "to settle and wind up its affairs." Article 6 concludes by stating that the board of trustees of the local church corporation may adopt whatever bylaws, rules and regulations they deem proper, subject only to the approval of the local congregation.

Although Maple Street's 1925 articles were not set to expire until 2024, due to case law developments and intervening revisions to state corporations statutes, the board of trustees thought it prudent to recommend the adoption of new articles, which then were drafted and adopted in 2004 by the congregation meeting as members of the church corporation. The new 2004 articles are substantially similar in most respects to the 1925 articles but, whereas the former articles made reference to the PCUS, the new articles make no reference to a denomination. The PCUS ceased to exist in 1983 and, since that time, Maple Street's articles had been anachronistic. By omitting denominational reference, it was thought that the new articles would maintain their currency even while Maple Street remained in voluntary affiliation with the PC (USA).

Upon congregational approval, the new articles were recorded with the state corporations office and in the property records of Shelby County. They also were furnished to the Presbytery of Memphis, together with the annual minutes of the session and congregational meetings, as required by G-9.0407 of the PC (USA) *Book of Order*.

As with all of the other many factors under the neutral principles of law approach, no one factor can be assumed determinative by itself on the question of whether a valid trust exists. The language in the property deeds certainly is significant, though, and in our fictional case study the local government assessment records list several assessments in metropolitan Memphis for Maple Street Presbyterian Church on the tax-exempt rolls. Those tracts were acquired in eight different deeds. Six of those deeds pre-date the 1982 addition of held-in-trust language.

None of those acquisition deeds, before or after the addition of held-in-trust language to the denominational constitution, contains any reference to any trust being created or that the property would be held in trust by Maple

Street for the benefit of a national denomination. Subsequent to the addition of denominational trust language in the PCUS and PC (USA) constitutions, Maple Street never filed "corrected" deeds. Though under no legal obligation to revise and file new deeds, the presence or absence of "corrected" deeds may be relevant to the question of intent. Significantly, Maple Street's property deeds list the titleholder only as "Maple Street Presbyterian Church of Memphis, Tennessee Inc." The deeds do not include, list, abbreviate, or otherwise refer to any denominational affiliation in identifying the titleholder.

Maple Street's intent and understanding of the 1982 changes to the PCUS *Book of Church Order* and the subsequent, related PC (USA) trust provisions may be evidenced by actions taken by the congregation in 1985. On May 1 of that year, following the "consummation of union" that established the PC (USA) but prior to the expiration of eight years following that establishment, the congregation timely approved the following resolution:

> ... to be exempt from all the provisions of Chapter VIII of said *Book of Order* of the Presbyterian Church (USA), in order that it may continue to hold title to all of its property and exercise its privileges of incorporation and property ownership, as provided in the *Book of Church Order* of the Presbyterian Church of the United States that is set forth therein in Chapter 6 prior to the establishment of the Presbyterian Church (USA).

Text of (fictional) property resolution approved at the May 1, 1985 Maple Street congregational meeting. The minutes of this congregational meeting reflect congregational uncertainty over what the PCUS intended by Chapter 6 but left it clear what the congregation intended in adopting the foregoing resolution. The minutes state:

> Elder Jones explained at the time of consummation of union all churches were given the option for eight (8) years to have the congregation vote if they wished for local church property to remain in control of the local church or have the property in control of the denomination as outlined in the new PC (USA) *Book of Order*. Elder Jones stated that the session was recommending that the congregation vote to retain its property under local control.
>
> Following a second and discussion, the congregation voted unanimously to approve the resolution. The minutes

were signed by the senior minister and the clerk of the session and subsequently submitted to the Presbytery of Memphis.[6]

The Application of Neutral Principles of Law

Civil courts following neutral principles of law are to consider both sides of the coin when asked to resolve church property disputes. On one side of the coin are denominational documents whose examination, without regard to other considerations, would lead readers to conclude that "held-in-trust" language is to be given effect. The official position of the PC (USA) attaches great weight to this denominational side of the coin. The denomination has prepared "The Legal Resource Manual for Presbyterian Church (USA) Middle Governing Bodies and Churches 2000-2003," which outlines its viewpoint.[7] This manual emphasizes the held-in-trust language in the PC (USA) constitution and advises local congregations to acknowledge denominational ownership of local church property. It suggests the preferred text for local church property deeds while also asserting that, in the absence of express trust language in property deeds, "secular courts have upheld the right of denominational units to succeed to the title on the implied trust theory. …"

Manual Operation

The manual lists factors that it says have been held determinative by civil courts in resolving property disputes: language in prior conveyances of property titles; the use of the name, customs, or polity of the PC (USA) such that the congregation in question becomes known in the community as a member church of the PC (USA); service in the congregation by a PC (USA)-ordained minister member of the presbytery; activity by the local congregation within the presbytery, such as participating in presbytery meetings; and

---

6 The text of the hypothetical 1985 property resolution and the hypothetical minutes of the May 1, 1985, Maple Street congregational meeting may be susceptible to differing interpretations. It may be argued, compellingly, that the text and minutes clearly indicate that the congregation of Maple Street understood that Chapter 6 of the 1982/83 PCUS *Book of Church Order* (immediately prior to the establishment of the PC (USA)) authorized local congregations to exercise full control over local church property without any trust – consistent with what arguably always had been the case before, where no express trust language had existed in the PCUS constitution and where no implied trust existed. See discussion of *Hull* and *Wolf, supra*. Those who oppose disaffiliation with property, however, may argue that the resolution and minutes only reflect an intent to invoke the language (whatever its meaning) of the held-in-trust provisos added to the 1982/83 PCUS *Book of Church Order*.

7 Located at www.pcusa.org/legal.

funding provided to the local congregation by the presbytery for the purchase of property or construction upon it.

The manual's list of factors is selective. Omitted is mention of several additional factors that courts have relied on when not giving effect to held-in-trust clauses and authorizing local congregations to disaffiliate with property, such as those factors noted in *Hull*, *Wolf*, *St. Luke's*, and *From the Heart*. The manual properly recognizes, though, that not all state courts have upheld denominational trust clauses, and offers the important caveat that, "Almost all property matters are governed by state law. ..." The manual further states that a state-by-state compendium of legal resources to be used by counsel for presbyteries seeking to enforce the held-in-trust language is in the process of being compiled by the denomination's legal staff.[8] The manual states that some denominational funds are available to underwrite, in part, presbyteries' costs in civil litigation involving title to church property. No amount is given.

While recognizing the existence of state court decisions that have not upheld denominational trust clauses, the manual asserts that those rulings do not give proper weight to the free exercise clause of the First Amendment which, the manual argues, when given proper weight should allow the denomination to determine its own polity and structure. This assertion, however, was rejected by the courts in *Jones v. Wolf*, *St. Luke's* and *From the Heart Church Ministries*, *supra*. Instead, those cases stated that undue deference by state courts to denominational documents would violate the establishment clause of the First Amendment. The conflict between the manual's statement in support of the free exercise clause and the statements in the cited case law in support of the establishment clause reflect the inherent and counter-balancing tension between the two clauses.

The Other Side of the Coin

Turning to the other side of the neutral principles' coin, local property documents and actions and state law, Article 2 of fictional Maple Street's 1925 articles of incorporation state the purpose of the local congregation and notes its "connection" to the PCUS. At the time of this incorporation, it may be noted, there was no express held-in-trust language in the PCUS constitution, and the historical evidence for the existence of an implied trust is very debatable. Notwithstanding the introductory statement of Article 2, Articles 3, 5 and 6 of Maple Street's 1925 articles of incorporation appear to grant autonomy to the local congregation over property matters, as do the

8 It cannot be determined from the Web site whether this compendium is complete or correct without keying in identifying information that could compromise anonymity.

parallel provisions in the 2004 articles. Although initially there was a general statement of "connection" to the denomination and presbytery, there was no specific provision expressing or implying that the board of trustees' authority on property matters was limited by or subject to any national or regional denominational rules.

Although the provisions in the new 2004 articles of incorporation adopted by Maple Street are enumerated differently, the new articles, like the former articles, contain no specific provisions expressing or implying the existence of a trust attaching to Maple Street's property. The omission of denominational reference subsequent to the 1982/83 adoption of express trust language by the denomination may be a further indication of intent and of Maple Street's understanding that continued membership in good standing with the PC (USA) is not mutually exclusive with a particular church's decision not to concur in the denomination's assertion of a trust over local church property.

Maple Street's property deeds do not contain held-in-trust language. Maple Street never has amended its articles to include held-in-trust language, nor has it ever filed "corrected" property deeds. While it has been under no legal obligation to amend its bylaws or "correct" its deeds, Maple Street has chosen not to do so despite published statements by the parent denomination encouraging local congregations to so act.

Neither the PC (USA), the PCUS, nor the Presbytery of Memphis ever contributed any funds for the purchase or construction of Maple Street property. Significantly, the property of Maple Street is, and always has been, titled in the name of the local church corporation only, without mention, listing or other reference to denominational affiliation or identification. On the other hand, Maple Street has been an active member of the Presbytery of Memphis and has called PC (USA)-ordained ministers to serve, subject to the presbytery's approval. Maple Street remained a member of the PCUS subsequent to the adoption of held-in-trust language in 1982 and has remained a member of the PC (USA) subsequent to the adoption of held-in-trust language in 1983. This apparent acquiescence may be offset, though, by the provisions of G-8.0700 of the PC (USA) *Book of Order*, the congregation's actions pursuant thereto on May 1, 1985, the presbytery's receipt without objection of the minutes of the May 8, 1985, Maple Street congregational meeting, and other factors indicative of intent.

In further support of the view that the Maple Street property is held without a trust is the general legal maxim that a member of a voluntary association is bound by amendments to the association's rules, but that such amendments shall not deprive the member of vested property rights without the member's explicit consent. See, e.g., *In Re Church of St. James the Less* (Pa.

J-18-2005) (decided Dec. 29, 2005); *Leatherman v. Wolf*, 240 Pa. 557, 564 (1913); *Marshall v. Pilot's Ass'n*, 206 Pa. 182, 183; and *Calabrese v. Policeman's Benevolent Ass'n*, 384 A.2d 579, 583 (N.J. Super. 1978).

EDITOR'S NOTE

With considerable erudition, Dr. Thomas C. Oden explains in Chapter Five that the current United Methodist Church trust clause has an unbroken line of historical antecedents dating to John Wesley's Model Deed of 1763. According to Dr. Oden, it has been the intention since the inception of American Methodism that local Methodist church property deeds include express trust clauses that are mandated by the denomination's governing documents. [Whether local deeds actually contain such language is, of course, subject to inspection.]

By contrast, express trust clauses were not added to the constitutions of major Presbyterian and Episcopal denominations in the United States until 1979-1983, and those denominational documents do not mandate that local churches amend their deeds to add trust language.

Dr. Oden also notes that, unlike the trust clauses in Presbyterian and Episcopal constitutions, the text of the United Methodist Church trust clause uniquely incorporates doctrinal standards to define the trust asserted. He therefore argues that the United Methodist Church trust clause, by incorporating doctrinal standards into the trust itself, guarantees the right to the use of church property only to those who are guardians of Methodism's established doctrinal standards.

He concludes that the United Methodist Church trust clause thus may be used by faithful congregations in Methodist ecclesiastical proceedings in opposition to denominational officials or agencies who have departed from those standards but seek to confiscate property from those who have rightly remained "in connection" with Mr. Wesley and his teachings. In effect, Dr. Oden suggests his preferred legal argument for use in the denomination's ecclesiastical courts: Demonstrate that, by its specific language, the United Methodist Church trust clause exists to preserve doctrinal standards, and demonstrate that it is the local church – and not wayward denominational officials – who are in faithful connection with those standards.

Dr. Oden writes as a theologian to urge doctrinal fidelity in the context of Methodist polity. He recognizes, though, that courtroom strategy is a separate endeavor and acknowledges that his recommended prescription is not without practical difficulty. It assumes a fair ecclesiastical forum, as well as a commitment by the bishop and ecclesiastical court officials not to default on their responsibility to uphold established points of doctrine. When a fair ecclesiastical forum is shown not to exist, he argues that faithful Christians, consistent with Scripture, may seek remedy in civil courts.

A second difficulty with Dr. Oden's prescription is that although a doctrinally-based argument may be apt in a Methodist ecclesiastical court, civil courts are barred from using the departure-from-doctrine rule to decide church property disputes. The establishment clause of the First Amendment prohibits the consideration of religious doctrine as a basis for a decision by civil courts when determining property rights.

In acknowledgement of this, Dr. Oden suggests additional causes of action, or legal bases for claims, that are within the subject matter jurisdiction of civil courts – e.g., unjust taking, fraud and violation of due process. Under prevailing U.S. Supreme Court jurisprudence, when the text of a denominational trust clause incorporates religious concepts that render the application of neutral principles of law impossible, civil courts are to follow the hierarchical/deference rule. Under that rule, civil court subject matter jurisdiction is limited only to review for potential fraud or collusion.

CHAPTER FIVE[1]

CONSIDERATIONS SPECIFIC TO METHODISTS

The issue of local church property rights is an active question for many believers in Presbyterian, Episcopal, Methodist and United Church of Canada traditions. Town by town, the question of who owns local church property is emerging as a painful, volatile dilemma. There is only one reason why it is a dilemma: The mainline leadership has refused to listen to its own laity.

This inquiry takes one case study of the history of a single tradition (Methodist, in this instance) of understanding the relation of local property rights to judicatory responsibilities. Many analogies are easily drawn with other communions.

Property Deeds and Established Doctrines

This is a "time bomb issue for many local churches whose governance is both connected with and disaffected by denominational commitments. This issue is arising with particular poignancy and passion among the rising voices of confessing Christians. It is intensified by the "stay or leave" dilemma. It remains highly contested and confusing, especially to lay leaders within the major mainline denominations.

This is an issue in which many laypersons, pastors, boards of trustees, judicatories, local church study groups and church councils will have to face, like it or not, and about which whey necessarily will have to be informed.

1 This chapter is an abridgement of "Who Owns Local Church Property," Part 6 of *Turning around the Mainline: How Renewal Movements are Changing the Church* by Thomas C. Oden (Grand Rapids, Mich.; Baker Books, a division of Baker Publishing Group; 2006). Reprinted with permission.

Multi-denominational Analogies

This argument is pertinent not for one denomination only, but by analogy for property issues in all the mainline traditions. Further, the interested parties in this dispute are not only those of the "mainline," but rather are generic, since the dilemma is felt in every quarter of North American Protestantism – whether evangelical or liberal or liturgical. The struggles and agonies in the mainline are bound to have a ripple effect upon non-mainline congregations that struggle with similar issues, especially in long-established denominations.

Settlement of local church property conflict differs widely among denominations, depending upon whether they are *congregationally* governed, as distinguished from what the law calls *hierarchically* governed, where the trusteeship of the local church property is entrusted by law to the denominational discipline or to some non-local legal entity.

Congregationally governed congregations own their own church property. Denominationally governed congregations operate under a church law or discipline or constitution that defines the terms of local ownership and trusteeship. Those in the former category will not be so directly affected by the ownership dilemma. Those in the latter category will be greatly affected by legal determinations of who owns the local church property, and to whom is it legally entrusted.

Although many details of what follows are relatively denomination-specific, the same generic issue persists in all church traditions. This chapter leaves it to others to grasp and reflect upon analogies with the history and polity of the diverse church bodies.

Why the Special Focus on the United Methodist Property Issue?

Since it is too much to try to deal with all the traditions of the mainline, we focus on only one in particular, in this case the Methodists, although it equally could have been Episcopalian or Presbyterian.

It is fitting to focus on trusteeship of local church property in the largest of the mainline Protestant denominations – the United Methodist Church. The choice to limit the discussion in this way does not make any assumption that the decisions made in Methodist circles will be valid for other denominations, but it does assume that there will be analogies in other denominations that will face the same urgent dilemma.

It is hoped that the argument could be examined without prejudice and fairly as a historical, legal and constitutional argument, and analogous reasoning applied to other similar situations. What follows is arguably a turnaround line of reasoning in the property-use arena. It could change the way of framing the question of church property by focusing on the constitutional history of local church deeds.

Regrettably, this sort of research has not been generally available. This argument and documentation could mean thousands of dollars of savings for local church boards of trustees for legal fees and opinions, and can be ignored only at their peril.

If the following argument seems complicated, it is necessary to spell it out accurately, and remember how important it is for thousands of local congregations. If not spelled out with precision, it might appear cavalier or tendentious.

Narrowing the Question

The question first must be narrowed to ask: What does the legal history of deed making (i.e., uniform deeds of trust of all local churches) in American Methodism clearly establish that impinges upon contemporary disputes over who owns the right to occupy and use United Methodist church property today? And how does this history correlate with other Protestant traditions?

The constitutional and disciplinary standards of this church tradition have been respected by the courts for over two centuries. Most observers remain confident that they will continue to respect them. It is on the basis of these constitutionally grounded doctrinal and disciplinary standards that the courts have reserved a generous and deferential space of freedom for church law. It is to be administered within church judicatories by due processes governed by the conferences of the denomination under their *Book of Discipline*.

The issue: Who owns title to local church property when that property long has been connected with a denomination that has become wayward in the doctrinal commitments that stand permanently at the legal authority of the denomination? Put simply, the legal problem is: Who owns title to United Methodist Church property – those who follow the United Methodist doctrine and discipline or those who do not? Do those who defy these standards have equal status with those who remain faithful?

The Model trust deed of 1773 formed the pattern for all American Methodist deeds of trust of local church property, and its relevance remains indisputably pertinent to contemporary church property issues.

Thesis

Although not widely recognized, there already exists a legitimate recourse under church law – the model trust deed in the American Methodist tradition, which for over 200 years has impinged upon civil court judgments on how the property of the local church is rightly to be governed and used. But its implications have not been adequately understood or applied.

The doctrinal and disciplinary standards embedded in these deeds are unmistakably clear. They are stated in every *Book of Discipline* and have been substantially and repeatedly stated since founding constitutional conferences in 1784 and 1808 without change, and without diminution.

When the guardianship trust vested in judicatory officials (whether ordained pastors, superintendents, conferences or boards of trustees) has been neglected or abandoned or disavowed, those parties do not have a self-evident clear or legitimate claim to the use of church property. Rather, those who support the doctrine and discipline of the United Methodist Church have reasonable legitimate recourse to the courts that they be allowed not only to use church facilities, but that they be protected from being denied access to these facilities.

Here, the inquiry necessarily becomes historical in nature. The argument that follows will show textually that the standards remain clear and binding.

Titles in Trust in Church Property – A Legal Duty within the Secular Order

First, it is widely conceded in church law that the church "exists in the secular world and that civil authorities may seek legal definition predicated on the nature of the United Methodist Church." (*Book of Discipline*, 2004, para. 139, 94, hereafter noted as Disc., 2004, para. 139, 94).pp. 93-4).

While the church is of God, it lives within the context of a civil society, and hence must duly account for its property as a matter of secular and civil accountability. The church's doctrine is protected from infringement by civil authorities, but the church's business practices and legal obligations cannot be exempt from civil responsibilities.

The Trust Clause Embedded in Every Local Church Property Deed

Every local United Methodist Church must have a property deed that places it under the authority of the historic *trust clause*. The title requirement is clearly stated in all Methodist *Disciplines*: "Titles to all real and personal, tangible and intangible property held at jurisdictional, annual, or district conference levels, or by a local church or charge, or by an agency or institution of the Church, shall be held in trust for the United Methodist Church and *subject to the provisions of its Discipline*" (Disc., 2004, para. 2501, 671, italics added).

The Discipline itself places clear constraints on what legislators and administrators can do. The provisions of the *Discipline* begin with a Constitution that enumerates the specific texts of the established standards of doctrine and discipline and their central importance for the use of property.

EVERY TRUST CLAUSE EMBEDDED IN EVERY LOCAL CHURCH DEED IS SUBJECT TO THE UNITED METHODIST CONSTITUTION AND DISCIPLINE

Local church properties cannot be held legally without reference to the Book of Discipline, which states: "All written instruments of conveyance by which premises are held or hereafter acquired for use as a place of divine worship or other activities for members of The United Methodist Church shall contain the following *trust clause*: In trust, that said premises shall be used, kept, and maintained as a place of divine worship of the United Methodist ministry and members of The United Methodist Church, *subject to the Discipline*, usage, and ministerial appointments of said Church as from time to time authorized and declared by the General Conference" (Disc., 2004, para. 2503.1, 671-72, italics added). This is the starting point for understanding property usage according to United Methodist doctrinal standards.

THERE ARE FOUR SPECIFIED HISTORICAL AND CONTEMPORARY UNITED METHODIST DOCTRINAL STANDARDS

The Plan of Union accepted by the Evangelical United Brethren and Methodist traditions in 1968 takes great pains to specify that the phrase "our present existing and established standards of doctrine" includes "as a minimum John Wesley's forty-four *Sermons on Several Occasions* and his *Explanatory Notes upon the New Testament*. Their function as "standards" already had been defined by the 'Large Minutes' of 1763, which in turn had been approved by the American Methodists in 1773 and 1785. To these *Sermons* and *Notes*, the Conference of 1808 added the *Articles of Religion*" (Disc., 1968, Preface, Part II, p. 35 and continuously sustained in subsequent editions).

After 1968, *The Confession* also was included in protected doctrinal standards, in reference to the Evangelical United Brethren Confession of Faith. So, there are four texts of doctrinal definition: three from The Methodist Church doctrinal tradition (*Articles*, *Sermons* and *Notes*) and one added to these from the EUB doctrinal tradition (*The Confession*).

Even Without an Explicit Local Trust Clause the Duty to Guard and Maintain These Four Doctrinal Standards Remains in Effect 'Subject to the Provisions of the Discipline'

Suppose, however, someone objects: "We have examined our local church deed and we do not see any explicit reference to the *Sermons, Notes, Articles*, or *Confession*. How could a trust clause be enforceable in doctrinal matters if there is no explicit reference to the texts of the doctrinal standards?"

The *Discipline's* answer is highly explicit and unambiguous. The trust deed functions precisely under accountability to the *Discipline*, which compacts into legislative and administrative language the cohesive and continuous historical correlation of doctrine and deed making. This history is a consistent and unabrogated tradition, as will be demonstrated. The *Discipline* specifies these doctrinal standards that are the very reason for writing the trust clause.

The absence of explicit reference does not legitimate ignoring the Constitution, which requires the doctrinal standards in the Book of Discipline. Thus, the lack of a trust clause with cited texts does not "absolve a local church or church agency or the board of trustees of either, of its responsibility and accountability to The United Methodist Church" (Disc., 2004, para. 2503.6, p. 673) which stands under the specific constraint of its established doctrinal standards.

If local trustees examine their local church deed, they will not see the trust clause appearing directly. But the Discipline explicitly states that this in no way excludes "a local church or church agency, or the board of trustees of either, from or relieves it of its connectional responsibilities to The United Methodist Church," which under its constitution is legally bound to guard and respect its own doctrinal standards embodied in the *Sermons, Notes, Articles* and *Confession.*

The Purpose of the Deed is not to Protect the Judicatory but the Doctrinal Standards

But why do Methodists have a doctrinal trust clause written into all their deeds?

> *The very reason for the trust clause in deeds is to protect the doctrinal standards, not the Conference. The Conference is legitimized only insofar as it protects the doctrinal standards. The Restrictive Rules as interpreted by the Plan of Union and subsequent Disciplines textually specify the documents of the*

doctrinal standards (Disc., 2004, para.103, 59-74).

Only on this basis can the local church be required to revert its property. Much of the remainder of this argument focuses on the next point, which will be meticulously documented textually.

USE OF PROPERTY UNDER THE TRUST CLAUSE IS SUBJECT TO THE DISCIPLINE'S DOCTRINAL STANDARDS

Title to all United Methodist church property, whether it is "taken in the name of the local church trustees, or charge trustees," is "held subject to the provisions of the *Discipline*" (Disc., 2004, para. 2504, 673), hence the doctrinal standards that the *Discipline* holds inviólable.

Title to real property is held in the name of the local church in trust for the benefit of the United Methodist Church *but always subject to its doctrinal and disciplinary standards.* To be "subject to the usages and the *Discipline* of The United Methodist Church" (Disc., 2004, para. 2503.5, 672) requires first of all to be subject to its Constitution, hence subject to the Restrictions on the General Conference in the Constitution, which limits the General Conference or any Conference from amending or negating the doctrinal standards found in the *Sermons, Notes, Articles* and *Confession.*

Since church property "shall be held, kept, maintained, and disposed of for the benefit of The United Methodist Church and subject to the usages and the *Discipline* of the United Methodist Church," (Disc., 2004, para. 2503.5, 672) there can *be no licit uses of the property that are not subject to the Discipline, and therefore the doctrinal standards.* "This provision [the trust clause] is solely for the benefit of the grantee" (Disc., 2004, para. 2503.1, 672). Who is the grantee? Precisely the United Methodist Church that is pledged to remain "subject to the *Discipline,*" which itself is pledged to guarantee the doctrinal standards.

Hence, no local or conference board of trustees that holds property in trust for the United Methodist Church can function legally apart from the constitutional guarantees of the Restrictive Rules that limit the General Conference and Annual Conferences concerning doctrinal standards. No property can be duly used apart from its being "authorized and declared by the General Conference," which stands under the constraints of these Restrictive Rules, which require the use of property to be restricted to responsible accountability to "our doctrinal standards" – namely, the standard *Sermons, Notes, Articles* and *Confession.*

No use of property is licit "that violates the right of the Church to maintain connectional structure." This recalls that the notion of connection for two and a half centuries has meant *connection with Mr. Wesley*, as defined in his writings, and notably in his standard *Sermons* and *Notes* (Disc., 2004, para. 2506, 674).

How the Plan of Union keeps the trust clause in constant application, even when not explicit in the local church deed

The Plan of Union (1968) is a legal instrument that defines the lawful status of the trust clause in property deeds of the successor organizations of the former Methodist Episcopal Church, Methodist Episcopal Church South, the Methodist Church, and the Evangelical United Brethren Church. All formerly devised deeds are legally folded into the Plan of Union, as specified in all subsequent *Books of Discipline.*

The Plan of Union maintains the manner and conditions of deeds apart without reference to "lapse of time or usage." A central feature of the Plan of Union is the provision stated explicitly in every United Methodist *Discipline*: "Nothing in the Plan of Union at any time after the union is to be construed so as to require any existing local church of any predecessor denomination to the United Methodist Church to alienate or in any way *to change the title to property contained in its deed or deeds at the time of union, and lapse of time or usage shall not affect said title or control.*" (Disc., 2004, para. 2504, 673, italics added; also protected in Section VIII of the Local Church on Protection of Rights of Congregations, Disc., 2004, para. 261, 182).

The stated purpose of this paragraph (2504) was to show the *continuity between the trust clauses before the Plan of Union and after,* and to make it easier under the conditions of proposed mergers to properly maintain and examine and prove merchantable titles after the Plan of Union in all jurisdictions.

The "time of union" was 1968. No trust clause written after that time can fail to be legally bound to the Restrictive Rule established in 1808 and confirmed in 1968, in reference to our doctrinal standards – the *Sermons, Notes* and *Articles* and, after 1968, the *Confession.*

Crucial to the argument is the next step.

The Plan of Union Confirms That the Four Doctrinal Standards Are Textually Specific

The Plan of Union (between Methodists and the EUB)of 1968 clearly specifies that the phrase "our present existing and established standards of doctrine" includes "as a minimum John Wesley's forty-four *Sermons on Several*

Occasions and his *Explanatory Notes upon the New Testament*" (Disc., 1968, Preface, Part II, 35). "In the present plan of Union ... the Confession, the Articles of Religion and the Wesleyan 'standards' are thus deemed congruent if not identical in their doctrinal perspectives and not in conflict" (Ibid., 36). These four documentary standards are protected by Restrictive Rules from revision or abrogation by any General Conference acting on its own authority or without amending the Exception of 1832. Title deeds from the beginning have been written in order to protect these doctrinal standards. This is what I will show textually in what follows.

The record of the proceedings of the General Conference of 1972 makes this continuity clear: "*We have tried to clarify the contextual relationships between the* Articles, *the* Confession, *and Wesley's* Sermons *and* Notes *and Rules in order to clarify the reference in the First Restrictive Rule about 'our present and existing and established standards of doctrine.' We have not altered these standards*" (1972 DCA, 291, italics added).

By 1980, this rule was further underscored and reinforced: "The *Discipline* seems to assume that for the determination of otherwise irreconcilable doctrinal disputes, the Annual and General Conferences are the appropriate courts of appeal, *under the guidance of the first two Restrictive Rules (which is to say, the* Articles *and* Confession, *the* Sermons *and the* Notes)" (Disc., 1980, para. 67, 49, italics added).

BINDING STANDARDS THAT AFFECT THE WRITING OF CHURCH PROPERTY DEEDS AND MORTGAGES

The Plan of Union cannot be circumvented licitly by any Conference, bishop, Committee of Investigation, or Judicial Council. It is intrinsic to the Constitution. If the right of a local church or pastor to teach according to United Methodist doctrinal standards is tested in any court, church or civil, the Plan of Union must be quoted directly as a legal instrument binding on all subsequent United Methodist polity and all subsequent General Conferences, since it belongs permanently and intrinsically to the Plan of Union: "Wesley's *Sermons* and *Notes* were specifically included in our present existing and established standards of doctrine by plain historical inference" (Disc., 1984, 49). The current *Discipline* states even more tersely that "Wesley's *Sermons* and *Notes* were *understood specifically to be included* in our present existing and established standard of doctrine" (Disc., 2004, para. 102, 58, italics added); hence, not just inferentially.

The once contested debate leading up to the General Conference of 1988 about the strength and purport of "plain historical inference" was settled by the 1988 General Conference, and remains textually embedded in all subsequent *Disciplines* to date as *Articles*, *Confession*, *Sermons* and *Notes* (Disc., 2004, para. 102, 58).

It is too late to revisit or revise the legally binding constitutional decisions made in the Plan of Union. Even if the terms of the Plan of Union do not appear in detail in a local church deed, that does not abrogate the terms of Union, as the *Discipline* makes clear. These were settled in 1968 as an act of civil law. A complex set of judicial challenges would follow from any attempt to revise the Plan of Union.

This legal clause constitutes a remarkable guarantee from the 1968 Plan of Union that the trust clause in deeds cannot be circumvented or changed from the conditions legally established in the Constitution (i.e., established in the 1808 General Conference with its Restrictive Rules for all future Conferences).

This means: Any future local title deeds that are legally written for any future local United Methodist Church stand accountable to the doctrinal standards of the *Sermons*, *Notes*, *Articles*, and *Confession*. Any future merger must respect the trust clause that limits the ability of any future General Conference to emend or revamp any of the established doctrinal standards. The Plan is clear and specific: "Title to all property of a local church, or charge, or agency of the Church shall be held subject to the provisions of the *Discipline*" (Disc., 2004, para. 2504, 673); hence, subject to the Restrictive Rules whose very purpose is to guard these textual doctrinal standards set forth in specific texts.

What if the Trust Clause is Violated?

The naked title for *ownership* of local Methodist Church property normally lies in the hands of the local church's board of trustees. Their *use* of the property is conditioned upon the trust clause.

First, *if the trust clause is violated by the local church*, the property can, through due process, revert to the Annual Conference Board of Trustees or an agency vested with accountability under the trust clause.

When asked to decide whether "the voluntary placement of a 'Trust Clause' on the title deed of real property" when discontinued or abandoned allows funds to be used "in another location," the Judicial Council held that they can, provided they are administered "through the Annual Conference Board of Trustees" (Judicial Council Decision, hereafter noted as JCD, 688, 1993).

Second, *if the trust clause is violated by the conference or agency or judicatory itself*, the judicatory officials could be liable to the charge of teaching contrary to doctrinal standards and discipline. Bishops and ordained conference members, who are solemnly and voluntarily pledged to defend these doctrinal standards, are subject to charges if they inveigh against these doctrines. The tide is now shifting in the direction of more attention to this second point, without diminishing the first.

There are ample precedents for the title of local church property to revert to the conference when the local church violates doctrine or discipline (the first point made above). But we still have ahead of us the challenge of argument for cases (on the second point), where the conference itself violates its own constitutional doctrine or discipline. There is nothing in historic or contemporary United Methodist *Discipline* to protect the Conferences or bishops from full accountability to the trust clause.

The consequences of these legal instruments have not yet been tested in detail in either church law or civil law but, to the extent that challenges occur, they likely will be tested in the light of more historical information than usually has been considered. All the documentary evidence is now, at long last, in place for a defense of constitutional standards of doctrine.

Suppose a judicatory, bishop, or Annual Conference publicly, flagrantly and repeatedly is determined to defy and resist official United Methodist doctrine and discipline. The local church laity, *remaining faithful to the connection*, have a right to be protected from flagrant doctrinal and disciplinary abuses and evasions, even and especially when done by a judicatory official.

This brings us to distinguish between two different types of connectionalism, faithful and unfaithful.

'Faithfulness to the Connection' means 'According to Established Doctrinal Standards'

What does it mean to be faithful to the connection? "*The connection*" is a crucial concept characteristic of Methodist history, doctrine and polity, and has been pivotal since the earliest Conference of 1744, where the ministers "*in connection with Mr. Wesley*" were brought together under his leadership to confer on doctrine and discipline. Although Mr. Wesley made the decisions on what would be entered into the Minutes, he listened carefully to the advice of preachers.

Faithfulness to the connection in the early Methodist tradition meant faithfulness to the teaching and direct pastoral care of Mr. Wesley, always under the authority of Scripture. Faithfulness to the connection in the present

Methodist tradition still means faithfulness to the teaching and patterns of pastoral care established by Mr. Wesley under Scriptural authority, but for some it has become so thinly diluted that it points merely to simple loyalty to the present institution and management. In either sense, faithfulness to the connection rightly understood means faithfulness to the doctrinal and disciplinary standards that are constitutionally defined first by Mr. Wesley, then refined and amended by the early American Methodists, and now are mandated for all who follow this *Discipline*. These are the doctrinal standards that are necessitated, taken for granted, meant, predicated, expected, entailed, and required in every title deed. This is a duty for anyone who administers United Methodist church property.

Unfaithfulness to the connection would therefore imply any form of teaching contrary to these doctrinal standards protected in every trust clause. This is a *chargeable offense* for anyone who has become ordained to sacred ministry (Disc., 2004, para. 2702.3.C and 2702.3.D), a binding, solemn and voluntary act.

The Difference Between Being Faithful and Unfaithful to the Connection

The issue here is not between congregational governance (which would make the local congregation the sole authority for local policy) versus connectional or denominational governance (which would make the constituted Book of Discipline the authority for local church policy).

All parties in Methodist conflicts must follow the rules of connectional polity. Most who wish to enter the arena of this discussion view themselves as already dedicated to connectional governance by virtue of their confirmation of their baptism.

This is an important point: The confessing movement is speaking from within the frame of reference of a faithful connectionalism, and in opposition to an unfaithful abuse of connectionalism. Readers who think exclusively in terms of congregational governance may stumble over this point. The confessing movement is not proposing to revert to congregational governance but, rather, to protect the innocent from those who abuse connectional governance.

Hence, there is no question whether a local church that is disobedient to doctrinal and disciplinary standards has a right to challenge the use of connectional church property apart from established church law. That is not a presumption here, nor is it even a contested question. The question, rather, is what happens when judicatory officials who have been authorized to guard the

Discipline default on that guardianship, or when they take measures against precisely those who faithfully uphold the doctrine and Discipline?

It may seem an anomaly that most voices in conflicted property situations consider themselves to be intensely faithful to the connection. Few voices among Methodists are arguing specifically for a purely congregational polity or against connectional polity. The issue, rather, is what constitutes doctrinal responsibility to the connection, and how is that related to the connection with Mr. Wesley and the authorized texts of his writings. The key question is: What right do denominational or judicatory officials have to act against established church law and doctrine? This is a question of unfaithful abuse of the connection in which unfaithful precisely means unfaithful to doctrinal standards.

So, the Methodist debate is occurring primarily within the arena of Methodist connectional polity, not outside it, and not on the premise of an alleged autonomous or congregational local authority. No traditional or orthodox or evangelical Methodist who knows Methodist history and polity could plausibly argue that the local congregation as such is the final legitimate source for determining Methodist doctrine. The reason for that is that each local church is an expression of the whole body of Christ in that locale. Baptism is not baptism into a local church, but into the church of Jesus Christ, into the one, holy, universal, and apostolic church. So, the form of polity under which the Methodist issue emerges is not congregational or synodal or charismatic, but Methodist and Wesleyan in its connectionalism, which means a direct relation to Mr. Wesley and his teaching. Although this distinction may seem like a parochial issue only for Methodists, there remain broad analogies with other forms of polity.

THE CONNECTIONAL ANOMALY

Those who are *unfaithful to the connection* and its doctrine have shown signs of being at times ready to disavow those standards of doctrine and discipline and yet still attempt to hold onto the property, and to administer its use against disciplinary standards. This is now being challenged as illicit.

Those who remain most *faithful to the connection* and its doctrine, and who seek to guard, protect, defend and embody the connectionally established doctrinal standards, have previously been forced into having to defend their faithfulness to the connection. That defensiveness has come to an end. They are now asking the courts of church law and, if necessary, civil law to strictly respect the repeatedly upheld constitutional history and the right to teach United Methodist doctrine. They are becoming more free to ask the courts to understand and respect the legal trust clause, and factor in its bearing upon the present use and administration of local church property.

This, as will be shown, is a continuing tradition with substantive continuity and cohesion and legal standing. But is it a binding requirement for pastors? This is our next subject.

What the Pastor is Required by Church Law to know about Doctrinal Standards

This is a crucial piece of the puzzle: Is the pastor as local administrator of church property responsible for knowing the standards?

Every ordained elder must answer formally the question: "Have you studied the doctrines of the United Methodist Church? After full examination do you believe that our doctrines are in harmony with the Holy Scriptures? Will you preach and maintain them?" (Disc., 2004, para. 331.d.8-12)

Failure to answer yes from the heart, *ex animo*, with sincerity, may call into question or jeopardize one's ministerial credentials and accountability. What is included in "the doctrines of the United Methodist Church?" It is clear: *Sermons, Notes* and *Articles* (and, after 1968, the *Confession*).

Are the Doctrinal Standards Settled Church Law?

The core of the doctrinal standards of the United Methodist Church have been clearly agreed to and established since the earliest deeds in 1773 and the founding Christmas Conference of 1784 and the constitutional Conference of 1808 (as further strengthened by the Exception of 1832). Since 1988, there has been no doubt about the meaning of "our doctrinal standards," textually defined and repeatedly reconfirmed. A leading constitutional expert, Bishop Holland N. McTyeire, summarized the standards this way: "American Methodists (1781) vowed to 'preach the old Methodist doctrine' of Wesley's '*Notes* and *Sermons*.' May, 1784, 'the doctrine taught in the four volumes of the *Sermons* and the *Notes on the New Testament*' was reaffirmed. The Deed of Declaration (February, 1784) legally established these standards in the present body. The Rule (1808) guards them equally with the Articles" (*Manual of the Discipline*, Nashville, Southern Methodist Publishing House, 1870, 20th edition, 1931, 131).

The question of "theological pluralism" (referred to in the *Discipline* of 1980, para. 69, 72) has been subsequently placed under strict limitation since 1988, when the General Conference voted to view theological pluralism as standing "*under the guidance of our doctrinal standards*" (Disc., 1984, para.

69, 72) – the *Sermons, Notes, Articles* and *Confession*, along with the General Rules. This core is a standard that stands as an immovable dictum in the Constitution, unamendable according to the Restrictive Rules.

Since we are here discussing only the core documents of our doctrinal standards protected by the Constitution and pertinent to the trust clause, we are not entering here into speculations about other documents that may lie beyond the penumbra of this core. These have been thoroughly discussed in my documentary history of *Doctrinal Standards in the Wesleyan Tradition* (Grand Rapids, Mich.; Zondervan;1988, hereafter DSWT). There one can find a more explicit discussion of ancillary issues on the penumbra: the number of sermons in the standard sermons, occasional pamphlets, the General Rules, the "Binding Minute," the Ward Motion, and other issues.

DOCUMENTING THE CONTINUOUS HISTORICAL RECORD: PROPERTY DEEDS ALWAYS ASSUME DOCTRINAL STANDARDS

The earliest American property deeds (1770-1784) followed in continuity with Wesley's "Model Deed" for meetinghouses of 1763. The sustained continuity and cohesion of this tradition can be demonstrated textually by six crucial documents:

• The *earliest recorded legal deeds* for use of Methodist church properties in America repeat verbatim the pivotal phrase in Wesley's "Model Deed:" Preach "no other doctrine than is contained in the said John Wesley's *Notes upon the New Testament* and his four volumes of *Sermons,*" as is found in the deed of trust of the John Street Methodist Church in New York City, Nov. 2, 1770.

• Identical language is found in the deed for *St. George's meeting house* in Philadelphia

(June 14, 1770, Bishop Thomas Neely, *Doctrinal Standards of Methodism*; New York; Revell; 1918; 139; hereafter DSM).

• *The Asbury Memorandum of 1773*. Francis Asbury wrote this memorandum on the first American Annual Conference (1773): "The following propositions were agreed to: 1. The old Methodist doctrine and discipline shall be enforced and maintained amongst all our societies in America. 2. Any preacher who acts otherwise can not be retained amongst us as a fellow-laborer in the vineyard" (*Journal and Letters* 1:85).

• *The Conference Minutes of 1780* legally formalized and confirmed the principle that "all the deeds shall be drawn in substance after that in the printed [then British] Minutes" (*Minutes of the Annual Conferences of the Methodist Episcopal Church for the Years 1773-1828*; New York; T. Mason and G. Lane;1849; hereafter MAC; 1780; 12; italics added).

• Preachers were required in *the Subscription of 1781* to subscribe to this Minute: "after mature consideration, close observation and earnest prayer, to preach the old Methodist doctrine, and strictly enforce the discipline as contained in the *Notes, Sermons*, and Minutes published by Mr. Wesley" (MAC, 1781;13; probably by signature).

• In *Mr. Wesley's letter of 1783 to the Conference*, he wrote: "To the Preachers in America:" "Let all of you be determined to abide by the Methodist doctrine and discipline, published in the four volumes of *Sermons*, and the *Notes Upon the New Testament*, together with the Large Minutes of the Conference" (*Letters of John Wesley*; 8 vols.; London; Epworth; 1931; 7:191).

None of these six documents had their context in Britain. All were American, all before 1784. All of them specified the *Sermons* and *Notes*, and three of them specifically showed the relation of the *Sermons* and *Notes* to the making of Methodist deeds in America.

From these documents and others, John Tigart, in *A Constitutional History of American Episcopal Methodism, 2nd ed* (Nashville; Smith and Lamar; 1904; hereafter CH; 113), the definitive study of Methodist doctrinal standards, concluded: "The American chapels and meetinghouses have been generally settled according to the form of the deed used in England since 1750" (Tigert; CH; 113). Bishop Ole Borgen agrees that "the earliest deeds of record in America followed Wesley's form of 1763" the "Model Deed" ("Standards of Doctrine in the United Methodist Church: Never Revoked, Altered or Changed?" Drew University lecture, Oct. 8, 1986; 2).

This shows beyond doubt that the standards of the Sermons and Notes were the central features of the earliest American Methodist property deeds. Hence, there is no discontinuity or ambiguity whatever in this earliest American tradition, which the story up to:

The Founding Conference of 1784

For the Founding Conference, Baltimore, Christmas, 1784, Mr. Wesley's abbreviation of the Thirty-nine Anglican Articles was included among the already established doctrinal standards for American Methodists. *The Articles did not supplant, but complemented the* Sermons *and* Notes. There is no evidence to the contrary, despite active attempts to discover some.

The reasons the Articles were needed harks back to the fact that the Anglican clergy had largely abandoned the colonies before the Revolutionary War. Mr. Wesley recognized the urgent need to free the Methodist preachers in America not only to preach the Word, but also to baptize and administer the Lord's Supper. He found the Thirty-nine Anglican Articles inadequate in several passages, so he edited them down into Twenty-four Articles, to which another was added by the Founding Conference (as Article XXIII) on the sovereignty and independence of the United States of America, making Twenty-five Articles for the American Methodists. The Articles obviously were not trying to define doctrine that was original to American Methodists but, rather, the opposite: to show the substantial continuity of Methodist teaching with the doctrine of the Church of England, despite the problematic phrases that were edited out. The *Discipline* of 1798 make it clear that these American Methodist Articles of Religion are the doctrines "maintained more or less, in part or whole, by every reformed church in the world" (Disc., 1798, Notes, Preface).

The *"binding minute" of 1784* (Conference Minutes; MAC; 1784; Question 2) showed that there had been no change of doctrine in the transition to America, and that Methodists in America were still firmly bound to the connection with Mr. Wesley and his teaching. To be "in connection" precisely means to be in connection with Mr. Wesley and his teaching. Consistent with this motivation, Methodist preachers continued to "be active in dispensing Mr. Wesley's books" (Tigert; CH; 27), a mandate repeated in all the *Disciplines* from 1784 to 1808. Mr. Wesley's sermons thereafter were regularly republished by the General Conference to make sure that these standards were not revised or issued without authorization (MAC; 1773; 5). Over sixty editions of *Wesley's Sermons on Several Occasions* were published in the years between 1784-1860! This is evidence that they were not, as some have imagined, neglected or set aside during this period between 1784 and 1808.

The Principle of Non-Abrogation

Throughout these developments, the legal rule applied that "laws not repealed are laws in effect." This is the "principle of non-abrogation," agreed upon by virtually all Methodist constitutional authorities (Curtiss, Wheatley, Tigert, Buckley, Harrison, Neely, Lewis and Outler).

There is no record of any abrogation of the basic form of the trust clause in Methodist deeds in America. If such an abrogation should have occurred, it surely would have left behind it a vast paper trail of controversy, and no such paper trail exists. Hence, arguments from silence (that some documents do not specifically name the standard texts) are unconvincing.

Constructive Theological Reflection Affirmed by the Standards under the Limitation of the Standards

These standards have never pretended to be an end to all theological or exegetical debate.

The 2004 *Discipline* strongly affirms that the present "theological task includes the *testing, renewal, elaboration and application of our doctrinal perspective*." This encourages "serious reflection across the theological spectrum" (Disc., 2004; para. 104; Section Four; 75; italics added), but never apart from or contrary to the texts of the doctrinal standards themselves. While critical and constructive theological work is encouraged, however, the textually specified documents embodying the doctrinal standards have not changed, and constitutionally will remain in place.

The current *Discipline* affirms that, "The United Methodist Church stands continually in need of doctrinal reinvigoration for the sake of authentic renewal, fruitful evangelism, and ecumenical dialogue," (Disc.; 2004; para. 102; 59). Yet, in the same paragraph, it adds, "The process of creating new 'standards or rules of doctrine' thus *continues to be restricted*, requiring either that they be declared 'not contrary to' the present standards or that they go through the difficult process of constitutional amendment." (Disc.; 2004; para. 102,58-59, italics added). The trust clause protects these standards.

How Deeds Function in relation to Doctrinal Standards

The purposes of the trust clause from its earliest inception have been quite clear, as stated by John Lawson: "(i) to secure that Methodist Trusts should everywhere be drawn up on a uniform and approved plan, and that the trustees be bound to administer them on behalf of the whole Methodist Church," yet conforming to varied local laws (*Selections from John Wesley's Notes on the New Testament*; ed. John Lawson; London; Epworth; 1955; Introduction; hereafter SWN). And "(ii) to secure legal power to exclude from Methodist pulpits any persons holding opinions alien to the genius of Methodism; (iii) to secure that if in any local Church a discontented section wishes to sever itself from the Methodist Church as a whole, and from Conference, it shall not have the power to take possession of the trust property" (SWN, Ibid.). For two centuries, the trust clause has exercised this steady service to connectional Methodism, as a rugged legal defense for the Wesleyan connectional system based on doctrinal standards, and a stumbling block to schism.

The Trust Clause Grants the Right to Property Use Only to Those Who Protect Doctrinal Standards

It is erroneously assumed by some that denominational officials, *whether faithful or unfaithful to the doctrinal standards,* have a right to direct the use of Methodist church property. The evidence proves the opposite. *It is only on the basis of faithfulness to the standards that one has a right to the use of the property.* One who abandons faithfulness to the standards has no right to the property. That is precisely what the deed says, and why it was written. Why else would these standards take the form of a deed, if not for legal purposes?

The crux of this argument: *The trust clause was not devised to protect the Conferences as such, but the doctrinal standards. The trust clause guarantees the right to use property only to those who are guardians of its established doctrinal standards.*

The choice to inveigh against the doctrinal standards may, under fair examination, disqualify the abuser from the legitimate right to use the property with impunity. Those who are determined to preach against the Trinity and Incarnation and the authority of Scripture have dubious legitimate right to the property because these teachings are prominent in the standards. It is yet to be decided the extent to which these standards will be applied to a wide range of moral issues such as the rite of marriage, man and woman in the order of creation, idolatry, witchcraft, paganism, sexual abuse, and the value of life. There is no doubt that all these subjects are touched upon, even if tangentially, in various places in the *Sermons, Notes, Articles* and *Confession.*

How the Trust Clause Affects Contemporary Church Property Usage

The trust clause entrusts the property to those who voluntarily follow Methodist doctrine and discipline. Lawson writes: "To have these considerable *legal powers in reserve* is a valuable and necessary factor in maintaining the life of our Church as an ordered connexion" (SWN; Ibid.; italics added). Those who preach Methodist doctrine have a right to use Methodist property. Those who choose to dissent from or inveigh against Methodist doctrine have no such obvious legal right, *prima facie*, for they have chosen to work apart from the connection with Mr. Wesley and his teaching, and contrary to Methodist doctrine and discipline.

From the viewpoint of the civil courts, the issue cannot be directly about church doctrine, but only about civil law. The courts will not enter the arena of doctrinal dispute, as they repeatedly have shown. Rather, the issue only can be about fiduciary responsibility under civil law, about covenants made and covenants kept, about rights of access, which are questions of civil law. This is why the trust deeds are so important. The trust clause in the property deed transmission is a legal guarantee in a court of law. That is what deeds are for – legal protection.

This brings us, however, to the present irony: Those who are *faithful* to the connection and its doctrines are ironically now having to contend *against* those who imagine that they have the right to *disobey* these very teachings in the name of connectionalism. This is why so many local congregations now are studying the history of property deeds. Many have expressed appreciation to learn that the trust clause embedded in every property deed in Methodism is not merely a sentimental piece of dated paper, but even today a binding legal instrument.

The Deed of Settlement (1796) Made Doctrinal Standards a Judiciable Matter of Civil Law

The next steps in showing the continuity of the *Articles, Sermons* and *Notes* for deed making are the legal bulwarks of protection for the doctrinal standards in America. They are found in the Deed of Settlement (1796), the Restrictive Rules (1808) and the Exception of 1832.

First, how did the Deed of Settlement (1796) make the doctrinal standards a judiciable matter of civil law? The Deed of Settlement provided the standard post-Revolutionary model of the title deed for local churches in America (*Journal of the General Conference*; 1796-1836; see 1796 minutes; New York Carleton and Phillips; 1855; hereafter JGC 1796, 9). This deed was a legal instrument that set aside properties for preaching in accord with and nothing contrary to Methodist doctrinal standards, standards firmly established prior to this time, and repeatedly reconfirmed.

By the Deed of Settlement and *all its successor deeds, the local trustees were granted the right to mortgage, buy, and sell, but not to change doctrine.* No preacher could join the connection without agreeing to "abide by the Methodist doctrine and discipline published in the four volumes of *Sermons* and the *Notes*" (*Minutes of the Methodist Conference Annually Held in America from 1771 to 1794*; Philadelphia; Henry Tuckness; 1795, 1783; cf. Jesse Lee, *History of the Methodists*; Baltimore; McGill and Clime; 1810). The Deed of Settlement provided a legal means by which American church properties in various states could conform to the various laws of the states, while reconfirming doctrinal unity with the entire previous connectional history of Methodism.

THE UNION OF THE CONNECTION WAS DEFINED BY THE DOCTRINAL STANDARDS IN THE DEEDS

There was a strong sense of *union* between British and American Methodist connections, despite the troubles of the Revolution. The very concept of "union" in the Methodist connection cannot be separated from doctrinal considerations. *The union was in order to preserve the doctrinal teaching, not vice versa.* The trust clause is provided *legally* to protect these local church properties from threatened abuses or offenses against established doctrinal standards.

When the various British Methodist traditions organically united in 1932 (Methodist New Connection, 1846; Bible Christians, 1863; United Methodist Free Churches, 1842-1864; and the Primitive Methodists, 1864), all of these church bodies were merged on the explicit doctrinal premise of *"the essential similarity of the trust deeds"* (*Notes on Wesley's Fortyfour Sermons*; ed. John Lawson; London; Epworth; 1946; italics added). As a point of law, it was the doctrinally-grounded trust deeds that legally held together the union, not the sentiment of union that legitimated the trust deed.

These three standards in American Methodism before the Plan of Union – *Sermons, Notes* and *Articles* – (remembering that the *Confession* was added after the 1968 Union) thus became "the non-compressible core of 'our present existing and established standards of doctrine' and it is still in legal force to this day" (Albert Outler; "The Methodist Standards of Doctrine," Perkins School of Theology; 1958; iv; 6; mimeographed copy of syllabus addendum). Virtually all major Methodist constitutional historians (N. Bangs, N. Burwash, H. McTyeire, G.L. Curtiss, T. Neely, H. Wheeler, J. Tigert and N. Harmon) agree on this point.

HOW WAS THE GENERAL CONFERENCE STRICTLY PROHIBITED FROM CHANGING THE DOCTRINAL STANDARDS BY THE FIRST RESTRICTIVE RULE OF 1808?

The central constitutional restriction on changing these standards was and remains the Restrictive Rules. The General Conference of 1808 devised and adopted the constitution of the Methodist Episcopal Church and its successor organizations. In the constitution it included what has come to be called "the First Restrictive Rule." Restrictive means that the Annual and General Conferences were placed under a restriction. The Rule put an absolute constraint on any future General Conference against establishing doctrinal standards contrary to those previously and presently established.

The *First Restrictive Rule* remains decisive for any judicial assessment of the usage of local Methodist church property. It states: *"The General Conference shall not revoke, alter or change our Articles of Religion, nor establish any new standards or rules of doctrine contrary to our present existing and established standards of doctrine"* (JGC; 1808; 89 and all subsequent editions of the *Discipline*). Under this Rule, even if the General Conference unanimously wanted to change doctrinal standards, it could not do so constitutionally. This would require a constitutional amendment with a much more rigorous process of consent. The stringency of the Restrictive Rule intends to protect United Methodists from doctrinal tampering, and especially to protect Methodist properties from being wrongly used. It protects the title deeds from abrogation. Thereafter, if the General Conference sought to modify the doctrinal standards, it would face the obstacle not only of the title deeds but the Restrictive Rule, which limits the power of the General Conference to act.

Distinguishing the Two Complementary Clauses of the First Restrictive Rule

In this restriction on legislation, there is *a two-fold prohibition*, first *against any revocation, alteration or change in the Articles of Religion*, and second, *against any new standard or rule contrary to "present existing and established standards;"* i.e., in reference to the same standards stated in the Model Deed (1763) and the Deed of Settlement (1796).

These two clauses confirm both ecumenical affirmations and Methodist distinctives, the two complementary dimensions of our doctrinal standards: The first clause addresses the teaching of the *Articles,* which were not intended to set forth distinctively Methodist teaching, but to indicate *what our doctrine shares with all Reformed Protestantism and with all ecumenical Christianity generally*. The second clause deals with *the distinctives of Methodist teaching that shine forth in the* Sermons *and* Notes *(on themes like assurance, holiness of heart and life, and perfect love not treated in the* Articles*)*. This same distinction is sustained in recent Judicial Council Decisions (see JCD 486; 1979; Decisions 358 and 468 refer to the first part as "Landmark Documents," and the second part as "the present existing standards of doctrine." These two questions are different in nature and must be considered and answered separately").

Note that the defining phrase "shall not be revoked, altered, or changed," applies to the text of the *Articles* (and, after 1968, the *Confession*), but not to the *Sermons* and *Notes*. For *there has never been any thought or active initiative for changing the text of Mr. Wesley's* Sermons *and* Notes, nor is one hardly imaginable. "The original distinction between the intended functions of the *Articles* on the one hand, and of the *Sermons* and *Notes* on the other, may be inferred from the double reference to them in the First Restrictive Rule (adopted in 1808 and unchanging ever since)" (Disc., 1984; 45). But there might at some point be proposed an attempt to change or amend the *Articles* or *Confession*.

The firm textual definition of this second part was consistently held to be the *Sermons* and *Notes*, but a definitive settlement of this question awaited the Plan of Union of 1968 and the *Discipline* of 1988 for its definitive confirmation and unambiguous textual definition. The General Conference of 1988 specified that the texts of "our present established standards of doctrine" include Mr. Wesley's *Sermons* and *Notes*. These are still listed as doctrinal standards in every *Discipline* (Disc., 2004; para. 103; 71).[2]

How is Continuous Binding Authority Established?

What protects the Articles, Sermons and Notes under the Restrictive Rule?

- Their inclusion in the Constitution.
- Their long history of consensual reception,
- especially their inclusion in the trust clause for property deeds; and finally
- the irrevocable Plan of Union as an instrument of civil law.

If the binding authority of these "present existing and established standards" had been questioned in any decade, it surely would have been actively debated and there would have been some written residue of the debate, but there is no such residue. A motion explicitly stricken from the record (as in the case of the Ward motion in the 1808 minutes) cannot be used as an argument, since it is merely an argument from silence. Exactly what was meant by "our present and existing standards of doctrine" in 1808 was clear to all Methodist preachers and ordinands because it was simply the continuation of the steady textual tradition written into every trust clause. "The Articles did not annul anything in the old standards and there was no act of abrogation (Bishop Thomas Neely; DSM; 207). These standard documents have repeatedly been confirmed without any hint of a record of

2 Referring to the first clause, there are several Judicial Council decisions (JCD 358, 1972; JCD 947; 1998; JCD 871; 1999) that speak of the Articles, Confession and Rules, not to "be revoked, altered, or changed." But the earlier Judicial Council ruling 358; 1972, clearly had divided the documents covered under the Restrictive Rules into these two parts: first, Articles, Confession and Rules; and second, "any new standards or rules of doctrine contrary to our present existing standards of doctrine" JCD 358; 1972. When this ruling was made, the Judicial Council elected not to rule on whether the 1968 Report of the Theological Study Commission on Doctrine violates the Restrictive Rules. Subsequently, the General Conference of 1988 did act to make this clear in all subsequent *Disciplines*.

dissent from the earliest times. The argument against their consistent historical confirmation remains a weak one – an argument from silence.

When the Judicial Council was asked to allow "deletion by the General Conference of provisions of the Constitution no longer relevant because of passage of time," the Council reaffirmed: "No portion of the Constitution ... may be amended or deleted by the General Conference without the required vote in the Annual Conference" (Judicial Council Decisions; hereafter JCD; 483, 1980). This is so difficult to obtain that it never has been challenged.

I have sometimes been asked what would ever cause me to leave the church that baptized and ordained me – surely there must be some limit. I always answer simply: "abrogation of the First Restrictive Rule." This is shorthand for "abrogation of doctrinal standards." Nathan Bangs, the pre-eminent nineteenth-century Methodist historian, showed why the First Restrictive Rule was written: "knowing the rage of man for novelty, and witnessing the destructive changes which have frequently laid waste the church by removing ancient land marks, and so modifying doctrines and usages as to suit the temper of the times, or to gratify either a corrupt taste or a perverse disposition, many had felt uneasy apprehensions for the safety and unity of the church and the stability of its doctrine" (*History of the M E. Church*; 4 vols.; New York; Carlton and Porter; 1859; 223-4). Hence, the First Restrictive Rule has become a constitutional bulwark.

How the Exception of 1832 Made Any Amendments to the Trust Clause in Property Deeds Even More Formidable

After 1808, the First Restrictive Rule has remained continuously in effect and, indeed, increased its force. This is clear from a decisive action in 1832. A resolute proviso was added that made the Restrictive Rule even more difficult to circumvent. This was a brilliant procedural defense to protect all Methodist pulpits and their property deeds legally from abuse or maladministration. It is somewhat analogous to the Bill of Rights.

What is the *Exception of 1832*? There, the General Conference set forth a daunting method for amending the Restrictive Rule, so demanding as to be generally perceived to be virtually impossible. According to the Exception of 1832, the Restrictive Rule could be changed only by these supermajorities: "*The concurrent recommendation of three fourths of all the members of the several annual conferences who shall be present and vote on such a recommendation, then a majority of two thirds of the conference succeeding*" (JGC; 1832; 378). Why such a double layer of safeguards? To protect the doctrinal standards.

This is the only method for changing the Restrictive Rule and, hence, the trust clause and, hence, the terms for legal property use. It is formidable and exacting. The provision for amending the Rule is a double process, as stated by Bishop Thomas Neely: "First it would be necessary to amend the provision for amendment by striking out the words 'excepting the first article.' This could be done by the .... action of two thirds in the General Conference and the concurrence of three fourths in the Annual Conference." (*A History of the Origin and Development of the Governing Conference in Methodism*; Cincinnati; Hunt and Eaton; 1892; 405).

This Exception still remains immovably fixed in the Constitution that governs every deed of local church property. There has never been any serious attempt in Methodist history to abrogate or amend the First Restrictive Rule, and very likely there will not be. The Restrictive Rules are the only portions of the Constitution subject to such strict defense against amendment.

Hence, no General Conference can amend the first and second Restrictive Rules on its own authority, without an insuperable "three-fourths majority of all the members of the annual conferences" (Disc., 2004; para. 57; 39). Any proposed amendment can occur only by this extremely demanding procedure that virtually insures its continuing effect.

This presents a formidable barrier, making the Rule virtually unamendable. Few today think the First Restrictive Rule can be changed. *It is the central fortress of the American Methodist constitutional system. But what is pertinent to this argument is that its doctrinal standards are guaranteed in every trust clause of every local church in all subsequent* Disciplines.

The Interweaving of Property Administration with Doctrinal Accountability

It has been demonstrated that there is an intimate interweaving between the Restrictive Rules and the trust clause The Restrictive Rules define and protect the inviolability of the texts of the doctrinal standards. The trust clause defines and protects the use of church property based on the doctrinal standards. These intermesh intrinsically. *These doctrinal standards are pertinent to the assessment of the work of any ordained minister or church leader, and to the proper use of church property, under the direct authority of the local church trust clause, as set forth in the* Discipline. Next, it is necessary to specify:

Who is Accountable?

The *Discipline* requires the bishops to take direct responsibility for "carrying into effect the rules, regulations, and responsibilities prescribed and enjoined by the General Conference and in accord with the provisions set forth in this Plan of Union" (Disc., 2000; para. 45; 35), which clearly specify these four doctrinal standards. If the Council of Bishops fails to carry into effect these responsibilities, the offending members of the Council could be liable to the charge of failure to provide episcopal supervision, for "The Council of Bishops is charged with the oversight of the spiritual and temporal affairs of the whole church" (Disc., 2004; para. 427.3; 288).

These doctrinal texts are constitutional standards not amendable by General Conference, and that do not depend upon approval from any Annual Conference or denominational executive or church leader or pastor because *all levels of United Methodist leadership* are strictly accountable to them.

No candidate for ordained *ministry* can ignore them, or be approved without answering the questions on willingness to preach United Methodist doctrine and implement United Methodist *Discipline* (Disc., 2004; para. 3330.4d.8-10.225; 214). If ordained ministers do not know or cannot in good conscience consent to the doctrinal standards they once voluntarily agreed to teach, then they may be subject to chargeable offenses, as well as vocational disingenuousness.

The Fourth Restrictive Rule (Disc., 2004; para. 20; 27), which provides the *right to fair trial* for both clergy and laity, does so under the assumption of accountability to the doctrinal standards protected by the First and Second Restrictive Rules. No judicatory or local church or person has the right to deny due process to those seeking to obey church law.

The General Conference Decision of 1988 on Doctrinal Standards

The clarity and firmness of the Plan of Union was one of the major reasons why the Committee on Our Theological Task in 1988 resisted an interpretation of the doctrinal standards that would privilege the *Articles* as more decisive. The argument for this approach (based upon a presumed motion that was subsequently *stricken* from the minutes of the 1808 General Conference) elicited a three-year debate that ended in 1988. That debated ended with a firm action of the General Conference. The idea of deleting the *Sermons* and *Notes* from constitutional protection was defeated. However stressful the debate was, it had one salutary effect: It made it necessary for the General Conference to make entirely unambiguous the protected status of the *Sermons* and *Notes* as "our doctrinal standards."

Hence, all *Disciplines* after 1988 confirm the textual definition of "Our Doctrinal Standards." "The headings of the current *Discipline* clearly list the texts of Our Doctrinal Standards and General Rules (Disc., 2004; para. 103;

59-74). They are the outcome of the 1988 decision. In order to avoid any confusion, they are listed by document title as follows: The Articles of Religion of The Methodist Church, The Confession of Faith of The Evangelical United Brethren, The Standard Sermons of Wesley, The Explanatory Notes Upon The New Testament, and The General Rules of The Methodist Church. Together, they define the standards.

All of these are important. The General Rules assert "the connection between doctrine and ethics" (Disc., 2004; para. 101; 49). They are sometimes treated under doctrinal standards, but more specifically as a bridge between doctrine and ethics. They, too, are protected by a Restrictive Rule, Article V (Disc., 2004; para. 21; 27). They "convey the expectation of discipline within the experience of individuals and the life of the Church. Such discipline assumes accountability to the community of faith by those who claim that community's support" (ibid.). Thus, it is a constitutional requirement that the doctrinal standards are expected to be understood by, and remain obligatory for, any church official.

FREE INQUIRY WITHIN DOCTRINAL GUIDELINES

The *Discipline* rightly protects "free inquiry *within* the boundaries defined by" our doctrinal tradition and standards, assuming that "*Scripture is the primary source and criterion for Christian doctrine*" (Disc., 2004;, para. 104; 78; italics added). "Our standards affirm the Bible as the source of all that is 'necessary' and 'sufficient' unto salvation (*Articles of Religion*) and 'is to be received through the Holy Spirit as the true rule and guide for faith and practice' (*Confession of Faith*)" (Disc., 2004; para. 104; 78).

For laypersons, there is no formal ascription to these standards, but they are binding upon all "who assume accountability" to the connection, and especially all who have been duly ordained to fulfill the teaching office. Our doctrinal standards do not demand of laity "unqualified assent on pain of excommunication," but the questions for ordination and the possible charges against elders place the ordained clergy under rigorous voluntary requirements. The standards are to be viewed as model sermons, exegetical notes and explicit condensed confessions, as guidelines "for the sake of authentic renewal" (Disc., 2004; para. 102, 59). But this does not give license to "'theological indifferentism' – the notion that there are no essential doctrines" (Disc., 1980; para. 69; 73). Other doctrinal summaries or theological interpretations may be licitly argued, but "*without displacing those we already have*" (Disc., 1980; para. 67; 50; italics added).

The Persistent Misstatement of the Trust Clause

The trust clause sometimes has been wrongly interpreted as an obstacle to the faithful who seek to protect their own church property from takeover or abuse. Some evangelicals have developed a mistaken habit of assuming that the trust clause was a stumbling block for them. It is the opposite. It protects the faithful from domination by the unfaithful. Laypersons have imaged that if they disagreed with the Conference leadership, they would be faced with the dire alternative of surrendering the local church property itself to an entity that itself is arguably unaccountable to the Discipline. In most cases where property has been surrendered, the local church has not known its constitutional rights under church and civil law. Their legal counsel often has not understood the history of deeds and its documentation.

Now the tables are turning. The reconsideration of these constitutional guarantees reflected in the trust clause places our property dilemmas in an entirely different light: Now the trust clause can be rightly understood to be a legal instrument to call the judicatory itself to account under its own constitution, based on a continuing unchanging tradition of both historical and contemporary documents that have juridical and binding import.

The very trust clause that sometimes has been abused so as to intimidate faithful local churches and threaten to wrest their very property from them may now be seen itself as a powerful argument in their defense. But all this assumes that they are well-informed, are rigorously faithful to doctrinal and disciplinary standards, and have not sought to withdraw from the church.

The most ill-advised decision that can be made by the local church is too quickly to declare itself independent of the church and its Discipline, the very instruments that seek to protect it from abuse. Attorneys for congregations need to be advised of this constitutional history, which still is in effect and embedded in their own property deeds.

Are These Legally Binding Standards Testable in a Court of Law?

But many doubt that these historic doctrinal standards are legally binding standards in a court of civil law. Are they not merely church law with no standing before the civil courts?

The civil courts have no jurisdiction whatever entering into doctrinal disputes or determining church law as such. They have a consistent record of not entering this privileged territory, commendably.

But they do have jurisdiction and valid interest in certain spheres of distinctively civil action (as distinguished from church law, doctrine or polity).

Here is a short list of ten of these arenas where civil court judgments do not infringe on the right to freedom of religion, but rather protect that right:

- Abuses of constitutional rights under the U.S. Constitution and Bill of Rights (such as limiting freedom of worship, speech, press, or assembly).
- The taking of property without just compensation.
- The due performance of contracts.
- The fair examination of evidences of fraud or malfeasance.
- Abuses of due process under civil law.
- Actions against public policy or actions disruptive of public order that offend public decency (such as the disruption of communities, the embitterment of long-standing peaceful communities of worship, or the pre-emptive exercise of questionable authority).
- The legal guarantee that organizations be allowed to operate under their own legal and constitutional constraints.
- The rights of laity who have paid for church property to use church property in accord with church *Discipline*; and especially
- The fair use of property under the trust clause in legal deeds.

The above points of law are all issues of *civil* law; hence, referable to civil courts if need be. These are not rights granted by the church constitution, but by the U.S. Constitution and state constitutions. There is little doubt that the trust clause in property deeds will have directive, judicial and legally binding authority enforceable under civil law in these civil justice arenas. It is along the lines of these civil issues that actions are almost certainly going to occur.

THE APPEAL TO THE TRUST CLAUSE OF PROPERTY DEEDS

The Judicial Council does not make church law; rather, it interprets it. Administration of church law is defined by the church constitution and by the due legislative entity acting under that constitution, not by the courts.

All remedies first must be sought through ordinary church law, but when those remedies fail, the only remaining remedy may be the appeal to the title deeds under which local church buildings and property are legally protected and duly constituted. Any remedy should be sought under strict disciplinary procedures and with due process, and only under extreme conditions in civil actions, if needed – never unnecessarily, but only if no other judiciable remedies are available within church law. The courts have no jurisdiction except in cases of flagrant repeated abuses of civil liberties, or in enforcing the contracts legally binding, or when title deeds that govern the use of local church property are ignored, or in cases where some of the civil guarantees require resolution (such as the constitutional right to freedom of assembly or speech or religion, or the taking of property without just compensation, due performance of contracts, fraud, malfeasance, or due process).

If faithful congregations are deprived of or threatened to be expelled from their church property, as they have been in some instances, they need not be afraid to ask that the civil rights of those faithful to the connection be protected. It is a civil right to receive due process under law concerning fair use of title deeds. The faithful have a civil right to have the constituting rules of order that have prevailed for over two centuries respected by their own clergy, Conferences and judicatories.

Answering the Three Most Common Objections

There are three common objections to this line of argument, familiar to any who have entered the threshold of this debate. They are:

"But we are not a doctrinal church." The most common objection to taking doctrinal standards seriously is the historically uninformed view that the church has no doctrine, or no textually defined church teaching. If the church lacks doctrine, why does it have the doctrinal standards written into its Constitution? Why does its Discipline guarantee them to be rigorously unchangeable? Why are clergy required to understand and consent to them and preach them in good conscience? Why would there be a provision for chargeable offenses when they are inveighed against?

We do, in fact, have doctrinal standards that are embedded in our daily use of church property. These doctrinal standards have enjoyed respect from the courts and laity for over two centuries of consent and continuity, with no abrogation. It is a specious assumption that any mainline church is without doctrinal constraints, or can define its own doctrine arbitrarily, apart from its constitution and history

"But we encourage theology based on experience." In fact, the Discipline instead calls the worshiping community to "interpret our experience in terms of Scripture" (Disc., 2004; para. 104; 81; italics added). Indeed, "We interpret experience in the light of Scriptural norms" (Ibid.; 82; italics added). Experiential theology is viewed as standing under the guidance of Mr. Wesley and his writings: "We follow Wesley's practice of examining experience, both individual and corporate, for confirmations of the realities of God's grace attested in Scripture" (Disc., 2004; para. 104; italics added.

Finally, it sometimes is objected that: "We are not a confessional church." The argument that we are entirely non-confessional is evasive. We actually do have a constitutionally-recognized Confession – the Confession of Faith (Disc., 2004; para. 103). If we are not a confessional church, why do we have a Confession? And why would we protect that Confession with an extraordinary bulwark of constitutional guarantees that cannot be revoked, altered, or changed (para. 17).

Confessing Christians are not cranks, not historically unsophisticated, and not divisive. They will not be intimidated. And they are going to stay within the church, with all its faults, and uphold church teaching. They understand that they no longer can keep silent, and will not be harassed or chased out of the church that baptized them and taught them to respect the integrity of due process.

CHAPTER SIX

CONSIDERATIONS SPECIFIC TO EPISCOPALIANS

The mother church of American Protestantism is the Episcopal Church. Today, this denomination has only 795,765 people who attend its 7,200 parishes and missions on an average Sunday, giving it a median average Sunday worship attendance of 75 souls per congregation.[1] Notwithstanding its few numbers today, however, the history of the Episcopal Church is the key to understanding much in the spiritual history of Protestant America.

The key to understanding the law of real property from an Episcopal Church perspective is to understand the history of the church since, as Oliver Wendell Holmes famously said, "A page of history is worth a volume of logic."

The colonial settlers of England who came to the Americas brought with them their faith. Numerous Anglican congregations were established in as many towns and villages as there were settlements from the mother county in the colonies of Massachusetts, Connecticut, New York and Virginia. The church congregations from the Church of England that were planted on the American continent were the first Christian worshiping communities in colonial America. Some were faithful to the Church of England, such as those who came to Jamestown in Virginia in 1609, and others were dissenters, such as those who settled at Plymouth in Massachusetts in 1620. By 1740, there were 246 Anglican churches in the colonies (almost 20 percent of the total of all congregations) and by 1776, there were 495.[2] But more significant than the numbers (which started to proportionally decline even before American independence was declared from England), Episcopalians have had a disproportionately large share of influence and money. There have been more American presidents, congressmen and Supreme Court justices who were

1 Report of the House of Deputies Committee on the State of the Church to the 75th General Convention (2006), p. 51, colloquially known as the Blue Book. This data is from compiled statistics for the calendar year 2004.

2 Noll, Mark A.; *America's God* (Oxford University Press; New York; 2002) p. 162.

Episcopalians than any other faith tradition.

When these English settlers brought Anglicanism to the colonies, though, they brought it in a changed format from what it was in England. They came with Anglican priests, the *Book of Common Prayer* and their laity, but they did not come with bishops. They came with notions of independence from the authorities they had left across the Atlantic. Massachusetts – from Plymouth, Boston and beyond – was settled by Puritan dissenters from the Anglican Church.

Virginia was strongly Anglican, with churches ruled by lay vestries of independent-minded men who learned the principles of democracy as they practiced them in their parishes before they brought them into the political area. In 1763, for example, prominent laymen George Washington and George William Fairfax were appointed church wardens of a small Anglican congregation in northern Virginia that today is known as The Falls Church. With no bishops in the colonies and few priests, strong laity such as Washington and Fairfax took the leadership roles by necessity and inclination. In Virginia, the vestries of laity ruled the church and effectively dictated how the parish was to be run, even to the clergy.

These notions of independence greatly influenced the political discourse of the fledgling colonies. They settled and established a church in America that, in theory, was episcopal; i.e., bishop-led; yet, the transplant of their church to America was without *the* single distinctive feature that made the English Church different from most of it Protestant brethren – bishops.

In theory, they had a bishop over them since the Bishop of London exercised jurisdiction over the Anglican church in the colonies.[3] But with a six-week, one-way trip some 3,000 miles across a stormy ocean in a small sailing ship between the bishop on one continent, and priests and parishes on another, meaningful ecclesiastical oversight was nonexistent. This state of affairs lasted for almost two centuries after the first Anglican worship came to America.

America got its first Anglican bishop after the end of the Revolutionary War. Samuel Seabury, an Episcopal priest from Connecticut, was consecrated a bishop in the Scottish Church in 1784 and then returned to America. But even after his arrival, it was lay leadership in the American church that distinguished it from its English mother church.

3 In the wake of General Convention 2003 and the consecration of a homosexual bishop in New Hampshire, several formerly Episcopal churches in the United States left the ecclesiastical oversight of their diocesan bishops and submitted themselves to bishops in Rwanda, Uganda, Bolivia, and other overseas ecclesiastical jurisdictions of the Anglican Communion in an ironic return to overseas bishops reminiscent of the earliest days of the American church.

Writing in the mid-19th century, the distinctively democratic polity of the Episcopal Church in America was criticized by an English cleric who compared it to the Church of England. He described the American Episcopal Church as a form of "polity, which was, in fact, copied, in the main, from the political institutions of the newly-founded republic, and rested, therefore, far too much upon the choice and self-government of all its members."[4] Rather than government from the bishops running things from the top down, this American church was completely different. The cleric's scorn of the democracy of the American church is clear in his description of it as he saw it:

> The title "parish" in America has a widely different meaning from that which it bears with us. [I]t was merely a set of persons who associated themselves together and agreed to act and worship together in a certain place, and under certain rules, because they preferred the episcopal form to any other. Their very corporate existence was the consequence of their own choice and will, and not the result of care taken for them; and this principle was present every where. After a time these men determined upon building a church; they built it, and divided its area into pews, which they took to themselves... ... [E]very year all the holders of the pews met together to elect by ballot a vestry, ... To this vestry the management of all the affairs of the parish was committed, and this lay body not only conducted its pecuniary concerns, but settled the payment of the minister, "engaged the services of a clergyman in cases of a vacancy." Thus by this system, not only was the pastor dependent on the offerings of his flock, but he derived his authority from them, and to them he was responsible.[5]

The diocese suffered from the same democratic disease, he scorned:

> Next to the parish comes the diocese, which consists of all the parishes within any one state, which, having organized themselves according to the rules of the general convention, have been admitted into union with it. Here again, the same faulty principle was present. ...[I]n America a diocese meant

4 Wilberforce, Samuel; *A History of the Protestant Episcopal Church in America* (James Burns; London; 1844) p. 241.

5 Id., p. 242-44.

> nothing more than a federal commonwealth of "parishes," associated on certain prescribed conditions with each other and the general convention. So far from dependence on one bishop defining its character and marking its limits, it might, and often must, for years, by the general canons of the Church, have no bishop at all.[6]

The logical conclusion from this over-reliance on democracy and the semi-necessary need for a diocese to have a bishop, according to the English commentator, is that:

> It fostered the very spirit of self-will and independence from which it sprang; for, by allowing the organization of a diocese without a bishop, it led practically to the undervaluing of the office of a bishop, to it being esteemed an ornamental part of the Church machinery, and not as the power of government and the instrument of a visible unity. The "convention," and not the episcopate, became really the ruling power. That is, while called Episcopal, the Church was, in fact, in a great measure Presbyterian.[7]

This lay-led polity of the American church had an impact on property law from the days of its formation. One of the largest and most prominent Anglican congregations in the new United States was King's Chapel in Boston. During the Revolution, many of the members of King's Chapel, being loyal to the King, fled the country – leaving the parish with a strong patriot congregation. This fostered an uneasy alliance with the traditional Anglican form of worship and animosity toward foreign bishops. Even when there finally was an American bishop, the free-spirited Bostonians of King's Chapel maintained their sense of independence. An uneasy mixed loyalty simmered for years over arguments about the proposed *Book of Common Prayer* and theology. The pleas of Bishop Samuel Seabury and others that a parish could not leave the Episcopal Church fell on deaf ears in Boston. The fact that Seabury had been sympathetic to the British in the American Revolution did not help matters either. Ultimately, the dispute between the congregation and the larger Episcopal Church culminated on November 18, 1787, when a lay reader of the parish was ordained as priest and installed as rector by the senior warden. King's Chapel, its church building and all, walked away from the

6 Id., p. 245-46.

7 Id., p. 249.

Episcopal Church and became Unitarian.[8]

The way colonial worshipers related to their churches encouraged a local sense of ownership. "Parish churches 'belonged' to the parishioners who had purchased pews. As proprietors, they handled the finances, made all the decisions, hired and fired the clergy." This scheme of ownership of a church by its members in some places lasted until the early 20th century and, "while it lasted it nourished a sense of congregational identity so strong that it could put any sense of diocesan identity in the shade."[9]

Another factor contributing to the lack of Episcopal authority over church buildings is the early 19th century tendency toward "community" churches. Today, we think of a community church as basically an independent, non-denominational church. The early community churches, though, were mixtures of people of various Protestant denominations who worshiped in a single building in one town or village that was too small for numerous churches. When common worship was held with the others, a vote of the majority determined the form of worship, be it Episcopal, Presbyterian, Methodist, or dissenters. Usually, Episcopalians (or Churchmen, as they were called) were in a minority, and got outvoted. Yet, the congregants tended to keep their own denominational identity. Such an arrangement hardly contributed to any bishop or diocesan authority over church lands.[10]

In Virginia, a different assault was made upon the property of the Episcopal Church. Englishmen settled Virginia and received their charters of land through the monarch, and their churches derived their charters and the title of their lands from the same English sovereign. They literally were "established" churches as they were in England, and supported by the public purse. Cutting the ties to England at the end of the American Revolution changed this. In the name of religious liberty, no longer would public monies be used to support the church. The Virginia legislature cut the purse strings, and "dis-established" the church.

On Jan. 24, 1777, the Virginia General Assembly passed a law that "repealed all the laws relative to the late Protestant Episcopal church" and directed that the church properties be sold. "The proceeds of the sale were

8 Loveland, Clara O.; *The Critical Years: The Reconstitution of the Anglican Church in the United States of America: 1780-1789* (Seabury Press; New York; 1956) pp. 19, 161-180, 226-27; Hodges, George; *The Religious History of New England, King's Chapel Lectures* (Harvard University Press; Boston; 1917) pp. 237-38.

9 Duffy, Mark J.; Editor; *The Episcopal Diocese of Massachusetts 1784-1984: A Mission to Remember, Proclaim, and Fulfill* (Episcopal Diocese of Massachusetts; Boston; 1984) p. 2.

10 Walker, Frances Moorman; *The Early Episcopal Church in the Amherst-Nelson Area* [of Virginia] (J.P. Bell Co., Inc.; Lynchburg, Va.; 1964) pp. 34-5, 37-8, 44.

directed to be appropriated to the poor of the parish, or to any other object which a majority of freeholders and housekeepers in the parish might by writing direct, provided that nothing should authorize an appropriation of it 'to any *religious* purpose whatever.'"[11] No parish or diocese could stand up against the popular will of the people embodied in these newborn state legislatures.

One way to determine which level of the church has authority over church property is to ask where the Episcopal Church falls on a continuum of church authority. Four possible forms of polity for a church have been identified. They range from the most democratic on one end of the church spectrum to the rule of a single religious figure from the top at the other end of the church spectrum. In that order, they have been described as 1) congregational; 2) synodical or presbyterian; 3) episcopal; and 4) papal.[12] If the Episcopal Church were purely congregational, the answer would be easy: The local parish would have unfettered control over the parish property. If it were papal, the equally easy answer would be the opposite. Unfortunately, such a simplistic approach does not tell us much since, as one modern commentator has concluded,, "the Church is in some ways congregational and presbyterian as well as Episcopalian."[13]

After the first bishop was consecrated beginning with Samuel Seabury in 1784, two more were added once peace was made with Britain and parliament authorized American bishops. In 1787, William White of United Church in Philadelphia and Samuel Provoost of Trinity Church on Wall Street in New York City were consecrated bishops in England and, hence, the General Convention's House of Deputies was complemented with a House of Bishops. These bishops continued to serve as rectors of their parishes, and their duties as bishops occupied their duties along with the usual pastoral duties of running a parish. As a practical result, most of the day-to-day duties of the early bishops were taken up with their duties as parish pastors, rather than handling the affairs of the diocese or the larger church.

Two of these early bishops of the Protestant Episcopal Church had differing views of how the church should be run. Bishop William White, being a patriot and supporter of the American Revolution, had a more democratic and congregational approach toward church government. Bishop Samuel Seabury, with Loyalist political leanings, favored a more English model that would have given far more authority to the bishops. The dispute

11 Hawkes, Francis L.; *Contributions to the Ecclesiastical History of the United States*; Volume I (Harper & Brothers; New York; 1836) p. 234.

12 Stevick, David B.; *Canon Law: A Handbook* (Seabury Press; New York; 1965) pp. 71-86.

13 Id., at p. 87.

threatened to split the early church just as it was being formed. Had that happened, today we might have had two rather than one Episcopal Church as the heritage from the Church of England.

But both sides were committed to unity, and both sides compromised to form one church. Basically, Bishop White's views carried the day, leaving the early American bishops with little authority over the parishes, their property and their rectors. Bishop Seabury won some concessions with a more high church, Eucharistic prayer in the *Prayer Book* and the right of the bishops rather than vestries to discipline the clergy.[14] This is a legacy that survives to the modern day.

The Episcopal Church as it was configured at its inception looked a little like the United States under the Articles of Confederation. The parish was the most important and fundamental unit of the church. Parishes were autonomous and quite independent from the diocese. Neither the parish nor the diocese had much sense of the broader church across the country except in name.

The Protestant Episcopal Church of the United States of America (often abbreviated PECUSA and later ECUSA) as a "national" church is very much a misnomer. While the various parishes assembled at the first General Convention to band together and adopt a constitution and canons, they did little more than establish a pattern of meetings every three years of deputies from each state, with each state being organized as a diocese. They also began the early steps to adopt a *Book of Common Prayer* that was an Americanized variation of the English prayer book.

Neither this General Convention nor any diocese owned any property or laid claim to any property of any parish in these formative years, nor was there any effort to regulate parish property. Parish property was a matter of local control completely unfettered by the diocese or the ECUSA. As far as real property was concerned, the ECUSA was purely congregational, except that the elected vestry of the congregation rather than the parish congregational meeting was in control of the real estate of the parish.

Beginning in 1789, the General Convention met every three years, but it did and said nothing with respect to church property for almost a century. It is clear from the historical record that the Episcopal Church – be it the diocese, or the General Convention, or the bishops – exercised virtually no control over parish property until after the American Civil War.

For the first 40 years, there still was no national Episcopal Church of any

---

14 See generally, *The Critical Years: The Reconstitution of the Anglican Church in the United States of America: 1780-1789*; op. cit.; for an excellent discussion of the politics and maneuvering that produced the Episcopal Church.

real sort. All that existed was a triennial meeting of bishops and deputies to hammer out church laws (called canons) and resolutions. The effect of these meetings and canons on real parish property was non-existent.

In 1821, this changed slightly when a special convention of the church was held that resulted in the New York legislature passing legislation to incorporate "The Domestic and Foreign Missionary Society of the Protestant Episcopal Church in the United States of America," which "Society shall be considered as comprehending all persons who are members of this Church."[15]

Even after that corporation came into existence, there was no overarching national church organization. There was just this New York corporation. It was ruled by a General Convention that met every three years, and in between times by a Board of Missions to which "shall be entrusted the supervision of the general missionary operations of the Church, with power to establish missionary stations, appoint missionaries, make appropriations of money, regulate the conducting of missions, fill any vacancies in their number which may occur, and also to enact all by-laws which they may deem necessary for their own government and the government of their committees."[16]

The stated purposes did not include any authority or supervision over parish property. The only purpose of this entity was to establish missions and supervise them. Once a "mission" made the jump to self-supporting "parish," the statement of its purposes as set forth in the 1821 Constitution of the Society asserted no claim to authority over the parish, and no claim over its property. The charter of the corporation was (and to this day still is) silent concerning parish property.[17]

Before 1979, there were only a few provisions of church canon law that sought to place regulations or restrictions on parish church property.

The first canons seeking to restrict parish property were adopted at the General Convention of 1868 under the general title "Of Dedicated and Consecrated Churches." The current wording of one of these canons says that:

> It shall not be lawful for any Vestry, Trustees, or other body authorized by laws of any State or Territory to hold property for any Diocese, Parish or Congregation, to

15 1821 Constitution of the Domestic and Foreign Missionary Society of the Protestant Episcopal Church in the United States of America, Articles I & II, reprinted in *Annotated Constitution and Canons for the Government of the Protestant Episcopal Church in the United States of America otherwise known as The Episcopal Church* (Volume I) by White & Dykman, Church Publishing Incorporated (1981) p. 216-18.

16 Id., Article IV, p. 216.

17 The current version of the Constitution of this corporation is found in Canon I.3 of the Canons of the General Convention (2003).

> encumber or alienate any dedicated and consecrated Church or Chapel, or any Church or Chapel which has been used solely for Divine Service, belonging to the Parish or Congregation which they represent, without the previous consent of the Bishop, acting with the advice and consent of the Standing Committee of the Diocese.[18]

The focus of this canon is to protect property that is a "dedicated and consecrated Church or Chapel." It does not apply to the church rectory, or any other real estate that a parish might happen to own. The *Book of Common Prayer* has a service titled "The Dedication and Consecration of a Church," which focuses on the sacred function of the buildings.[19] It also contemplates protection of property that has "been used *solely* for Divine Service," (emphasis supplied) and not property with multiple use for worship, and also used for other functions. Hence, the concern of this canon appears to be a limited protection of dedicated and consecrated sacred space used solely for worship.

Another canon adopted at the same time pertains to "the building and the ground on which [a church or chapel] it is erected" and regulates what property may be "consecrated" by the bishop.

> No Church or Chapel shall be consecrated until the Bishop shall have been sufficiently satisfied that the building and the ground on which it is erected are secured for ownership and use by a Parish, Mission, Congregation, or Institution affiliated with this Church and subject to its Constitution and Canons.[20]

The emphasis of this canon is on what property a bishop may consecrate, not on the restriction of parish property generally.[21]

---

18 Canon II.6.2 of the Canons of the General Convention (2003). *Annotated Constitution and Canons for the Government of the Protestant Episcopal Church in the United States of America otherwise known as The Episcopal Church* (Volume I) by White & Dykman, Church Publishing Incorporated (1981) p. 478.

19 *Book of Common Prayer* (1979) p. 567-579.

20 Canon II.6.1

21 Related to Canon II.6.1 is Canon II.6.4, which also mentions "Any dedicated and consecrated Church or Chapel." Canon II.6.4 was proposed in 1979 along with Canon I.7.4 (the so-called "Dennis Canon") and directly references it. Canon II.6.4 suffers from the same procedural defect in its enactment as Canon I.7.4, as noted in *Annotated Constitution and Canons for the Government of the Protestant Episcopal Church in the United States of America otherwise known as The Episcopal Church* (Volume I); op. cit.;

In this era of shrinking church attendance in the Episcopal Church, many parishes are closing their doors and the property is being sold. While there is no service in the *Prayer Book* for the de-consecrating of a church or chapel, services of de-consecration are becoming common, especially in dioceses where church attendance is forcing the closing of parishes. Once that service is performed on a church or chapel, these canons place no restrictions on the parish's use or disposition of the property.

There is a canon (also originally added in 1868) that contemplates the de-consecration of a church or chapel. That canon requires the consent of the standing committee of the diocese before a dedicated and consecrated church or chapel can be torn down.[22] Again, it is apparently the concern for sacred space rather than a general restriction on parish real estate that undergirds this canon, as well as the canons discussed above.

The only other canon that deals with church property is a canon that restricts the ability of any parish to "encumber or alienate [real estate] or any part thereof without the written consent of the Bishop and Standing Committee of the Diocese of which the Parish, Mission, Congregation, or Institution is a part, except under such regulations as may be prescribed by Canon of the Diocese."[23] This provision of the church canons dovetails with the laws of most states that seek to place restrictions on the mortgage or sale of church property and often requires court approval for such transactions.[24] There is little textual history to determine the precise purpose behind this canon. However, it is apparently a canon that seeks, as do the numerous similar state statutes requiring court consent to sell church property, to protect religious corporations from being fleeced by unscrupulous buyers of church lands who would give an inadequate price for the property.

Even with these canons of the General Convention, the vestry was left in control of all parish property. Under canon law, "the Vestry shall be agents and legal representatives of the Parish in all matters concerning its corporate property and the relations of the Parish to the Clergy."[25] There is a provision of canon law that gives the rector of the parish "use and control of the Church and Parish buildings."[26] But there is nothing in canon law giving the bishop, the diocese, the General Convention, or The Domestic and Foreign

p. 480, discussed later in this chapter. Hence, while Canon II.6.4 appears in the book of the canons, it apparently was not enacted.

22 Canon II.6.3 of the Canons of the General Convention (2003).

23 Canon I.7.3 of the Canons of the General Convention (2003).

24 New York Religious Corporations Law §12, Consolidated Laws of New York (2005), is one example of such state statutes.

25 Canon I.14.2 of the Canons of the General Convention (2003).

26 Canon III.9.5(a)(2) of the Canons of the General Convention (2003).

Missionary Society any authority over any parish property, other than the consent needed of the diocesan bishop and standing committee to sell or mortgage.

This was the state of Episcopal Church canon law in 1979 when a problem was brewing. Three years earlier, the General Convention adopted a proposed *Book of Common Prayer* with a more ambiguous and liberal theology than the 1928 *Prayer Book* that the church had been using. There also was dissatisfaction with the ordination of women priests in the Episcopal Church. Between the conventions of 1976 and 1979, there were 32 parishes "in which substantial schism occurred" and 11 "attempts to alienate property" away from the Episcopal Church.[27] These circumstances, along with the issuance of a U.S. Supreme Court decision, inspired defensive measures at the 1979 General Convention to prevent parishes from leaving with their property.

The Supreme Court decision was *Jones v. Wolf*, released by the court on July 2, 1979.[28] The Episcopal Church General Convention was scheduled for September of that year. *Jones v. Wolf* decided that "neutral principles of law" could be constitutionally used to resolve disputes between a local Georgia Presbyterian church and the denomination from which it sought to secede. In making such a determination under "neutral principles of law," a civil court could look to several things. Those things include "the language of the deeds, the terms of the local church charters, the state statutes governing the holding of church property, and the provisions in the constitution of the general church concerning the ownership and control of church property."[29] It was this last clause of itemized factors ("the provisions in the constitution of the general church concerning the ownership and control of church property") that caught the attention of those at the highest councils of the Episcopal Church who were alarmed at the prospect of local parishes leaving the denomination and taking their property with them.

On Sept. 13, 1979, during the General Convention, the House of Bishops adopted House of Bishops Resolution #76, the so-called "Dennis Canon," named after Bishop Walter Dennis.[30] This proposed canon contained two parts, adding the following material to Canon I.7:

> Sec. 4. All real and personal property held by or for the benefit of any Parish, Mission or Congregation is held in

27 *Journal of the General Convention of the Protestant Episcopal Church of the United States of America otherwise known as the Episcopal Church* (1979), p. AA-282.

28 443 U.S. 595 (1979)

29 *Jones v. Wolf*, 443 U.S. 595, 603 (1979)

30 *Journal*; op. cit.; at p. B-60-61.

> trust for this Church and the Diocese thereof in which such Parish, Mission or Congregation is located. The existence of this trust, however, shall in no way limit the power and authority of the Parish, Mission or Congregation otherwise existing over such property so long as the particular Parish, Mission or Congregation remains a part of, and subject to, this Church and its Constitution and Canons.
>
> Sec. 5. The several Dioceses may, at their election, further confirm the trust declared under the foregoing Section 4 by appropriate action, but no such action shall be necessary for the existence and validity of the trust.

Since the General Convention is a bicameral legislature, both the House of Bishops and the House of Deputies must pass the exact same resolution for the action to pass the convention and become part of church canon law. The official record of the General Convention is the *Journal*, and actions passed by both houses are listed under "concurrent actions" in the *Journal*.

The *Journal* shows an entry on Sept. 19, 1979, which was the second to last day of the General Convention. In the records for the House of Deputies, the *Journal* reports "recommended concurrence with the House of Bishops Messages #75 and #76. The House Concurred (See pg. C-150)."[31] However, on page C-150 of the *Journal*, there is no reference to this proposed canon, but there is a reference to a different but somewhat related canonical change. Since all actions by both the House of Bishops and the House of Deputies are listed under "concurrent actions" in pages numbered with a "C," it appears that the official record of the convention indicates that the House of Deputies never concurred in the resolution of the House of Bishops to the "Dennis Canon." This apparent defect in the convention proceedings is noted in the authoritative and most recent edition of the *Annotated Canons of the Church* published by the official publishing house of the church.[32]

The "Dennis Canon" is found in all of the official printed copies of the Canons as Canon I.7.4 and Canon I.7.5. The book has been reissued every three years after the General Convention, and these "Canons" have been included in the published text. But it is not the publication of a law in a law book that makes it a valid law. It is the proper adoption of the law by lawfully

31 Id., at p. D-154.

32 *Annotated Constitution and Canons for the Government of the Protestant Episcopal Church in the United States of America otherwise known as The Episcopal Church* (Volume I); op. cit.; p. 296.

constituted procedures that makes it valid.

How does one decide whether this canon was properly adopted? The official *Journal* of the convention is the one and only authoritative source of what happened there. The fact that the "Dennis Canon" is in the latest published copy of the canons says nothing about its validity. If it never was adopted by both Houses, it is not a canon of the church. The official *Journal* of the convention's proceedings does not show it as having been adopted as a concurrent action of both Houses. Hence, the most reasonable legal conclusion one can draw is that the published book of the canons contains two proposed canons that were never adopted.[33]

Even if one were to conclude that the canon was validly adopted and is a part of the canon law of the church, the civil courts have not been uniform in their rulings in cases in which dioceses have asserted the "Dennis Canon" against a parish in disputes over the parish property.

In decisions rendered between 1986 and 2003, courts in Colorado, Connecticut, New York and Massachusetts have implied trusts in favor of the diocese and the ECUSA in the property of parishes based on the "Dennis Canon".[34]

Contrast the decision of the California Court of Appeal, which applied "neutral principles of law" in ruling that three of four parishes that had left the ECUSA and were sued for their property by the Diocese of Los Angeles owned their property free of any claim by the diocese. In so holding, the court refused to imply a trust and found that the evidence did not support a finding of express trust.[35] In three recently decided cases also in California, the trial court found in favor of parishes that had left the ECUSA.[36]

In each of these three cases (now on appeal by the Diocese of Los Angeles), "neutral principles of trust law" were discussed and considered as the court

33 See also, FN 21, *supra*, for a discussion of Canon II.6.4 which suffers from the same procedural defect as Canon I.7.4

34 See, *Bishop and Diocese of Colorado v. Mote*, 716 P.2d 85 (Colo. 1986); *Trinity-St. Michael's Parish, Inc. v, Episcopal Church In the Diocese of Ct.*, 224 Conn. 797, 620 A. 2d 1280 (1993); *Trustees of the Diocese of Albany v. Trinity Episcopal Church of Gloversville*, 250 App. Div. 2nd 282, 684 N.Y.S.2d 76 (3d Dept. 1999); and *Episcopal Diocese of Mass v. Deirdre Devine*, 797 N.E.2d 916 (Mass. 2003). The issues concerning the valid adoption of the "Dennis Canon" were not raised in any of these cases because that defect in the adoption procedure was not identified until late 2005.

35 *Protestant Episcopal Church in the Diocese of Los Angeles v. Barker*, 115 Cal. App. 3rd 599, 171 Cal. Rptr 541 (1981).

36 *Adair v. Poch* (Los Angeles Superior Court No. BC321101)(2005); *O'Halloran v. Thompson* (Los Angeles Superior Court No. BC321102) (2005); and *Rasmussen v. Bunyan* (Orange County Superior Court No. OC04CC00647) (2005); all of which cases are presently on appeal by the unsuccessful Diocese of Los Angeles.

rejected the claims of the diocese. This is consistent with another thoughtful application of principles of trust law in an unrelated church property dispute decided in 2004, also by the California Court of Appeal, in which a United Methodist parish successfully defended its claim to its property free of the claims of the United Methodist Church.[37] In that case, the court ruled among other things that a Dennis-like rule of the Church, if it did impress a trust, was revocable by the parish. In that case, the court asked rhetorically how someone who had no ownership interest in property could have the power to create a trust as to that property and make itself a beneficiary of that trust.

It is worthy to note that in the litigation in the Diocese of Los Angeles that currently is on appeal (see footnote 36), the ECUSA had attempted to intervene at the trial court level, asserting an interest in itself in the parishes' property under the "Dennis Canon." The court dismissed the ECUSA's complaints in intervention on the ground that the "Dennis Canon" did not give the ECUSA a claim to any interest in the property of the parishes.

May a parish using "neutral principles of law" enunciated in *Jones v. Wolf* leave the Episcopal Church and take its property with it? White & Dykman, the official commentary on the canons of the Episcopal Church, suggests that this is precisely what that case means. In its discussion of *Jones v. Wolf*, the commentary on Canon I.7.3 states that:

> This approach gives great weight to the actions of controlling majorities, and would appear to permit a majority faction in a parish to amend its parish charter to delete all references to the Episcopal Church, and thereafter to affiliate the parish – and its property – with a new ecclesiastical group.[38]

On the other hand, if a parish does not leave its diocese or the Episcopal Church, the "Dennis Canon" has no effect. By its own terms, it has no effect if a parish "remains a part of, and subject to, this Church and its Constitution and Canons." In such an instance, the vestry still controls the parish property.

Further intrigue involving the "Dennis Canon" comes from the Presiding Bishop of the Episcopal Church. In a recent statement carried by the online publication *The Living Church* titled "Dennis Canon Diocesan Issue, Presiding

37 *California-Nevada Annual Conference of the United Methodist Church v. St. Luke's United Methodist Church,* 17 Cal. Rptr 3rd 442 (Cal. Ct. App. 2004).

38 *Annotated Constitution and Canons for the Government of the Protestant Episcopal Church in the United States of America otherwise known as The Episcopal Church* (Volume I); op. cit.; p. 301.

Bishop," this issue is referenced with the following statement:

> Virtually all legal disputes over the ownership of parish property are internal diocesan matters and there is nothing in the so-called Dennis Canon that prevents a diocesan bishop from reaching an amicable settlement with a congregation that wants to leave the Episcopal Church and retain its building, according to Presiding Bishop Frank Griswold, who led separate question-and-answer forums for clergy and laity in the Diocese of Western Louisiana May 11, [2006] at St. James' Church, Alexandria. ... Bishop Griswold told the Western Louisiana clergy gathering that bishops and other diocesan leaders are primarily responsible for deciding how to respond to disputes over property ownership, and that there have been instances in which such disputes have been resolved amicably. The Episcopal Church Center in New York City becomes involved in a legal dispute only after it has been invited by the diocese, Bishop Griswold said.[39]

This may be a signal that the "Dennis Canon" is a dead letter, and that the ECUSA will leave any fights with parishes to the dioceses.

A few years before *Jones v. Wolf*, the U.S. Supreme Court issued a decision in which it ruled that, "the First and Fourteenth Amendments [of the United States Constitution] permit hierarchical religious organizations to establish their own rules and regulations for internal discipline and government, and to create tribunals for adjudicating disputes over these matters. When this choice is exercised and ecclesiastical tribunals are created to decide disputes over the government and direction of subordinate bodies, the Constitution requires that civil courts accept their decisions as binding upon them."[40]

Some have claimed that the Episcopal Church is a "hierarchical religious organization" and, hence, it can tell each of its parishes that they cannot leave the denomination. As indicated earlier in this chapter, the ECUSA alternatively partakes of congregational, presbyterian and episcopal polity, depending on which aspect of the denomination is being discussed. The denomination, however, never acted to "create tribunals for adjudicating disputes over these matters." There are courts in the Episcopal Church, but their function by canon is limited to church discipline of bishops, priests

39 The Living Church Foundation, Web site (5/15/2006).

40 *Serbian Orthodox Diocese v. Milivojevich*, 426 U.S. 696, 724-25 (1976).

and deacons.[41] The church courts have no authority over parish disputes with the diocese or the ECUSA. The General Convention and the diocesan conventions are legislative bodies, but there are no judicial bodies.

Nor is there an executive of the denomination other than the office of the Presiding Bishop, or the diocesan bishops. The Presiding Bishop is not given by constitution or canon the authority to tell diocesan bishops what to do, much less any parish with its property. Diocesan bishops have enumerated powers and duties, but not in the area of parish property, which by canon are reserved to parish vestries, other than as discussed, *supra*, to approve the sale or mortgage of parish property. Hence, from a parish property perspective, the denomination looks more congregational than hierarchical.

Shortly after General Convention 1979, a few of the more than 100 dioceses around the country adopted their own form of the so-called Dennis Canon. These local canons differ from diocese to diocese, but basically they claimed to establish a trust in favor of the Episcopal Church and the diocese as against any parish property of a parish seeking to split from the diocese or the ECUSA.

These diocesan canons usually resemble the ECUSA canon. The Dennis-type canon for the Episcopal Diocese of Virginia is a typical example of what these diocesan canons are like.

> All real and personal property held by or for the benefit of any church or mission within this Diocese is held in trust for the Episcopal Church and the Diocese of Virginia. The Vestry of every church and, when authorized by the bishop, the Vestry Committee of a Mission, shall elect trustees for appointment pursuant to law to hold title to such property.[42]

Generally, the diocese seeking to assert this trust will claim in litigation that the language of the "trust" canon (which was added to the canons after 1979) merely codifies a longstanding understanding of the right of the diocese to parish property upon a parish seeking to leave the denomination. Finding either authority or practice to substantiate such a claim is problematic and, as a consequence, parishes deny its validity.

If the Episcopal Church or any diocese wanted to clearly establish a claim of trust in parish property, it might consider the manner in which the Wesleyan Church handles this issue. That denomination has within its *Book of Disci*pline explicit rules that state that all deeds to property must contain trust

41 See generally, Title IV of the Canons of the General Convention (2003).

42 Canon 15, Section 1 of the Canons of the Protestant Episcopal Church in the Diocese of Virginia (2005)

language.[43] The failure of the Episcopal Church to have had such requirements in its canons at the time existing parishes were established, combined with the lack of any trust language in Episcopal Church deeds, supports the conclusion that the claim of trust in the "Dennis Canon" is an afterthought, bootstrap argument to justify an otherwise non-existent claim to parish property.

In addition to adding trust claims to the diocesan canons in the days after General Convention 1979, the Episcopal Church persuaded many state legislatures to enact similar language of trust in favor of the diocese and the ECUSA into the state statutory scheme for Episcopal churches. There is no typical state statute, since all state church law frameworks are so different, but New York's statute is an example of one of these statutes:

> [S]ubject always to the trust in which all real and personal property is held for the Protestant Episcopal Church and the Diocese thereof in which the parish, mission or congregation is located, the vestry or trustees of any incorporated Protestant Episcopal parish or church, the trustees of every incorporated governing body of the Protestant Episcopal Church and each diocese are authorized to administer the temporalities and property, real and personal, belonging to the corporation, for the support and maintenance of the corporation and, provided it is in accordance with the discipline, rules and usages of the Protestant Episcopal Church and with the provisions of law relating thereto, for the support and maintenance of other religious, charitable, benevolent or educational objects whether or not conducted by the corporation or in connection with it or with the Protestant Episcopal Church.[44]

It is one thing for a church to set up canons, bylaws, or rules of priority of one level of the church over the other, but it is quite a different matter for the government to do so. The First Amendment to the U.S. Constitution says that, "Congress shall make no law respecting an establishment of religion. …" The establishment clause covers not only the federal government, but also is applied today to states.[45] On its face, there would seem to be no more obvious

43 The Discipline of the Wesleyan Church, ¶¶4590, 4610 (2004).

44 New York Religious Corporations Law §42-A, Consolidated Laws of New York (2005).

45 See *Cantwell v. Connecticut*, 310 U.S. 396 (1940) wherein the U.S. Supreme Court applied the free exercise clause of the First Amendment to the states.

violation of the establishment clause than a statute passed by a state legislature seeking to declare the diocese to be the winner *a priori* in litigation with a parish.

In light of the current theologically-driven disputes within the Episcopal Church today, property issues likely are to remain at the forefront of the denomination for some time to come. It also is likely that unless some form of amicable separation can be arranged for parishes leaving the ECUSA, litigation over property will continue.

In that litigation, the "Dennis Canon" and claims by the ECUSA and its dioceses of a trust interest in parish property are likely to continue to be asserted for the immediate future. There may be, however, a trend toward the purer application of "neutral principles of trust law" as we have seen in the California litigation, which would bode well for parishes leaving the denomination and poorly for their dioceses and the ECUSA.

CHAPTER SEVEN

THE CHURCH INCORPORATED: STATE TRUST AND CORPORATION LAW

The resolution of church property disputes includes not only the consideration of denominational texts and the property-related documents and actions specific to a local church, but also the laws of the state in which the local church property is situated – in particular, state trust and corporation law.

This chapter highlights selected aspects of each that are particularly important for lawyers, church pastors, officers and trustees to understand. If what is at issue is the existence of a trust, obviously the provisions of state law setting forth the requirements for the valid establishment of a trust are of great importance. Just because one party asserts the existence of a trust may not determine the issue under the governing trust law of the state in which the contested property is located. Similarly, state corporation law has much to say about the authority of a nonprofit corporation over corporate property – provisions that may be especially relevant when denominational constitutions permit, encourage or mandate local church incorporation.

Trust but Verify

The concept of a "trust" may be unfamiliar to some readers. According to the traditional legal definition, a "trust" includes:

> A legal entity created by a grantor for the benefit of designated beneficiaries under the laws of the state and the valid trust instrument. ...
>
> A confidence reposed in one person, who is termed trustee, for the benefit of another, who is called the *cestui que* trust, respecting property which is held by the trustee for the benefit of the *cestui que* trust.

> Any arrangement whereby property is transferred with the intention that it be administered by the trustee for another's benefit. …
>
> Essential elements of trust are a designated beneficiary and trustee, a fund sufficiently identified to enable title to pass to trustee, and actual delivery to the trustee with intention of passing title.

Black's Law Dictionary, 6th Edition (West Publishing Company, 1990) (citations omitted).

This basic definition also has been codified in the *Restatement of Trusts* 3d, a national model of persuasive value to courts in the absence of specific state trust laws. It explains the concept of trust:

> A trust, as the term is used in this Restatement when not qualified by the word 'resulting' or 'constructive,' is a fiduciary relationship with respect to property, arising from a manifestation of intention to create that relationship and subjecting the person who holds title to the property to duties to deal with it for the benefit of charity or for one or more persons, at least one of whom is not the sole trustee.

Restatement, Third, Trusts § 2.

Most states, however, have defined by case law or statute the specific requirements for a valid trust in that state. Those provisions may vary from state to state on important particulars, but all hold in common these basic definitional concepts.

Accordingly, to correctly analyze whether a local church's property is subject to an enforceable trust, and whether any such trust is revocable, one must determine what is required under state trust law in order for a valid and enforceable trust to come into being. Assuming a validly created trust, does state law presume its revocability or irrevocability, and how can any such presumption be overcome?

The answers to these important questions may vary from state to state, so it is necessary to consult with legal counsel familiar with the law of the state wherein any property of concern is located.

For the purposes of illustrating how neutral principles of law might apply to a particular situation, the hypothetical scenario of "Maple Street Presbyterian Church of Memphis, Tennessee" was presented in Chapter Four (applicable to other denominations with national trust clauses). To further illustrate how state trust law might bear on the issue, the following hypothetical state trust law also is posited. The reader should not confuse the statutes discussed below with actual Tennessee law, or that of any particular state. Rather, the trust law provisions described and applied are a fictional amalgam. They represent a sampling of the kinds of very real provisions that may be found in whole or in part in some states. Though hypothetical, the point of this exercise is to illustrate the real impact a state trust statute might have in determining the existence of a valid trust.

Let us now turn to the salient provisions of hypothetical state trust statutes and their application to Maple Street Presbyterian Church:

DEFINITIONS

Hypothetical statute § 101 defines a trust as the relationship resulting from the transfer of title to property to a person who administers it as a fiduciary for the benefit of another. The circumstances of Maple Street and the Presbyterian Church (USA) do not fit this definition. If there was a transfer of title as a result of the creation of a trust, it would have been from Maple Street, as owner, to the Presbyterian Church (USA) after its 1983 merger with the Presbyterian Church in the United States. Under the case law discussed in Chapter Three, Maple Street would be the "settlor." The Presbyterian Church (USA) may argue and assert that it is the beneficiary even though it was not actually involved in the original acquisition or ownership of the property. It may argue that because of the doctrine of the universal church and the related connectionalism of Presbyterian polity, the denomination has a mystical, *a priori* claim on all property for which local churches might hold title.

The denomination also may argue that it is by virtue of a "trust" created by the Presbyterian Church in the United States in 1982 and carried over after 1983 by the Presbyterian Church (USA) that the title therefore is allowed to be held by the local church, which then administers the property as trustee for the benefit of the denomination.

The hypothetical facts of Maple Street Presbyterian Church, though, do not square with this scenario. This argument also was rejected as "self-dealing" by the California court in *St. Luke's*, discussed in Chapter Three. Moreover, the application of theological arguments to interpret property documents is inconsistent with neutral principles of law and are not considered by civil courts.

Required Format

§ 102 sets forth the mandatory form requirements for a valid, non-testamentary trust. It requires an authentic act or an act under private signature in the presence of two witnesses, duly acknowledged by the settlor or by affidavit of one of the attesting witnesses. In the present case, there does not appear to be a written trust instrument of any kind (unless one argues it is the constitution of the Presbyterian Church (USA) or the Presbyterian Church in the United States). In any event, under the hypothetical scenario of the Maple Street church, there is no written trust instrument that conforms to these form requirements.

Clear Intent

§ 103 provides that although no particular language is required to create a trust, it "must clearly appear that the creation of a trust is intended." The Presbyterian Church (USA) may argue that the acts of conveyance of the Maple Street property created a trust. That argument should fail, however, since there is no intent expressed or implied in any of the deeds that the vendor was transferring property in trust. Of course, a trustee of a previously and validly created trust may acquire property from a seller for full value being given, and that property then vests in the trustee pursuant to the trust for the benefit of the beneficiary. That, however, did not occur with any of the real property deeds in our hypothetical scenario, and this argument likewise should fail.

As to other property acquired by Maple Street through donation – including cash and movable property – in furtherance of its general or specific purposes, the Presbyterian Church (USA) may have a stronger argument in saying that the donated property was received in trust by Maple Street under the "held in trust" provisions, at least as to donations made after the effective date (1982) of the Presbyterian Church in the United States' provisions. Those opposed to disaffiliation with property may place heavy emphasis on the fact of Maple Street's continued membership in the Presbyterian Church in the United States following the 1982 amendments and its continued membership in the Presbyterian Church (USA) since 1983. Maple Street, it will be argued, has acquiesced to the "held in trust" language. This argument of acceptance-of-a-trust-by-acquiescence, however, does not address the threshold inquiry of proper form requirements in the establishment of a trust. Moreover, as noted above, one cannot generally lose vested property rights without explicit consent.

This argued acquiescence by Maple Street also may be offset, as previously noted, by the presbytery's acquiescence to the congregation's 1985 vote and other, subsequent congregational actions. The minutes of the May 1, 1985, congregational meeting were customarily delivered to the Presbytery of Memphis, which accepted them without objection. Opponents of disaffiliation with property will dispute the interpretation of the 1985 vote and what was intended by it, arguing that the congregation only was invoking the "held in trust" language in the 1982/83 Presbyterian Church in the United States' *Book of Church Order*. The text of the minutes of the 1985 congregational meeting, however, place control in "the local church" and, thus, appears strongly indicative of intent.

ACCEPTANCE OF A TRUST

§ 104 provides that the trustee may *accept* the trust in the trust instrument or in a separate instrument. This statute differs from the *Restatement of Trusts* 3d. In contrast to our hypothetical trust code, the *Restatement* 3d indicates that acceptance may be implied by a trustee's words or conduct. Section 114 of our hypothetical trust code indicates that a trust is created upon the execution of the trust instrument without regard to the trustee's acceptance. Section 115 says that if the trustee was not a party to the trust instrument, he must accept the trust *in writing* within a reasonable time after its creation. …

§ 105 states that an addition of property in an existing trust must be made in one of the forms required for making a donation of the same type free of trust. A trustee's acceptance must be in writing.

WHO IS (OR CAN BE) THE TRUSTEE?

§ 106 defines the trustee as the person to whom the title to the trust property is transferred and who administers the trust property as a fiduciary.

§ 107 states that a trustee must be either a natural person with capacity to contract …, or a bank or trust company organized under Tennessee or federal law and domiciled in Tennessee. Neither Maple Street, the Presbytery of Memphis, the Presbyterian Church (USA), or the Presbyterian Church in the United States fit any of these categories.

REVOCABLE OR IRREVOCABLE?

§ 108 states that a trust is irrevocable unless the settlor has reserved the right to revoke the trust in whole or in part or has reserved an unrestricted right to modify the trust. [Readers are reminded that this provision, as are all listed here, is an amalgam, or sampling, of trust provisions often seen in state statutes. Specific provisions will vary from state to state. Express trusts may be revocable or irrevocable by act of the settlor (donor or owner), depending upon state law. In California, for example, where a trust instrument is silent as to the settlor's intent, state law presumes the trust is revocable. By contrast, Pennsylvania state law presumes irrevocability. In both cases, the presumption can be rebutted. The *Restatement of Law of Trusts* (3d) § 63 (2003) states that if the written terms of the trust do not include whether the settlor has reserved the right to revoke, extrinsic evidence may be introduced to prove the settlor's intent as to revocability. If the settlor has retained an interest in the trust, then the presumption is that the trust is revocable.] It should also be noted that individual ministers, trustees, or church officers cannot create or revoke an express trust on the property of a church corporation. Corporate action is required, either by recital in the corporate charter or bylaws, or by resolution or by accepting or recording a deed or other legal instrument reciting a trust on corporate property.

A Change of Circumstance

§ 109 pertains to a change of circumstance. If there are circumstances not known to a settlor or anticipated by him such that the continuance of the trust would defeat or substantially impair the purposes of the trust, then a proper court may order the termination or modification of the trust. Section 109 does not appear applicable to the hypothetical Maple Street scenario. Some may argue that, if a trust was created, the circumstances have changed since 1982/83 because the Presbyterian Church (USA) has strayed from the doctrines of its founders. Civil courts, however, lack subject matter jurisdiction to rule on doctrinal matters. Moreover, the language in the denomination's *Book of Order* simply states that the property "held in trust" is for the benefit of the Presbyterian Church (USA), and the denomination continues to exist. That circumstance has not changed.

Recordation Required

§ 110 states that if a non-testamentary trust includes immovables or other property, the title to which must be recorded in order to affect third parties, a trustee shall file the trust instrument for record in each parish in which the property is located. In the present case, no trust instrument has been filed in Shelby County to our knowledge.

Charitable and Benevolent Purposes

§ 111 describes the scenario for a non-testamentary donation to a trustee for the benefit of educational, charitable or benevolent institutions. The circumstances described therein theoretically may pertain to some specific donations to Maple Street Presbyterian Church or to a separate Maple Street Foundation, but not for the Maple Street property as a whole.

§ 112 defines the term "trust" specifically for charitable or benevolent purposes and limits the term to express *or* implied trusts created for educational, charitable or religious purposes where all, or a substantial part of the corpus thereof, shall have been contributed *by the local beneficiaries.* . . ." Section 112 further defines "local beneficiaries" as those who shall have contributed (or whose predecessor beneficiaries shall have contributed) "all or a substantial part of the corpus of the trust ... and who shall locally, immediately and directly enjoy the benefits of such trust." The congregational members of Maple Street and their predecessor members contributed the corpus and it is they who locally, immediately and directly enjoy or have enjoyed the benefits. If an implied trust thus exists at all under this provision, it is in favor of the local congregation of Maple Street rather than the Presbytery of Memphis or the Presbyterian Church (USA).

§ 113 When one has donated money or other property and has dedicated it for a charitable or benevolent purpose, it is irrevocable as long as there is a competent person or institution to administer it and the donor has not expressly reserved in the dedication the right to dissolve or abolish the trust or the dedication made. As mentioned in commenting on Section 111, this does not seem to contemplate the present set of facts concerning Maple Street property generally, but may apply to specific donations to Maple Street or similar donations to the Maple Street Foundation.

To sum up, under the facts of our hypothetical scenario, there does not appear to be a valid trust under the sample trust code. There is no written trust instrument that conforms to the form requirements. The trustee does not fall within any of the categories authorized by Section 106. No trust instrument has been filed in Shelby County. Nor does there appear to be a trust for the benefit of the Presbytery of Memphis or the Presbyterian Church (USA) under our hypothetical state trust provisions pertaining to charitable or benevolent purposes. While these provisions permit implied trusts, the only implied trust therein recognized appears to be the one in which Maple Street members/contributors would be the settlors and beneficiaries rather than the Presbytery of Memphis or the Presbyterian Church (USA).

The Church Incorporated

State corporation law also is relevant to questions of property ownership and control. Denominational constitutions typically require or encourage member churches to incorporate. For example, G-7.0401 of the Presbyterian Church (USA) *Book of Order* provides:

> Whenever permitted by civil law, each particular church shall cause a corporation to be formed and maintained. Only members on the active roll of a particular church shall be members of the corporation and eligible for election as trustees. … Any particular church which is not incorporated may select trustees from the members on the active roll of the church. The power and duties of such trustees shall not infringe upon the powers and duties of the session or the board of deacons.

Significantly, by effectively requiring in the *Book of Order* that most (if not all) local Presbyterian churches form a corporation that will be the titleholder to property, the denomination's constitution purposefully defers in such corporate matters to the civil laws of the state of incorporation. This is consistent with the application of neutral principles of law in those states that have adopted that method of church property dispute resolution.[1] Therefore, it is worth noting not only what denominational texts state about the local church as a corporation, but also what state corporation statutes generally say.

The Presbyterian Church (USA) *Book of Order*, at G-7.0402, states:

> The corporation so formed, or the individual trustees, shall have the following powers: to receive, hold, encumber, manage, and transfer property, real or personal, for the

---

1 In those states that have adopted the hierarchical method, however, courts would continue to defer to the determinations of the highest ecclesiastical court to which the matter had been referred. In light of G-7.0401 in the *Book of Order,* one might argue in that ecclesiastical court that the denomination's constitution requires that the denomination itself, in electing to defer to state law on corporate matters, has imposed upon itself the application of neutral principles of law when addressing questions concerning corporate property. If this view is not adopted by the ecclesiastical court, failure by the ecclesiastical body to follow its own regulations arguably would make its determination of property use or ownership arbitrary. There appears, though, to be little remedy for this in an appeal to a civil court. The subject matter jurisdiction of civil courts in hierarchical states precludes review for potential arbitrariness. Review is limited to potential fraud or collusion. See the discussion, *supra*, in Chapter Three, n. 12.

> church; to accept and execute deeds of title to such property; to hold and defend title to such property; to manage any permanent special funds for the furtherance of the purposes of the church, all subject to the authority of the session and under the provisions of the Constitution of the Presbyterian Church (USA); provided further that in buying, selling, and mortgaging real property, the trustee shall act only after the approval of the congregation granted in a duly constituted meeting.

In other words, the denominational constitution not only effectively mandates incorporation, but also provides that the corporation thus formed be the titleholder of record of the local church property. Significantly, nowhere does the denominational constitution mandate that the local corporation be identified with the denomination in the text of its articles of incorporation, or that the name of the titleholder of record refer to or identify itself with the denomination in the deed language.[2]

The Book of Order essentially is a *religious* document. Its fundamental purposes relate to the spiritual life of the denomination. The denominational constitution recognizes, though, that a separate civil realm also exists, for which the application of state corporation law is appropriate – even mandated. Distinguishing the spiritual realm from civil authority, G-9.0102 of the *Book of Order* notes:

> Governing bodies of the church are distinct from the government of the state and have no civil jurisdiction or power to impose civil penalties. They have only ecclesiastical jurisdiction....

Because denominational constitutions encourage or require local church incorporation, and local church property typically is titled in the name of the corporation, the salient features of corporation law as found in most states are relevant to note.

Corporations 101

A "corporation" is an artificial or juridical person (as distinguished from a natural person) or legal entity created by or under the authority of the laws

2 Methodist and Episcopalian readers should consult the text of the *Book of Discipline* and the *Canons,* respectively, for related provisions on these corporate matters.

of the state. It ordinarily consists of an association of numerous individuals, but is regarded in the law as having a personality that exists distinct from that of its several members. State law generally addresses for profit and nonprofit corporations separately. The powers of nonprofit corporations under state law typically include all power to perform any acts necessary or proper to accomplish the purposes of the corporation, as those purposes are expressed or implied in the articles of incorporation, or any powers that may be incidental to those purposes. Nonprofit corporations' statutes usually specify that the corporation either may have perpetual existence or shall be of limited duration for a specified period of time (often 99 years); that the corporation has authority to sue and be sued in its corporate name; and that the corporation has the authority to elect and appoint officers, make bylaws, provide for indemnification, enter into contracts, *and acquire, hold, use, encumber or dispose of property of any kind.*[3]

Membership in the corporation, the frequency of meetings of the corporation, and any required notice of meetings to be given to members of the corporation can be set by statute, but often also are set forth in the articles of incorporation or bylaws. The members of the corporation usually are defined as those listed on the active rolls of the congregation. The notice requirements for a meeting of the corporation may be different from those set forth in a denominational constitution for a congregational meeting but, so long as both sets of notice requirements are timely observed, one meeting usually can suffice as both an annual congregational meeting and an annual meeting of the corporation.

A Critical Decision: Naming the Corporation

For churches that have incorporated, it is the corporation that typically is named as the titleholder of the church's property. How the local church is identified in its articles of incorporation – the name given to it – therefore can have important ramifications when resolving questions of property ownership or control. The name or identity of the corporation (and titleholder) may or may not include the name of the denomination, depending on the decision of the local incorporators.

---

3 The exercise of corporate authority under the statutes and articles of incorporation should be in harmony with the provisions of the relevant denominational constitution, provided that those provisions do not unilaterally assert claims of ownership or trust in a manner that impinges on the vested property rights of the local corporation. If a denominational constitution makes the sale or encumbrance of local church property contingent on the congregation's approval, for example, the articles of incorporation likewise should make such sale or encumbrance contingent on the approval of the members of the corporation.

The phrase "name of the denomination" is used here not in the sense of whether the local church is Presbyterian or Methodist or Episcopal but, rather, refers to whether the specific national body with which the local church may be affiliated also is included in the corporate name. In the hypothetical scenario discussed in earlier chapters, it is the difference between incorporating as "Maple Street Presbyterian Church of Memphis, Tennessee" or incorporating as "Maple Street Presbyterian Church of Memphis, Tennessee, *PC(USA)*."

Should the local church decide to include the identification of its denominational affiliation in its corporate name and in the name of the titleholder to its property, the case law discussed in Chapter Three indicates that this could measurably weaken if not defeat the local church's claim of full ownership and control, free of competing claims by a third-party denomination. In general, there is no requirement in state law that the name of a local nonprofit church corporation include in its articles of incorporation reference to the denomination with which it may be affiliated, nor is there any general requirement in state law that property acquired and titled in the name of the local church corporation include mention of its identification or affiliation with a denomination.

Whether inclusion of the name of the denominational organization in local church articles of incorporation or property deeds is mandated by a denominational constitution is a matter for examination under the relevant constitution. As noted previously, though, the Presbyterian Church (USA) *Book of Order* does not include any requirement that a local church include, as part of the name of the local church corporation, identification with the "Presbyterian Church (USA)." Nor is there a requirement in the *Book of Order* that the corporate titleholder of record for local church property include a reference to or identification with the "Presbyterian Church (USA)." Thus, such omission is not an act of disaffiliation. The omission of denominational reference in ownership or corporate documents is not inconsistent with the denominational constitution.

Whether to Adopt/Amend

For local churches that have not yet incorporated, there are several advantages to doing so, such as: protecting church property from potential legal judgments against individual church staff and officers, and providing for the indemnification for officers and staff who act in "good faith" and in a manner they reasonably believe to be in, or not opposed to, the best interests of the corporation (and also, with respect to any criminal action, providing indemnification when these officers and staff had no reasonable cause to believe that their conduct was unlawful).

Incorporating also provides an opportunity to potentially strengthen or clarify the status of local church property ownership – by forming the local church corporation and titling any church property only in the name of the local church corporation, without including in the local articles of incorporation or deeds the name of the affiliated denominational organization as part of the actual name of the corporation and titleholder. This may be particularly appropriate under circumstances where local church property was acquired only with contributions by local members and where the date(s) of the acquisition of local church property precede(s) the date of the adoption of an express trust clause in the relevant denominational constitution.

For local churches that already are incorporated, there may be a benefit to amending and restating their articles of incorporation to take advantage of changes in state corporation law – concerning indemnification, for example – since the date of prior incorporation. Amending the articles also may provide an opportunity to remove anything that has become anachronistic. Most churches in the Presbyterian Church (USA) were incorporated prior to 1983 and the articles of incorporation for many of these churches may not have been updated since. Even if the name of the corporation does not include a reference to denominational affiliation, the articles elsewhere may make some reference to either the Presbyterian Church in the United States or the United Presbyterian Church in the United States of America, entities whose existence was extinguished upon the formation of the Presbyterian Church (USA) in 1983. A similar situation may be present concerning Methodist congregations whose original incorporation predates the merger that formed the United Methodist Church in 1968.

If a local church so chooses, it may include mention of its denominational affiliation elsewhere in its new or amended articles of incorporation (i.e., other than as part of the name of the local church corporation, in whose name corporate property is to be titled), but the articles should prudently state that such affiliation is voluntary, and set forth the corporation's understanding of the terms and methods by which any decision to disaffiliate and identify with a different national body are to be determined. The articles also should state the corporation's position on determining the identity of the corporation, ownership of corporate assets, and right to use of the corporate name. On this score, the articles should be consistent with any applicable provisions of the corporation statutes of the state where the property is located, provisions that typically are more equitable and democratic than those found in some denominational constitutions.

In so stating, the provisions of the articles of incorporation should be consistent with any applicable statutory provisions of the law of the state in which the corporate property is located. Those statutory provisions may differ from the corresponding provisions in the denominational constitution, but in those denominations that mandate incorporation it can be argued that the civil laws of the state of incorporation should be given controlling effect.

CHAPTER EIGHT

NOW WHAT DO WE DO?
PRACTICAL POINTS AND LESSONS LEARNED

All of the contributors to this volume wish that peace would prevail in the church, centered on a consensus on the historic beliefs that long have defined the Christian faith. That deep theological divisions mark much of the American mainline church is a cause for sorrow. There is no joy in exploring the law that governs the resolution of church property disputes.

Sadly, however, circumstances make discussion of this subject necessary. In some situations, it may be the ethical, moral or legal obligation of those charged with responsibility for local church property to pursue legal remedies. The presence of such obligations, and if or when such obligations can ever be pursued in civil courts in a manner consistent with the witness of Scripture, is discussed in the next, concluding chapter. This chapter, however, addresses some practicalities to consider as legal remedies are explored.

Readers concerned with local church property issues may well be asking themselves at this point, "What do we *do* with the information gleaned from this book?"

For local pastors, church officers and trustees who are considering whether to retain legal counsel to advise them, what factors should be considered or what instructions should be given? For the attorneys retained, what process can be followed to evaluate in a cost-effective manner the strengths or weaknesses of their client's claims to property ownership and control? What actions should be taken?

This chapter offers some specific, concrete steps to take and notes some of the important issues that one should be aware of along the way. Broadly described, the process to be followed by a church client and its counsel consists of education, evaluation, documentation and implementation.

Education

The first step in addressing any questions about local church property is to educate one's self about the law that applies in resolving issues concerning local church property ownership and control. Such information provides the necessary framework to make valid evaluations and sound decisions.

Many people have read the text of their denominational constitutions, which assert a trust in favor of the denomination over local church property, and they may have accepted at face value such assertions as binding. Likewise, many people have read the provisions in denominational constitutions that assert a right by the denomination to determine the ownership of local church property and assumed that such provisions always were conclusive. The law has much to say, however, about whether such assertions and provisions are legally enforceable in different states and under different scenarios.

An essential first step, then, is to educate one's self about the law that applies to these matters. Readers of this book will have taken an important step in obtaining that necessary education.

Although the contributors to this book hope that this volume will be of substantial, practical benefit to readers, the education that a church client and its counsel need is incomplete without additional, state-specific research. A state-by-state analysis of the case law in all 50 states is beyond the scope of this volume. Therefore, the next step in acquiring the needed education is to learn what the law is in the particular state in which the property of concern is located.

Has your state supreme court, or any appellate court in your state, for example, adopted the neutral principles of law method for resolving church property disputes? If this method has not been adopted in your state, is it because it has been considered but rejected in favor of the hierarchical method? Alternatively, is the situation in your state akin to that of Texas (discussed in Chapter Three), where the court adopted the hierarchical method subsequent to the 1872 U.S. Supreme Court decision in *Watson v. Jones,* but has not yet had occasion to revisit the issue in the aftermath of the Supreme Court's 1979 decision in *Jones v. Wolf*? Or has your state adopted a third method by adopting a statutory scheme that specifically addresses the resolution of church ownership? Such statutes may be intended to relieve courts of inquiries into matters of theology or religious doctrine. However, as written or applied, a statutory scheme may or may not be constitutionally permissible. At least one California trial court reportedly has opined that a California statute is an unconstitutional attempt by the state to support a denomination and cannot preclude the courts from following a neutral principles analysis.

Therefore, after reading this book (and sharing it with your local church attorney), the client should ask its legal counsel to perform the additional research needed to determine the method followed in your state. This research may require a few hours to several days of legal work, depending upon how extensive, nuanced or complex the body of case law is in your state and depending on the knowledge and experience level of your legal counsel.

It is appropriate for the client to request a preliminary cost estimate from its attorney before the research is performed. The cost of legal services generally is a function of the number of hours of work required multiplied by the attorney's hourly rate. Rates vary widely from one part of the country to another, and often are graduated according to the years of experience or level of expertise an attorney has. Many attorneys consider legal work for smaller churches to be part of their public service (*pro bono*) and, thus, may be able to offer their assistance to those churches at a special or reduced billing rate.

Such a projected cost, though, can be substantially reduced through two or more local churches sharing the financial responsibility for preliminary legal research and counsel – because this initial assessment of the law is state-specific but not church-specific. Accordingly, multiple churches in one state collectively can retain the same counsel and share the cost. An attorney will need to know, of course, which individual church is the financially responsible party of record, and the participating churches can enter into private arrangements for partial reimbursement among themselves. The relevant state case law can be accessed by computer from anywhere in the United States so, at this stage, the required work can be performed either by local counsel or by an attorney elsewhere in the country who is familiar with these issues and who can provide the client, or the client's local counsel, a written analysis.

In performing this state-specific research, counsel should take care to avoid focusing exclusively on the issue of a property trust. Denominational conversations, and much of the media coverage about church property issues, have focused on whether an asserted property trust is valid and enforceable under state law and the facts presented by a particular church. A separate but related issue, however, often has been overlooked. Sometimes lost in all of the attention on whether a valid property trust exists is the key issue of ultimate ownership and control of church property.

Many denominational constitutions contain provisions by which national or regional denominational authorities may assert a right to determine, irrespective of local majority vote, which faction of a local congregation constitutes the "true church" – i.e., the membership of the church corporation (if the church is incorporated).[1] As shown in Chapter Three, the case

---

1 In the Presbyterian Church (USA), for example, such a provision is found at G-8.0601of the *Book of Order*. Readers are counseled to examine the texts of their respective denominational constitutions for comparable provisions.

law distinguishes disputes between a united local church and a parent denomination and disputes between competing factions within a local church. If a local Presbyterian church were to prevail in court on the issue of there being no trust in favor of the denomination, for example, it may be a pyrrhic victory if its presbytery – under G-8.0601 of the *Book of Order* in the Presbyterian Church (USA) – were still able to designate by fiat a "loyalist five percent" as the true local corporate representative and, thus, the titleholder to the property. Winning a property trust battle is small consolation if one loses the ownership war.

In understanding the distinction between the property trust issue and the property ownership issue, it may be helpful to recall that under the neutral principles of law approach, for example, a two-stage analysis is followed. *First,* a civil court applies neutral principles of law to determine whether the property titled to the local church is held in trust for the denomination with which the local church is affiliated. In seeking to determine mutual intent, courts that apply neutral principles do not stop with the text of the denominational constitution that asserts a trust.

Courts also consider such things as the text of local property deeds, articles of incorporation, local resolutions, minutes, correspondence, and relevant provisions of state statutory law. If the court determines that a valid and enforceable property trust attaches to the local property, then the court will grant effective control over the use of that property to the governing ecclesiastical body of the general church, whether it be a presbytery, conference, or diocese. If, on the other hand, the court determines that no valid and enforceable property trust attaches to the local property, then control over the use of that property is granted to the local congregation.

Second, if the local congregation is united by a 100 percent vote, then ordinarily the matter is effectively concluded.[2] If there is a division or "schism" within the local congregation, however, then the next stage of analysis is required. Here, the court is called upon to determine which of the competing local factions should control the property; i.e., which faction may properly be identified as the valid titleholder. The authors recommend that the issue of ultimate property ownership be addressed by pertinent language in the local church's articles of incorporation that is consistent with the nonprofit corporation laws of the state in which the local church property is located. Whether or not ultimate ownership is so addressed, however, the question remains whether state law or the denominational constitution will be given effect by the civil courts. This issue will be decided by state law, which may

2 See *Presbytery of the Covenant v. First Presbyterian Church of Paris*, 552 S.W.2d 805 (Tex. Civ. App.-Texarkana 1977, no writ), discussed in Chapter Three.

vary from state to state.

Some states will defer the question of identity and, hence, ownership to the ecclesiastical hierarchy, or church courts, for decision. Other states may provide for a different method of determination (see the discussion in Chapter Three). Readers should seek the advice of legal counsel on the law in their state, whether a court of competent jurisdiction has addressed this issue and, if so, whether the law of their state defers to religious authority in determining the identity of the true owner in the event of a local church split or whether state law provides for an alternative means of determining ownership. If your state has adopted pertinent statutes for determining questions of ownership, those statutes may set forth different requirements for churches that are incorporated than those for unincorporated religious associations. What does your state law say concerning incorporated churches? Concerning unincorporated churches? If a state has adopted statutes to address this issue, they generally require a certain vote – whether a majority or a super majority – which is more democratic than an ecclesiastical edict. Articles of incorporation that address ownership determination should track the language of the pertinent state statute.

As indicated in the preceding chapter concerning state corporation and trust law, an important aspect of any state-specific research is learning if there are relevant state statutes that address the requirements for the valid establishment of an enforceable trust, as well as any related provisions concerning revocation. A discussion of such statutes may not always be included in the reported case law, particularly if the parties did not think to raise the application of such statutes. Courts generally do not address issues or defenses not raised by the parties. Therefore, thorough research on a state's statutory law, as well as state case law, is advisable.

Evaluation

Once one has a firm grasp on the law of the state in which the property of concern is located, the next step is to evaluate the circumstances of the particular church – by applying that law to the facts at hand, as evidenced in the local church's property-related documents. While the cost of the initial state law research easily can be shared by churches within the same state, this step of examining and evaluating individual church documents presents cost-sharing problems. In some states, the results and advice cannot be disclosed to anyone other than the authorized representatives of the particular church client without risking a waiver of the attorney-client privilege.

Such a waiver can make attorney-client communications disclosable to potentially adverse parties. Ordinarily, therefore, the cost of this evaluation must be borne by the particular church alone. It is possible, though, under some circumstances, to establish a collective legal expense fund to which contributions can be made from several sources, and a mechanism established to partially underwrite and defray the expenses of churches participating in the fund. Costs also can be reduced if the client has gathered all of its own local church property-related documents and already has a good grasp of its local church property history that it can convey to its counsel.

Local church representatives should gather all relevant church property-related documents in order to minimize the attorney time required to perform the necessary legal evaluation. These documents include, but are not limited to: 1) the current articles of incorporation and corporate bylaws and any prior versions of the articles of incorporation and bylaws that no longer are in force; 2) abstracts of title or title insurance certificates and all property deeds showing precisely how each parcel of real estate is titled and whether there are any reversion, remainder, or trust provisions of record; and 3) any minutes of trustee, session or congregational meetings at which resolutions were proposed, decisions made, or actions taken concerning denominational affiliation or disaffiliation, property ownership or use, or the adoption, rejection or application of property-related provisions in the denominational constitution.

Many of these documents should be found in local church archives and current files. Certified copies of articles of incorporation, past and present, usually can be obtained from the Secretary of State's office of the state in which the property is located. Similarly, certified copies of all relevant property deeds can be obtained, usually with the assistance of the Registrar of Deeds, County Clerk, or whatever government office maintains mortgage and conveyance records in the county in which the property is located. Alternatively, these records can be assembled for you for a fee by a local abstractor or title insurance company.

It is possible, from a sampling of the relevant case law, to glean the factors that often are persuasive or determinative and to which the courts have attached some weight. These factors help create a checklist of property questions that counsel should ask when evaluating the strength or weakness of his or her client's position. With all of the local corporate and property-related documents in hand, they then must be reviewed and evaluated against your state's law. The attorney for the local church and the local pastor, president of the board of trustees or other knowledgeable client representative should consider at least the following questions:[3]

---

3 This sampling of questions is not exhaustive. No answer to any single question may

• Has the use of the local church's name, its customs and its policy been such that the local church is known in the community as a member of a specific denomination?

• Has the hiring of the local church's ministers been contingent upon the appointment or approval by the denomination?

• Has the denomination (the presbytery, conference, diocese, or other regional body) had knowledge, whether actual or constructive, of the recorded deeds, local articles of incorporation, or records of relevant local congregation and corporate proceedings such as resolutions or minutes?

• At the time of the original affiliation or identification of the local church with the denomination, was there an express trust proviso in the denominational constitution?

• What trust clause, or set of trust clauses, is relevant to your local church? Presbyterian congregations, for example, find such provisions in the PC(USA) *Book of Order* or the PCUS *Book of Church Order* or the UPCUSA *Book of Order* as amended immediately prior to the 1983 formation of the PC(USA). Did the local church whose property may be at issue timely exercise the "opt out" provision of G-8.0700 of the PC(USA) *Book of Order*? If so, what does the text of the relevant resolution or minutes say in explanation?

• Is the property at issue held *by* the local church or *for* the local church by a third-party entity such as a foundation?

• When was the property at issue acquired by the local church – before or after the addition of express trust language in the relevant denominational constitution?

---

determine whether a binding property trust on local church property in favor of a denomination has attached to local church property, whether such a trust may be revoked or how questions of ownership are resolved. Viewed collectively, however, the answers to these questions will provide a strong indication of the relative strength or weakness of the client church's position.

• Was the property acquired by contributions exclusively from local church members, by contributions from a regional ecclesiastical body (presbytery, conference, or diocese), by a denominational mission agency or by some combination thereof? If acquired in whole or in part by contributions from non-members, what is the current approximate dollar value of all such contributions in relation to the total current value of the local property?

• Did the regional ecclesiastical body guarantee any loans or lines of credit necessary for the local church to acquire the property?

• How is the titleholder of the property described in the property deed(s)? Is the owner (as in the earlier hypothetical case) simply "Maple Street Presbyterian Church of Memphis, Tennessee?" Or do the title documents also specifically describe the church as "PCUS," "PCUSA," etc.?"

• Have the property deeds ever been amended to add, delete, or change a denominational reference, and were any such amended deeds recorded?

• Do the deeds contain reversion, remainder or trust language in favor of a denomination?

• What do the local church's articles of incorporation (charter) say about the disposition of property upon the dissolution of a local church corporation?

• Do the articles of incorporation state that, upon dissolution, the local property would be placed in trust for the denomination?

• Prior to the addition of an express trust proviso in the relevant denominational constitution, was there an indication in the relation of the two parties (the local church and the denomination) of an agreement on an implied trust? If so, was there any understanding whether such a trust was revocable or irrevocable?

• What do the articles of incorporation say about determining the identity of the corporation, ownership of the corporation's assets, or the right to the use of the corporate name, and are all such provisions consistent with the provisions of the non-profit corporation law of the state in which the property is located?

• Do the articles of incorporation include any mention of denominational affiliation with the current denomination or a predecessor denomination, or are they silent concerning a denominational affiliation? Have the articles of incorporation ever been amended to add or change a reference to a denominational affiliation or to delete a reference to a denominational affiliation?

• Do the articles of incorporation contain language that prohibits the local church from ever disaffiliating with a denomination? If so, can any such language be amended under your state's corporation law?

• Do the articles of incorporation grant plenary power concerning property matters to the board of trustees of the local church corporation, subject only to appropriate approval by the congregational governing body and/or the members of the corporation; i.e., the voting members of the local congregation?

• Do the articles of incorporation limit the authority of the board of trustees by subjecting their authority to a congregational board of elders, administrative council or vestry or to any regional or national church rules or bodies?

• Does the denominational constitution impose any limitations on the authority of the local corporate trustees?

• Has the local church continuously maintained its affiliation with a denomination subsequent to the adoption of express trust provisions in the relevant denominational constitution?

• Has the local church ever taken any action that can be construed as explicit consent to the relinquishment of vested property rights? Has it ever explicitly accepted a trust upon property titled in the local church?

• What are the requirements under your state's trust laws for the creation of a valid trust by a non-profit corporation or by an unincorporated body?

• Who is the "settlor," who is the beneficiary and who is the "trustee?"

• Do the laws of your state impose any requirements regarding form and/or recording in order for the creation of a valid trust? For the acceptance of a validly created trust?

• Do the trust laws of your state require that intent be clear and explicit in order to create a valid trust?

• Do the trust laws of your state require that a trustee be of a certain category, such as a natural (not juridical) person or an authorized financial institution?

• Assuming a validly created trust under the laws of your state, does your state's law presume that such a trust is revocable or irrevocable? Is any such presumption rebuttable? If so, how is the presumption to be rebutted?

Documentation

Whether it is an attorney evaluating the strengths or weaknesses of his or her client's position, the parties negotiating a mutually acceptable resolution, or a court rendering a judgment on the respective property rights of the parties, evidence is key. Evidence can be direct or circumstantial, testimonial or documentary. This section will discuss documentary evidence, which carries special weight in property matters.

The text of a denominational constitution cannot be ignored or altered by a local congregation. It says what it says. Likewise, the historical record of the minutes of past meetings of the congregation or local church boards stand as they are. However, articles of incorporation and bylaws can be newly adopted or amended as appropriate, new meetings of the congregation and corporation can be held and resolutions passed to clarify or modify a local church's position with respect to its property, and corrective deeds can be filed, if consistent with state substantive law.

If a local church is not already incorporated, it undoubtedly should be for the reasons described in Chapter Seven. (Sample articles of incorporation are included for review in an appendix to this volume. However, they must be reviewed, and modified if necessary, to comply with any applicable provisions in the corporation statutes of the state in which the property is located. For churches that already are incorporated, this appendix includes language that churches may wish to consider when deciding whether to amend their current articles.) Any articles that are adopted or amended should be filed in the appropriate governmental offices. The applicable denominational constitution may require the filing of congregational and corporate documents and minutes with denominational authorities.

The name of the local church corporation and the name of the titleholder to property contained in the property deeds should be the same. Any adoption or amendment to the articles of incorporation that establishes or revises the name of the local church corporation should be coupled with any necessary, parallel amendments to the property deeds. If the former articles and property deeds refer to an entity that no longer has legal existence,[4] for example, those references can be deleted in the revised articles and deeds. As previously noted, those amended deeds should be recorded in the mortgage and conveyance records in the Clerk of Court's office in the county in which the property is located, and any newly adopted or amended articles should be filed with the Secretary of State's office of the state in which the property is located.

Some denominational agencies are encouraging (and, in some instances, reportedly pressuring) local churches to amend their articles of incorporation and file "corrected" property deeds that include a specific reference to the denomination as part of the name of the local church corporation and titleholder to local church property, and include a reference to the denomination's trust clause. Before a local church makes any such amendment or "correction," however, it should first determine whether its denominational constitution requires this (the *Book of Order* in the Presbyterian Church (USA), for example, does not). If, perchance, the denominational constitution

4 The Presbyterian Church in the United States, the United Presbyterian Church in the United States of America, the Methodist Episcopal Church, the Methodist Episcopal Church South, the Methodist Church, and the Evangelical United Brethren Church all ceased having a separate existence upon mergers that formed new denominations.

asserts such a requirement, it should be determined whether this requirement is legally enforceable since such a requirement could interfere with vested property rights. As a general proposition, a member of a voluntary association is bound by any amendments to the association's rules – but any amendments to those rules cannot deprive the member of vested property rights without the member's explicit consent.

The adoption of articles of incorporation, or any amendments thereto, typically requires congregational approval. In addition to adoption by the corporate board of trustees and/or the local church governing body, therefore, a requisite congregational vote of approval must be obtained at a properly noticed meeting of the congregation/corporation. Even if not legally required before bringing the matter to the congregation, it may be prudent to also have the concurrence of the local church board (session, administrative council, or vestry). Although tensions within a congregation may be heightened because of theological divisions and a consequent concern about valuable property, it is still possible to bring the recommended articles of incorporation to the congregation for consideration and a vote in a low-key, normal course of business manner. This can be done at an annual or special congregational/corporate meeting by coupling any possible recommendation to change the name of the local church corporation, which may be thought needed to clarify property ownership, with other more routine changes. Such other changes might include the adoption or amendment of articles to provide for indemnification, remove anachronisms or otherwise take advantage of developments in state law since the date of the church's founding or the adoption of the original articles.

There also may be merit to creating an additional document that recites and clarifies the local church's history and position regarding its property. While not necessary to be submitted to the congregation for approval, it may be useful for understanding any proposed changes. It also could be filed as part of the official corporate records and in the local property records.

Having undertaken the foregoing steps to educate and evaluate, the local church officers and legal counsel should able to readily prepare a resolution that synopsizes or digests the local church's property history. This resolution can include various recitals that memorialize the facts concerning the history of the local church's property and which reaffirms the local church's understanding and intent concerning that history and the local church's property. The resolution can be presented to the board of trustees (if the local church is incorporated) and the local church's governing board (session, administrative council or vestry) for adoption.

Because the resolution does not require any action to be taken, no congregational vote on the resolution may be required by the relevant denominational constitution. As a public record of the local church, however, it can be made available to any interested member and attached to the minutes of the meeting of the board of trustees and the minutes of the meeting of the local church's governing board. Upon adoption of the resolution by the board of trustees and the local church's governing board, the resolution can be recorded in the county property records. As an attachment to the minutes and records of the local church, it will be subject to review by the regional ecclesiastical body in the usual course of business.

Readers are reminded that courts that follow a neutral principles of law approach consider the totality of circumstances in ascertaining the mutual intent of the parties. Consequently, what is important is the intent of a party as reflected over the course of time in its property-related records. Any articles of incorporation that are adopted, any amendments thereto, and any property deeds filed or resolutions passed will have greater evidentiary value if they are consistent with the other local property-related documents accumulated over the life of the local church and if they clarify or reaffirm prior intent.

By contrast, articles, amendments or resolutions that suddenly reverse course and take a position markedly different from the rest of the accumulated local property's history are unlikely to be accorded the same degree of evidentiary weight. The preparation, adoption and recordation of articles, deeds and resolutions may serve as further evidence of local intent to the degree that they are consistent with the aggregate history of the local church's property.[5] It also is important that review and correction of church corporate and property documents be accomplished before a local church attempts to sever its affiliation with its denomination, if such is its chosen path. Actions taken in the ordinary course of business usually are accorded greater evidentiary weight by courts than actions taken on the eve of litigation or while a dispute is pending.

Implementation

It is the hope of all who have contributed to this book that the theological discord that has roiled the American mainline church would subside and in its place would arise a more unified church that is grounded in consensus around the historic doctrines that have defined the Christian Church for

---

5 A sample resolution is included as an appendix to this volume. Of course, the specifics of the local church's history – the content of the various recitals in a resolution – and the particulars of state trust law will vary from local church to local church and from state to state.

two millennia. If that hope does not materialize, however, and if those who have pursued a separate agenda continue to press their case to the point of impasse, then those congregations that adhere to the traditional doctrines of the faith may be compelled by events beyond their control to take affirmative steps to protect their vested property rights and clarify the competing claims to ownership and control of local church property. In addition, some denominational actions may have the effect of placing a cloud on an otherwise merchantable or marketable title, therefore prompting local church trustees – in fulfillment of their fiduciary obligation – to obtain civil court declaratory relief or quiet title remedies and obtain a binding judicial declaration of the rights of the respective parties.

The Episcopal diocese for North Carolina, for example, has announced plans to file a "Declaration of Intent" in the county property records throughout the state to record the Episcopal Church (USA)'s claim under the "Dennis Canon" of a trust for the benefit of the denomination over all local church property. In similar fashion, the Presbytery for Eastern Oklahoma has filed in the county property records of every county within its jurisdiction an affidavit that reproduces the text of the Presbyterian Church (USA)'s trust clause found in G-8.0201 of the *Book of Order*, and other property-related provisions in the denominational constitution. Attached to the affidavit are the property descriptions of the 62 churches within the bounds of that presbytery and to which the presbytery asserts that the property trust and other provisions apply.

Such precipitating actions may compel many local churches to file a legal challenge to contest the efficacy of those actions. Negotiated settlements, of course, are always preferred, especially between Christians. Disaffiliation from a denomination may become necessary to fully protect local church property from the long-term adverse effects of such precipitating actions. In such circumstances, if prospects for good faith negotiations are dim, litigation to invoke the protection of "the civil magistrate" may be unavoidable.

It also is true that some parties are unwilling to negotiate seriously until they are persuaded that the other side is prepared to litigate if necessary. For this reason, it often is said that many cases only "settle on the courthouse steps." Filing suit and preparing for trial may therefore actually facilitate negotiations.

If a denominational constitution specifies a procedure to follow when a local church seeks permission from the regional ecclesiastical body to disaffiliate from the denomination with its property,[6] those procedures

6 In the Presbyterian Church (USA), for example, see generally G-11.0103i and G-11.0103y of the denomination's *Book of Order*.

should be followed, if litigation is not thought necessary to insure a fair forum is available to protect vested property rights and impartially consider defensible claims by the local church to property ownership or control. As discussed below, injunctive or declaratory relief from a civil court also may be necessary to protect and preserve local church governance from a takeover by denominational bodies or agents during attempted settlement negotiations.

In conjunction with any negotiations, a "settlement notebook" can be a useful tool to facilitate discussion. The notebook should set forth the local church's property history and specify the facts supporting the local church's claim of ownership without a denominational trust. It should cite, but need not include copies, of all relevant documents, such as any resolutions, articles of incorporation, bylaws, property deeds, minutes and copies of relevant denominational texts and judicial opinions. Certain key documents should be excerpted or attached.

There is no hard and fast rule to structuring a buyout settlement. The projected cost of litigation should be weighed by both sides. The denomination should consider the pros and cons of cessation by the local church of all per-capita and mission giving, which likely will occur if a settlement is not reached. The denomination probably will consider the size of the local church's budget, the amount of voluntary annual per-capita and mission giving to the regional and national ecclesiastical bodies, and the percentage of the regional body's budget represented by the giving of the particular local church. The congregation's per capita and other donations normally given to the higher ecclesiastical bodies could be redirected by the local church to fund any necessary litigation. The national denomination probably has a litigation fund to assist the regional governing bodies. If the local church's property is heavily mortgaged, the regional ecclesiastical body may have no financial incentive to block the local congregation from disaffiliating from the denomination with its property intact.

In Presbyterian Church (USA) settlements of which the authors are aware, it appears that various presbyteries have demanded approximately 10 percent of the current value of the congregation's property as the price to exit from the denomination.

Whether or not litigation is pending, good faith negotiations occur when both parties are on a level playing field. Consequently, any suit seeking declaratory relief may have to be accompanied by a request for injunctive relief to preserve the status quo between the parties while the litigation is pending. A claim for declaratory judgment or relief does not seek monetary damages but, instead, seeks a binding judicial declaration of the respective rights of the parties. A claim for injunctive relief would enjoin or stay the hand of the regional ecclesiastical body from taking any steps, by act of the bishop or the appointment of an administrative commission, to remove or displace the pastor, the governing board of the church, the local church corporation's board of trustees, or otherwise interfere with the congregation's continued use and enjoyment of the property while the litigation is pending.[7]

Prior to the commencement of any settlement negotiations that the local church must enter into with a potentially hostile or unfair regional governing body, it would be prudent to prepare for all contingencies and to consider instructing the local church's counsel to draft the appropriate pleadings to be ready for filing with the court on a moment's notice just in case quick action is later thought necessary to protect the local church while it pursues good faith negotiations.

The cost of litigation can be greatly reduced if the parties agree to enter into a mutual or joint stipulation of facts. The facts of the local church's property history that ought not to be reasonably contested can be stipulated, and both sides should agree on the authentication or validity of most of the documentary evidence. Pre-trial discovery (often the most expensive phase of litigation) can be substantially reduced through such common-sense agreements, and the matter perhaps can be submitted to the court for decision upon the stipulated facts without any, or very limited, time-consuming live testimony. The parties' legal briefs, stipulation of facts, affidavits and oral argument may provide an adequate record for a court's decision. At a minimum, an agreed-upon stipulation of facts will shorten the length of any trial and will reduce the costs to all parties.

The legal work involved in educating, evaluating, documenting and implementing can be performed either by local counsel or by counsel in another state who may have special expertise and thus may be able to use time with greater efficiency and help reduce costs. The same is true for negotiations. The filing of pleadings in civil court, however, requires the retention of local counsel licensed to practice in the state where the property at issue is located. If desired, co-counsel residing elsewhere in the United States can be retained to consult with local counsel, and can actively participate in the preparation and trial of the matter itself when admitted to the local bar *pro hac vice* (for one particular occasion).

In Chapter Nine, theological and ethical concerns are presented that

7 The Presbytery of Charlotte (N.C.), for example, appointed an administrative commission to take over governance of Harrisburg Presbyterian Church and sought congregational approval to amend the local articles of incorporation to provide for denominational ownership or control over local church property in the event of the local church's dissolution.

conscientious Christians should examine in determining if and when civil court litigation is appropriate or necessary. The Apostle Paul was not reluctant, when extraordinary circumstances warranted, of appealing to the authority of Roman procedural law to protect the call Christ had given him. The civil magistrate is a part of God's plan in a world not yet fully redeemed. Sincere Christians today rightly may view equal justice under law – a system of civil courts under a form of constitutional, representative self-government – as part of God's providential protection for property entrusted to local congregations for the proclamation of the Gospel and the preservation of the faith that was "once for all delivered to the saints." Still, resorting to the civil courts should only be pursued after much prayer, consideration of one's obligations and careful self-examination of motive.

CHAPTER NINE

THE RIGHT AND WRONG OF CHRISTIANS IN CIVIL COURT

This book began in Chapter One with a discussion of theology. Succeeding chapters have focused on legal precepts and issues. This concluding chapter returns to matters of theology and ethics. The primary Scriptural truths about property, as discussed in Chapter One, are:

Humankind is the steward of God's creation; God 'holds title' to all property, real and personal.

> The earth is the LORD's and the fullness thereof. …
>
> Psalm 24:1

Humankind was given dominion over the earth by God.

> And God said, 'Let us make man in our image, after our likeness. And let them have dominion over the fish of the sea and over the birds of the heavens and over the livestock and over all the earth and over every creeping thing that creeps on the earth. …
>
> Genesis 1:26

Christians are to hold material things subject to God and his revealed will, for which they are accountable to him.

> For it will be like a man going on a journey, who called his servants and entrusted to them his property. … Now after a long time the master of those servants came and settled accounts with them.
>
> Matthew 25:14-30

As those redeemed in Christ, Christians are to live out the above principles of the moral law in their fullest meaning. Therefore, followers of Christ should look to the Bible for its particular teaching about a Christian's attitude toward possessions and how to handle disputes about them. Members of churches with a hierarchical connection have bound themselves not only to live under the provisions of Scripture, but also their denomination's constitution or other covenants that do not conflict with state or federal law or vested rights. This dual responsibility, in some instances, will generate tensions or conflicts for officers. Decisions by the governing board of a congregation regarding its property have to be made in light of these duties imposed by Scripture, denominational promises and civil law. This chapter will thus explore the theology and ethics of Christians employing civil court remedies to resolve church property disputes.

First, we will look at several passages of Scripture that address property disputes between individual Christians. *Second*, we will consider how those passages apply when the situation deals not with the personal possessions of an individual, but with the common property of a worshiping congregation.

The Biblical Teaching on Proper Motive

In his Sermon on the Mount (Matthew 5-7), Jesus had much to say about law, righteousness, conflicts, and possessions. He said that he came to fulfill the law of God, not to destroy it, and that those who want to enter the Kingdom of Heaven must have a greater righteousness than that exhibited by the scribes and Pharisees. In 5:21-42, Jesus set out five commandments and contrasted the superficial observance of the letter of the moral law approved by the Pharisees with the true obedience that God always intended and continues to expect from his people. Those whose hearts have been regenerated by the Holy Spirit are called and enabled to live as disciples in Christ's Kingdom now.

Jesus first addressed the attitude that his people should have toward those with whom they are in conflict. He condemns the nursing of anger toward a brother (Matthew 5:21-26). Jesus faithfully interprets "not murder" to show that we are not to bear anger with a murderous attitude that breaks out either in physical violence or the emotional violence of insult, verbal, abuse, or contempt. Rather, we are to promote agreement and brotherly kindness, even leaving the sanctuary to effect reconciliation (v. 21-24) and going out of our way to end disputes and promote good will (v. 25-26).

Jesus then speaks to the real meaning of the law on retaliation (5:38-42). The rule of "an eye for an eye" was for the law courts to limit reaction to injuries, to institute a just sense of proportionality. It was not to serve as a model for private revenge. Jesus forbids the repayment of evil. Christ's followers are to forget evils done to them so that they do not respond in hatred, malice or vengeance.

The examples of offenses that Jesus sets out for his disciples to bear patiently do not rise to the level of lethal danger – a slap across the cheek, a lawsuit, carrying a burden. Being struck on the cheek is an act that most often is meant more for insult than physical harm. Being inconvenienced by a spurious lawsuit over a cloak or by having to tote baggage – a Christian can deal with those without striking back in anger or revenge. Furthermore, the examples given do no involve danger to or abuse of a third party. Jesus does not counsel inaction when harm to others is involved, nor abrogates the role of the secular law in dealing with violent behavior. Instead, he instructs his disciples to be magnanimous in foregoing *their individual* rights with regard to *personal* possessions or "honor" in the interest of reconciliation and checking strife. When the situation involves harm and loss to other persons or property that has been entrusted into a congregation's care, these Scriptures cannot be applied without careful consideration of the whole counsel of the Bible.

Christ summarizes his teaching of radical self-denial in Matthew 5:21-42 with the command of 5:43-48 – "love your enemies and pray for those who persecute you so that you may really be the children of your Father in heaven ...." John Calvin comments:

> [T]he man who brings his mind to love those who hate him will readily restrain himself from taking any revenge, he will endure their hurts, he will be far more ready to aid the afflicted.

Calvin, John; *A Harmony of the Gospels of Matthew, Mark and Luke*; A.W. Morrison, translator; David W. Torrance, Thomas F. Torrance, editors (Eerdmans Publishing Company; Grand Rapids, Mich.; 1972) Vol. 1; p. 198.

Jesus continues his instruction about righteousness by addressing a believer's proper regard for material things in Matthew 6:19-34. We are told not to lay up treasures on earth, where they will deteriorate or be stolen, but to store up treasures in heaven: "Seek first the kingdom of God and his righteousness; and all these things will be added unto you." We cannot serve two masters – God and money. In the Lord's Prayer, we are taught that our physical needs are provided for daily by our heavenly Father: "Give us this day our daily bread" (Matthew 6:9-13). We are to trust God; he will supply us with all things.

The Effect of Christian Behavior on The Witness to the Community

Another major passage teaching Christians about property and lawsuits occurs in Paul's response to the problems of the church in Corinth. Its members apparently were taking personal disputes between them to the public courts. In 1 Corinthians 6:1-12, Paul cites three great harms that their litigation in the courts is causing. Two of the grounds of Paul's condemnation are similar to those stated by Jesus in Matthew: rather than fight in court, they should bear injuries patiently and suffer wrong if they cannot settle their grievances within the church (I Corinthians 6:4); and that their motives in bringing the suits are wrong – they are trying to rob their brothers (I Corinthians 6:8-12).[1]

The third ground of Paul's disapproval, however, spotlights a concern about the effect of court cases on the church's mission. Going to public trial elevates the wisdom of unbelieving judges above that of the saints who, in the end times, will be exercising judgment over the whole world. He also implies that the airing of disputes before unbelievers shows the world that Christians cannot govern themselves in brotherly love and forbearance as they are supposed to.

In Matthew, Christ places his commands under the summary principle of loving our enemies. In Corinthians, Paul places both the unrighteous deeds in the first six chapters and the righteous deeds in Chapter 12 under the summary principle in Chapter 13 of love's "more excellent way:"

> Love is patient and kind; love does not envy or boast; it is not arrogant or rude. It does not insist on its own way; it is not irritable or resentful; it does not rejoice at wrongdoing, but rejoices with the truth. Love bears all things, believes all things, hopes all things, endures all things.
>
> 1 Corinthians13:4-7

This emphasis on love by Paul echoes Christ's emphasis on brotherly love from the Sermon on the Mount and from John 13-17. Jesus instructs his disciples that we are to love each other as he loves us, that loving him means keeping his commandments, and the world will know whether we are his disciples by our love for each other.

1 The use of the Greek word for "defraud" indicates that these disputes involve keeping another's property.

DOES THE BIBLE TEACH THAT CHRISTIANS MAY NEVER BRING A LAWSUIT IN CIVIL COURT?

State and federal courts deal with two kinds of cases. The first are criminal cases brought by government officials for violations of criminal laws, such as causing bodily harm or theft of property. The second are civil cases brought by a private citizen or entity against others for causing injury to persons or property or for protecting the rights and property of others. The Biblical texts noted above discuss situations that would arise in civil cases, not criminal ones, and circumstances that pertain to the individual rights of the litigants rather than circumstances necessitating the protection of the rights and interests of others. Therefore, as we continue to examine the principles of these passages we must remember that their teachings may be tempered if not intended to apply fully when the interests of third parties are at stake.

Jesus and Paul set a very high threshold for Christians contemplating civil legal actions against one another, within the "household of faith," whether the Christian is initiating a lawsuit or defending one. John Calvin, himself a lawyer by training, gives helpful commentary on these texts.

In considering the teaching in Matthew 5:21-26 about not nursing anger, Calvin says:

> Christ reproves that obstinacy [to flatter ourselves that we are in the right even when we are not] and enjoins his own people to cultivate moderation and justice, and to make some abatement from the highest rigor, that, by such an act of justice, they may purchase for themselves peace and friendship. ... But, as it is scarcely possible but that differences will sometimes happen, Christ points out the remedy, by which they may be immediately settled; and that is, to put a restraint on our desires, and rather to act to our own disadvantage, than follow up our rights with unflinching rigor. ... [I]t is usually advantageous for us to come to an early agreement with adversaries, because, with quarrelsome persons, their obstinacy often costs them dear.

Calvin, John; *A Harmony of the Gospels of Matthew, Mark and Luke*; Translated from the Original Latin and Collated with the Author's French Version by the Rev. William Pringle, Volume One; Christian Classics Ethereal Library; Grand Rapids, Mich.; Matthew 5:23-26, v. 25.

With respect to the Matthew 5:38-42 passage about being ready to yield our jackets, Calvin's comments keep Jesus' teaching from absurdity:

> None but a fool will stand upon the words so as to maintain, that we must yield to our opponents what they demand, before coming into a court of law: for such compliance would more strongly inflame the minds of wicked men to robbery and extortion; and we know, that nothing was farther from the design of Christ. … Christians are not entirely prohibited from engaging in law-suits, provided they have a just defense to offer. Though they do not surrender their goods as a prey, yet they do not depart from this doctrine of Christ, which exhorts us to bear patiently 'the spoiling of our goods' (Hebrews 10:34).

Ibid; Matthew 5:38-42, v. 40.

Calvin's observation about motives, noted in the I Corinthians 6 passage, is similar:

> [T]he reason why Paul condemns lawsuits is, that we ought to suffer injuries with patience. Let us now see whether any one can carry on a lawsuit without impatience; for if it is so, to go to law will not be wrong in all cases, but only … for the most part. I confess, however, that as men's manners are corrupt, impatience or lack of patience … is an almost separable attendant on lawsuits. … Let us therefore bear in mind, that Paul does not condemn lawsuits on the ground of its being a wrong thing in itself to maintain a good cause by having recourse to a magistrate, but because it is almost invariably accompanied with corrupt dispositions; as, for example, violence, desire of revenge, enmities, obstinacy, and the like.

Calvin, John; *Commentaries on the Epistles of Paul the Apostle to the Corinthians*; Christian Classics Ethereal Library; op. cit.; I Corinthians 6:1-8, point 7.

Thus, Calvin does not conclude that Scripture bars Christians from civil courts. He spells out four justifications for litigation:

> [I]t is useful for many reasons to show that [a lawsuit] is not evil in itself, but is rendered corrupt by abuse:
>
> *First*, that it may not seem as if God had to no purpose appointed courts of justice;
>
> *Secondly*, that the pious may know how far their liberties extend, that they may not take anything in hand against the dictates of conscience. For it is owing to this that many rush on to open contempt of God, when they have once begun to transgress those limits;
>
> *Thirdly*, that they may be admonished, that they must always keep within bounds, so as not to pollute by their own misconduct the remedy which the Lord has permitted them to employ;
>
> *Lastly*, that the audacity of the wicked may be repressed by a pure and uncorrupted zeal, which could not be effected if we were not allowed to subject them to legal punishments.

Ibid.

This last reason cited by Calvin certainly is a purpose that non-believing citizens, as well as Christians, recognize to be valid. The parable of the talents in Matthew 25:14-30 reveals the master's displeasure when the lazy servant reported no increase from the monies given to him. Imagine what the master's reaction would be if the servant reported that he had surrendered it without challenge to the master's rival!

In sum, a Christian on either side of a personal property dispute who wants to take the issue to court, or defend a matter brought against him or her in court, is taught to examine his or her motives very closely and consider the potential cost to the good name of Christ in the opinion of the public. If there is any doubt, the Scriptures seem to counsel that individuals should choose to suffer personal wrong and loss rather than to violate the rule of love.

Vindicating Personal Rights Versus Protecting the Rights of Others to Whom a Duty is Owed

These Scriptural understandings about *individual* property matters, however, cannot be directly applied to the issues of *congregational* property without the consideration of other significant factors. Under Biblical principles, local church officers take on a further obligation of stewardship:

They are answerable to God not only for the use of possessions given to them individually but are also answerable for the protection of possessions entrusted to them by donors, living and dead (See Exodus 22:10-15). Those moral responsibilities not only involve the wise use for benefit to the Kingdom, but also prevention from ungodly use.

Under state corporation laws, officers of a congregation also have legal duties that require them to guard the assets of the church. Legal title to property may rest with a congregation in its capacity as a corporation or an unincorporated association, or with trustees, according to the statutes or common law of the state where it is located. Indeed, denominational constitutions tacitly recognize such duties by requiring or permitting local congregations to become incorporated pursuant to state civil law. (See the discussion of the provisions of the Presbyterian Church (USA) constitution in Chapter Seven, *supra.*)

By requiring each Presbyterian church, for example, to form a corporation to hold its property, the Presbyterian Church (USA) knowingly subjects its ordained officers and the congregation's trustees to the civil corporate law of the state of incorporation.

The civil law and corporate codes of all states uniformly impose high fiduciary duties on corporate officers and directors or trustees. They owe the duties of utmost loyalty to the corporation, complete candor and absolute integrity in dealing with corporate assets, and faithful protection of the corporate assets from waste or misapplications to any use inconsistent with the corporation's purpose and mission.

Given these civil law duties, officers of local church corporations rightly may determine that the most faithful decision they can make is to defend and protect the local church's property against a denomination that no longer is faithful to the clear commands of Scripture.

The attempt by national denominations to impose by fiat in their constitutional documents a trust interest on local congregational property for the benefit of the national denomination presents a clear conflict of duties for the congregation's officers. On the one hand, the denomination purports to create a trust (to which the congregation has not expressly consented) over congregational property that the denomination does not own. On the other hand, state civil law duties clearly require that the officers of the corporation must protect and preserve the church corporation's assets. Ultimately, the officers of the congregational corporation must consider whether their obedience to Christ's authority would be compromised by some act of obedience to the lesser and conflicting authority of their denomination. They must grapple with the question: Who ultimately owns all church property?

Who is the ultimate beneficiary of the property God has entrusted to the local body of believers?

If an individual or group comes to the point that good conscience impels them to separate, there is no question that they have the liberty in Christ to do so. When that decision is accompanied by a claim to property to which a congregation holds title, Scripture requires all parties claiming an interest to examine their motives and manner of doing so. Christ commands us to resolve the differing claims in a way that honors him and our brothers and sisters in Christ, that the world "may see your good works and glorify your Father who is in heaven" (Matthew 5:16).

Christians should remember that the "them" on the other side in a conflict is really "us." Whether the dispute is with a group of other members in a congregation who want to leave with property or with the larger church represented by a presbytery, conference, or diocese, all are to be treated as brothers and sisters in Christ despite deep divisions in theology and practice, and mutual recognition that neither side is entirely innocent. Sadness rather than anger, love rather than hate, generosity rather than greed, friendliness rather than enmity, forgiveness rather than revenge, the spirit of mercy rather than the letter of justice – should characterize any steps to resolve disagreements between Christians and conflicting claims over property dedicated to Christ's glory. Such qualities are not necessarily incompatible, however, with invoking the authority of civil courts when proper motive, witness and moral or legal responsibilities to others are present.

There are, of course, ways of peaceably settling disputes between Christians without resorting to the civil courts – counseling, mediation and arbitration. "If it is possible, as much as lieth in you, live peaceably with all men" (Romans 12:19). However, such means of "alternative dispute resolution" (ADR) are not without difficulty. Some ADR methods may be non-binding or require forfeiture of all rights to appeal. Still, all avenues for resolving a property dispute short of filing a lawsuit merit thoughtful consideration. Several Christian organizations offer these services directly or can refer parties to people in a local area.[2]

2 There are organizations that offer helpful Bible studies and other resources to think about the issues involved in church disputes, as well as refer parties to persons trained in mediating or arbitrating those disputes and, if necessary, appropriately litigating them. Any referral by such organizations does not constitute an endorsement by the publisher of any recommendation. Each person seeking services must evaluate the qualifications of those to whom they may be referred by examining, for example, the credentials and peer-reviewed ratings listed in the *Martindale-Hubbell Legal Directory*. Organizations offering resources and referrals include:

The following list of questions[3] may be helpful to individuals, congregations, church boards, and trustees that are considering whether to bring or defend a lawsuit to protect or preserve personal or corporate interests.

16 Questions To Ask Before Going to Court

1. What action by me is likely to bring the most glory to God? (1 Corinthians 10:22-23)

2. With only six months to live, how much of my time would I spend in litigation? (Psalms 90:12)

3. What are the true motives for getting involved in litigation? Is it a desire for revenge or security? (1 Corinthians 13; Matthew 5:38-48; 7:1-5)

4. Is there a principle or issue at stake that is broader than my personal interests? (Acts 5:17-32)

5. Will the action I take compromise my witness before other Christians? Will I be a stumbling block? (Romans 14:13; 1 Timothy 4:12)

6. Will the action I take compromise my witness before non-Christians? Will I be a hindrance to their receiving the Gospel? (1 Corinthians 6:1-8; 10:32-33; Romans 15:1-3)

The Christian Legal Society
8001 Braddock Road
Suite 300
Springfield, Virginia 22151
(703) 642-1070
www.clsnet.org

Peacemaker Ministry
PO Box 81130
Billings, MT 59108
(406) 256-1583
www.Peacemaker.net
www.hispeace.org

The Rutherford Institute
112 Whitewood Road
P.O. Box 7482
Charlottesville, VA 22906-7482
(434) 978-3888
www.rutherford.org

American Center for Law and Justice
1000 Thomas Jefferson Street, N.W.
P.O. Box 90555
Washington, D.C. 20090-0555
(757) 226-2489
www.aclj.org

3 Suggested by Sam Ericsson, former executive director of the Christian Legal Society, and used by permission.

7. Will the action I take compromise my witness before the other party, their counsel, or my counsel? (Romans 15:1-3)

8. Will the action I take compromise the testimony of the Church or other Christians? (1 Corinthians 6:1-8; 10:32-33)

9. Will my action have potentially damaging consequences on "innocent" third parties? (Matthew 18:1-6; Mark 9:42, Luke 17:1-5)

10. Does Scripture expressly forbid the action I plan to take? (e.g., Matthew 5:31-32)

11. Does Scripture expressly endorse the action I plan to take? (Acts 25:1-12)

12. Does the dispute affect my obligations to my family and household? (1 Timothy 5:8)

13. Am I most concerned about my name, reputation and feelings? (Matthew 5:38-42)

14. What are my alternatives? (Matthew 5:25-26; 6:8-15; 18:15-18)

    (a) Is forgiveness appropriate? (Always!)

    (b) Is [*sic*] settlement and compromise appropriate?

    (c) Have I met with the person one-on-one to discuss my views and listen to his or her views?

    (d) Have I sought out counselors or mediators to assist in reconciliation?

15. Am I as eager to forgive and be reconciled as I am to assert my rights? (Matthew 6:12-15)

16. In whom have I placed my real trust? (Matthew 6:19-34)

Additional Questions to Ask When Fiduciary Responsibilities and Duties to Others are Present

The following list of additional questions may also be of particular help to congregations, church boards and trustees as they decide how to handle church property disputes that involve the interests of others, such as past and present donors and spiritual heirs to come:

1. Q. Who owns the church?

A. God, who gives stewardship to his people.

2. Q. Who are his people?

A. Those who use God-given resources to buy and maintain property for ministering in Christ's name for Christ's purposes – making disciples of all nations (Matthew 28:18-20). Those who have been entrusted by previous generations to carry on faithful use of the property, through the local congregation and larger church governing bodies.

3. Q. What are the two usual kinds of disputes over church property?

A. Those in which two substantial groups within the church disagree with each other over the control and direction of church ministry and property; those in which the vast majority of the congregation disagrees with a higher governing body over the control and direction of church ministry and property.

4. Q. Is it ever faithful for a congregation to leave a denomination?

A. Each congregation must decide after prayer and the study of Scripture and denominational covenants.

Just as an individual can decide in good faith to renounce membership in a congregation or denomination, a congregation can reach such a decision that is faithful to Scripture, to Christ and to covenants made with a denomination.

A denomination is a manifestation of the Church, which is the body and Bride of Christ, but leaving a denomination for a different expression of the body cannot be equated with an unfaithful leaving of "The Church." Covenants in a denominational relationship have commitments made by both parties, and the breach by the denomination of a fundamental understanding may so far compromise the Scriptural truths undergirding the compact that a congregation is required by its conscience to withdraw from the broken agreement.

5. Q. If it can be faithful for a congregation to leave a denomination, can it be faithful to claim the church property as belonging to the congregation?

A. Each congregation must decide after prayer and the study of Scripture and denominational covenants.

It can be faithful for a congregation to claim property as its own. The first condition would be that the congregation paid for the property and has no unresolved debts to a higher governing body. The second condition would be that the congregation's claim is motivated by a wish to use the possessions in a ministry faithful to Jesus Christ; the claims could not arise out of un-Biblical desires to nurse anger, seek revenge or satisfy greed.

6. Q. If it can be faithful for a congregation to leave and to claim property, can it be faithful for the congregation to defend its claims against the denomination in civil court?

A. Each congregation must decide after prayer and the study of Scripture and denominational covenants.

It is hoped, of course, that the congregation and the denomination first try to come to agreement without resort to civil courts, that representatives meet personally in good faith, using mediation or arbitration if needed. Those discussions may result in an amicable and private settlement of differences.

It may be, however, that no agreement can be reached and that a lawsuit is filed. Is it faithful for either party to contest the issue in court?

It can be faithful to take the case to court or to defend in court claims made by a denomination against local church property. Besides passing the Scriptural tests for individuals discussed earlier (a just claim with no improper motive), the congregation may calculate the effect of the dispute on its witness to the community and conclude that the duty to repress wickedness or injustice exceeds the exhortation to suffer loss patiently. The local church should act in a manner consistent with any moral and legal duties owed to others, duties that are imposed by the Bible and state law.

A Concluding Word

As said initially in the Introduction, this book is offered in humble service. The contributors would prefer that discussion of the legal issues involved in church property disputes would be unnecessary and that a peace and unity centered on a common and historic faith would prevail.

Addressing the realities of a world not yet fully redeemed, however, the contributors pray that their meager offering would be used by God for the edification of the Church. It is our hope that this volume will be useful in achieving equitable solutions for resolving competing claims to church property.

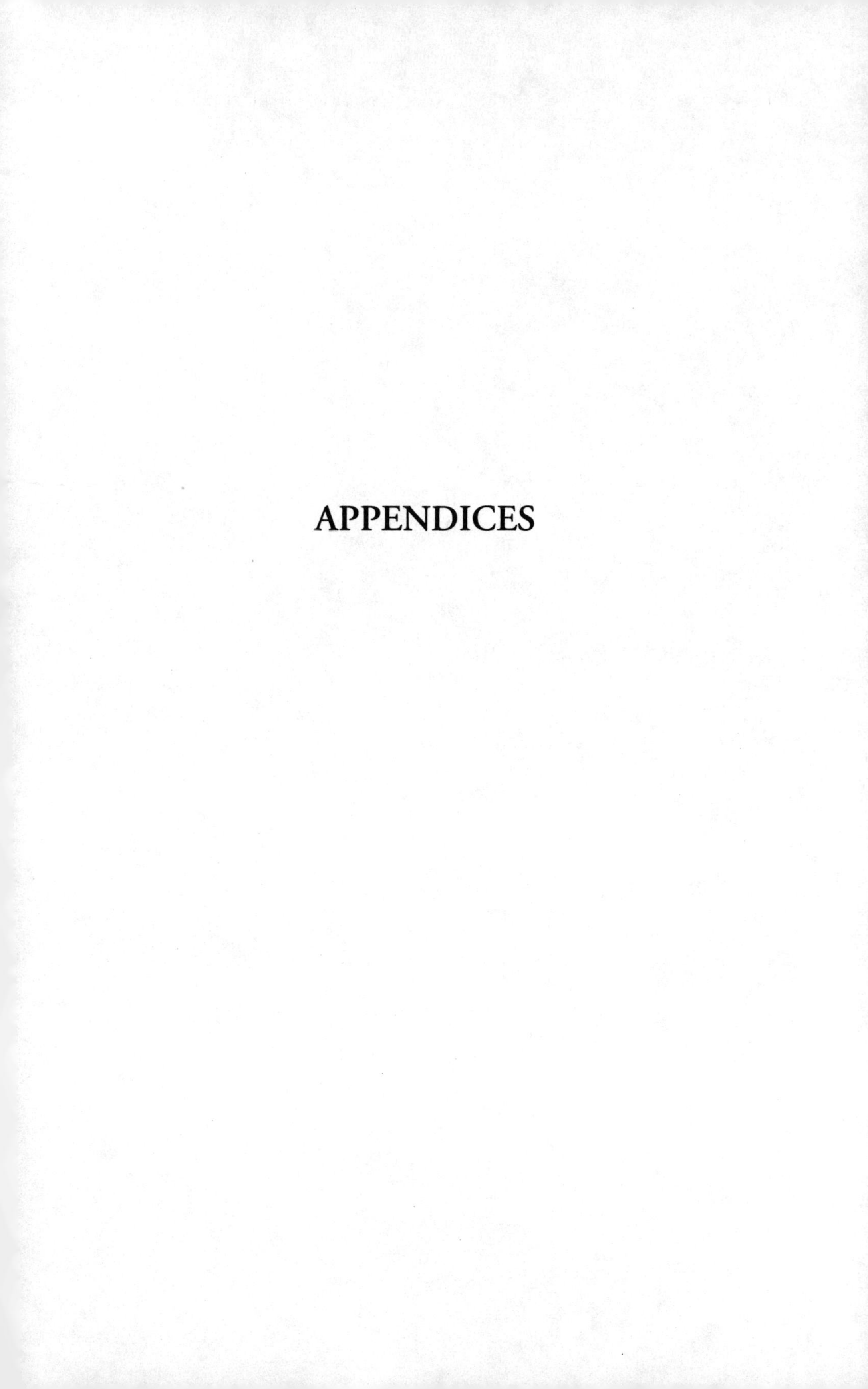

APPENDICES

APPENDIX A

SAMPLE ARTICLES OF INCORPORATION

OF

______________________ ______________________

CHURCH[1]

STATE OF ________________
COUNTY OF ________________

BE IT KNOWN, that on this _____ day of __________________, 200_, before me, the undersigned Notary, in and for said county and State, duly commissioned and qualified, personally came and appeared the undersigned President and Secretary of _______________ ___________ Church (the "Corporation"), and in the presence of the undersigned competent witness and availing themselves of the provisions of the __(state)__ Non-Profit Corporation Law (insert statutory citation), they do hereby execute and file the following Articles of Incorporation. Appearers declare and certify that these articles of incorporation of the Corporation were duly adopted by the vote of the members of the Corporation, namely, those individuals listed as members on the active rolls of the local congregation of the ______________ _ _________ Church (the "Church"), entitled to vote at a duly called, noticed and held meeting of the members, held on ________________, 200_, in __(city), (state)__, at which meeting a quorum was present and voting, and _____ members voted in favor of the resolution adopting the amendments as set forth herein, and ________ members voted against said resolution.

---

1 These sample Articles should be reviewed and modified as necessary to comply with any applicable provisions in the corporation statutes of the state in which property is located.

Amended and Restated Articles

Article I

Name

The name of the Corporation is:

__________________ __________________ CHURCH
(the "Corporation")

Article II

Duration

The duration of this Corporation shall be perpetual.

Article III

Object, Purpose and Powers

This Corporation is a non-profit corporation organized for religious purposes and may engage in any lawful activity for which religious non-profit corporations formed under the provisions of __(state)__ Non-Profit Corporation Law (insert statutory citation) may exercise, including particularly, to operate and continue a church called the ________________ ___________ Church located on ____________________ in __(city)__, __(state)__, for the conduct of worship, the proclamation of the Christian Gospel, and the witness of God's love for the world through service and mission, and further, this Corporation shall have full power and authority to receive, hold, encumber, manage, and transfer property, real or personal, for the Church, and to accept and execute deeds of title to such property, and to have and exercise all other incidents of ownership without limitation on behalf of the Church; to establish one or more churches at different locations, and to borrow money and to mortgage, pledge, assign, grant security interests and otherwise hypothecate the same, and to exercise all other rights, powers and privileges granted to non-profit corporations pursuant to the provisions of the of __(state)__ Non-Profit Corporation Law, (statutory citation), including particularly (statutory citation), as that law may be amended from time to time. [Any property held by or for the Corporation or titled in the name of the Corporation shall be for the use and benefit of the Corporation only, without a trust in favor of any other entity, provided, however, that any property deemed to be held in trust shall be held in a revocable trust, unless expressly stated otherwise in a written instrument describing said trust, and accepted and agreed to in writing by the trustees of the Corporation. The Corporation is further authorized to voluntarily associate with one or more churches and/or with a denominational body, such as the ___________ ______________, as may be deemed appropriate by the members of the congregation to carry out the dictates of conscience under the authority of Holy Scripture and in furtherance of the greater purposes of Christ's Church; provided however, any such determination to so voluntarily associate may be terminated or changed upon a two-thirds affirmative vote of the members present at a meeting duly called for such purpose.][2]

Article IV

Registered Office and Agents

The location of the Corporation's current registered office is ______________________, and its current post office mailing address is ____.

The name and addresses of the Corporation's current registered agents are:

____

____

____

____

____

____

____

____

____

2 This bracketed language is not intended to differ substantively from the rest of the text of these sample Articles but is offered as alternative phrasing.

The Board of Trustees may by resolution change the above location of its registered office and its mailing address, as well as remove any registered agent and/or appoint new registered agents.

Article V

Membership

This corporation is organized on a non-stock basis. The Corporation (i) is owned by its members and has only one class of members. The qualifications to become and be a member are as follows:

Each member of the Corporation must be an individual/natural person, who is listed as a member on the active rolls of the congregation of the Church, as determined by the governing body of the local congregation of the Church. The membership of any individual member of the Corporation shall cease and terminate if and when that individual's name is removed from the active rolls of the congregation of the Church.

Certificates of membership (membership certificates) are not and will not be issued.

Article VI

Board of Trustees/Members Meetings Powers of Board of Trustees

All corporate powers of this Corporation shall be vested in the Board of Trustees, which shall be composed of five (5) "trustees" who are members of the Corporation, as may be elected by the members of this Corporation from time to time for three year terms, which terms may be staggered, if so directed by the Board of Trustees, and any trustee may be re-elected for successive terms without limitation.

The Board of Trustees shall have the authority to make and alter by-laws, including the right to make and alter those fixing their further qualifications and terms of office, but subject to the power of the members to change and/or repeal the by-laws so made. All trustees shall hold office until their successors are elected and qualified.

The general annual meeting of the members of the Corporation shall take place at the registered office of the Corporation on the first (1st) Sunday in February each year, unless and until the place and/or time of the meeting shall be otherwise provided for in the by-laws, if any, or by resolution of the Board of Trustees. Thirty (30) days' notice in writing of each annual and/or special meeting shall be personally delivered to each member or shall be mailed to each member by U.S. Mail, postage prepaid, at his last known address, as shown on the records of the Church, which notice shall be complete and conclusively deemed delivered when mailed. In addition, notice of each such meeting shall be announced from the pulpit of the Church for two successive Sundays prior to the date of the meeting. Each member shall be entitled to one vote, and he must vote in person at the meeting. There shall be no voting by proxy.

Article VII

Officers

The Board of Trustees shall elect officers of this Corporation which shall be a chairman of the board, a president, a vice president, a treasurer and a secretary, and such other officers and agents as may deemed necessary by the Board of Trustees from time to time, including assistant secretaries and assistant treasurers. The chairman, president and secretary shall be trustees, and other officers may be, but are not required to be, trustees.

All officers shall be elected (or re-elected) by the Board of Trustees within two (2) weeks after the annual meeting of the members of the Corporation; provided, however, all officers so elected shall serve until their successors have been elected and qualified, unless terminated earlier.

Article VIII

Limitation of Liability

No trustee or officer of the Corporation shall be liable to the Corporation or to its members for monetary damages for breach of his fiduciary duty as a trustee or officer, provided that the foregoing provision shall not eliminate or limit the liability of a director or officer for (a) any breach of his duty of loyalty to the Corporation or its members; (b) acts or omissions not in good faith or which involved intentional misconduct or a knowing violation of law; (c) liability under (statutory citation), or (d) any transaction from which he derived an improper personal benefit.

No trustee or officer of this Corporation shall ever be held liable or responsible for contracts, debts or defaults of this Corporation, nor shall any mere informality in organization have the effect of rendering these articles of incorporation null, or of exposing any trustee or officer to any liability other than as provided above.

Article IX

Indemnification

The Corporation shall indemnify any person ("Indemnitee") who was or is a party or is threatened to be made a party to any action, suit or proceeding, whether civil, criminal, administrative or investigative, including any action by or in the right of the Corporation, by reason of the fact that he is, or was, a pastor, elder, or deacon of the Church, a trustee or officer of the Corporation or is or was serving at the request of the Corporation as director, officer, employee, trustee or agent of another entity, including foreign or non-profit corporations, partnerships, joint ventures, limited liability companies, trusts or any other enterprise against expenses (including attorneys fees), judgments, fines and amounts paid in settlement actually and reasonably incurred by him in connection with such action, suit or proceeding if he acted in good faith and in a manner he reasonably believed to be in or not opposed to the best interest of the Corporation and with respect to any criminal action or proceeding had no reasonable cause to believe this conduct was unlawful; provided that in causes of actions by or in the right of the Corporation the indemnity shall be limited to expenses (including attorneys fees and amounts paid in settlement not exceeding, in the judgment of the Board of Trustees, the estimated expenses of litigating the action to conclusion) actually and reasonably incurred in connection with the defense of settlement of such action and no indemnification shall be made in respect of any claim, issue or matter as to which such a person shall have been adjudged to be liable for negligence or misconduct in the performance of his duty to the Corporation, unless and only to the extent that the court shall determine upon application that despite the adjudication of liability but in view of all the circumstances of the case he is fairly and reasonably entitled to indemnity for such expenses which the court shall deem proper.

The determination of any action, suit or proceeding, judgment, order, settlement, conviction or upon plea of nolo contendere or its equivalent shall not of itself create a presumption that the person did not act in good faith or in a manner which he reasonably believed to be in or not opposed to the best interest of the Corporation and with respect to any criminal action or proceeding had reasonable cause to believe that his conduct was lawful.

To the extent that a trustee or officer or other Indemnitee of the Corporation has been successful on the merits or otherwise in defense of any such action, suit or proceeding or in defense of any claim, issue or matter therein, he shall be indemnified against expenses (including attorneys fees) actually and reasonably incurred by him in connection therewith.

The indemnification hereunder, unless ordered by the court, shall be made by the Corporation only as authorized in a specific case upon determination that the applicable standard of conduct has been met. Such determination shall be made 1) by the Board of Trustees, by a majority vote of the quorum consisting of the trustees who are not parties to such action, suit or proceeding, or 2) if such a quorum is not obtainable and the Board of Trustees so directs by independent legal counsel, or 3) by the members.

Expenses incurred in defending such an action, suit or proceeding shall be paid by the Corporation in advance of the final disposition thereof if authorized by the Board of Trustees in the manner provided for in this Article, without regard to whether the participating members thereof are parties to such action, suit, or proceeding, upon receipt of an undertaking by or on behalf of the trustees to repay such amount unless it shall ultimately be determined that he is entitled to be indemnified by the Corporation as authorized in the Article.

The indemnification and advancement of expenses provided by or granted pursuant to this Article shall not be deemed exclusive of any other rights to which the person indemnified or obtaining advancement of expenses is entitled to under any bylaw, agreement, vote of members or trustees, regardless of whether trustees authorizing such indemnification are beneficiaries thereof, or otherwise, both as to action in his official capacity and as to action in another capacity while holding such office, and shall continue as to a person who has ceased to be a trustee or officer, and shall inure to the benefit of his legal heirs and legal representatives; however, no such other indemnification measure shall permit indemnification of any person for the results of such person's willful or intentional misconduct.

The foregoing provision of this Article shall be deemed to be a contract between this Corporation and each officer, trustee and other Indemnitee who serves in such capacity at any time while this Article is in effect, and any repeal or modification thereof shall not affect any rights or obligations then existing, with respect to any state of facts or theretofore existing, or any action, suit, or proceeding theretofore or thereafter brought or threatened based in whole or in part upon any such state of facts.

The Corporation shall have power to procure or maintain insurance or other similar arrangement on behalf of any person who is or was a trustee, officer, employee, or agent of the Corporation or is or was serving at the request of the Corporation as a trustee, officer, employee, or agent of another entity or enterprise, including for profit, non-profit or foreign corporations, partnerships, joint ventures, trusts or any other enterprises against any liability asserted against or incurred by him in any such capacity, or arising out of his status as such, whether or not the Corporation would have the power to indemnify him against such liability under the Non-Profit Corporation Law of __(state)__.

Without limiting the power of the Corporation to procure or maintain any other kind of insurance or similar arrangement, the Corporation may create a trust fund or other form of self-insurance arrangement for the benefit of persons to be indemnified by the Corporation and may procure or maintain such insurance with any insurer deemed appropriate by the Board of Trustees regardless of whether all or part of the stock or other securities thereof are owned in whole or in part by the Corporation. In the absence of actual fraud, the judgment of the Board of Trustees as to the terms and conditions of such insurance or self-insurance arrangement and the identity of the insurer or other persons participating in a self-insurance arrangement shall be conclusive, and such arrangement for insurance shall not be subject to voidability and shall not subject the trustees approving such arrangement to liability, on any ground, regardless of whether trustees participating in approving such insurance arrangement shall be beneficiaries thereof.

ARTICLE X

DISSOLUTION/MISCELLANEOUS

The Corporation shall be dissolved (i) through the authorization by a vote of two-thirds of the members of the Corporation (being those individuals listed as members on the active rolls of the Church) voting at a meeting of members to consider dissolution, or (ii) upon an order of judicial dissolution in accordance with (statutory citation). Upon the dissolution of the Corporation by the members, one liquidator selected by the members shall settle the Corporation's affairs in accordance with (statutory citation). In addition, the identity of the Corporation, the ownership of the Corporation's assets, and the right to use of the name ______________ ____________ Church shall be determined at a duly noticed annual or special meeting of the members by a two-thirds vote of the members present and voting, in accordance with the provisions of the __(state)__ Non-Profit Corporation Law, unless otherwise provided herein.

End of Articles

- -

We, ______________________, President, and __________________________, Secretary of ________________ ______________ Church ("Corporation") certify that the above and foregoing Articles of Incorporation of the Corporation were duly adopted by resolution in accordance with the articles and bylaws of the Corporation by the affirmative vote of ______ members (with only ____ members voting against the resolution) at a duly called, noticed and held meeting of members at which a quorum was present and voting held on ________ ___, 200__, and we further certify that pursuant to said resolution the undersigned were authorized to execute this act and file the same with the __(state)__ Secretary of State.

THUS DONE AND SIGNED in (city), (state), on the date first written above, in the presence of the undersigned competent witnesses, who hereto sign their names with the appearer and me, Notary, after due reading of the whole.

WITNESSES:

______________________________	______________________________
Printed Name____________________	______________________, President
______________________________	______________________________
Printed Name____________________	______________________, Secretary
______________________________	______________________________
Printed Name____________________	Printed Name__________________
______________________________	______________________________
Printed Name____________________	Printed Name__________________
______________________________	______________________________
Printed Name____________________	Printed Name__________________

____

______________________________, NOTARY PUBLIC

Bar Roll #__________________

APPENDIX B

Sample Resolution[1]

WHEREAS, in anticipation of and in connection with the adoption in _____ of amended and restated articles of incorporation of the __________ __________________________ it is appropriate to memorialize the significant facts in the history of ______________ property, as follows:

1.) __________ was founded in ______, incorporated in ______, and reincorporated in ______. The ______ articles provide that the Board of Trustees shall exercise all powers of this corporation; the ______ articles of incorporation grant without limitation in Articles ___ through ___ full authority on all property matters variously to the local __________ Board of Trustees and congregation. The ______ and ___ ___ __________ articles of incorporation do not contain any provision imposing or accepting any express or implied trust upon the property of __________ in favor of a national denomination. Said articles were not amended to add such a proviso, and neither the Board nor congregation have adopted a corporate or congregational resolution creating or accepting a trust pertaining to property held by __________, and;

2.) All real property held by __________ consists of or are situated on tracts acquired in ___ different deeds, dating from ______ to ______, which acquisitions were made exclusively from contributions by members of __________. All deeds were originally titled to and at all times have remained titled to the corporation "__________________

1 This sample resolution should be modified to conform to the specifics of a local church's property history and the particulars of the trust or corporation laws of the state in which property is located.

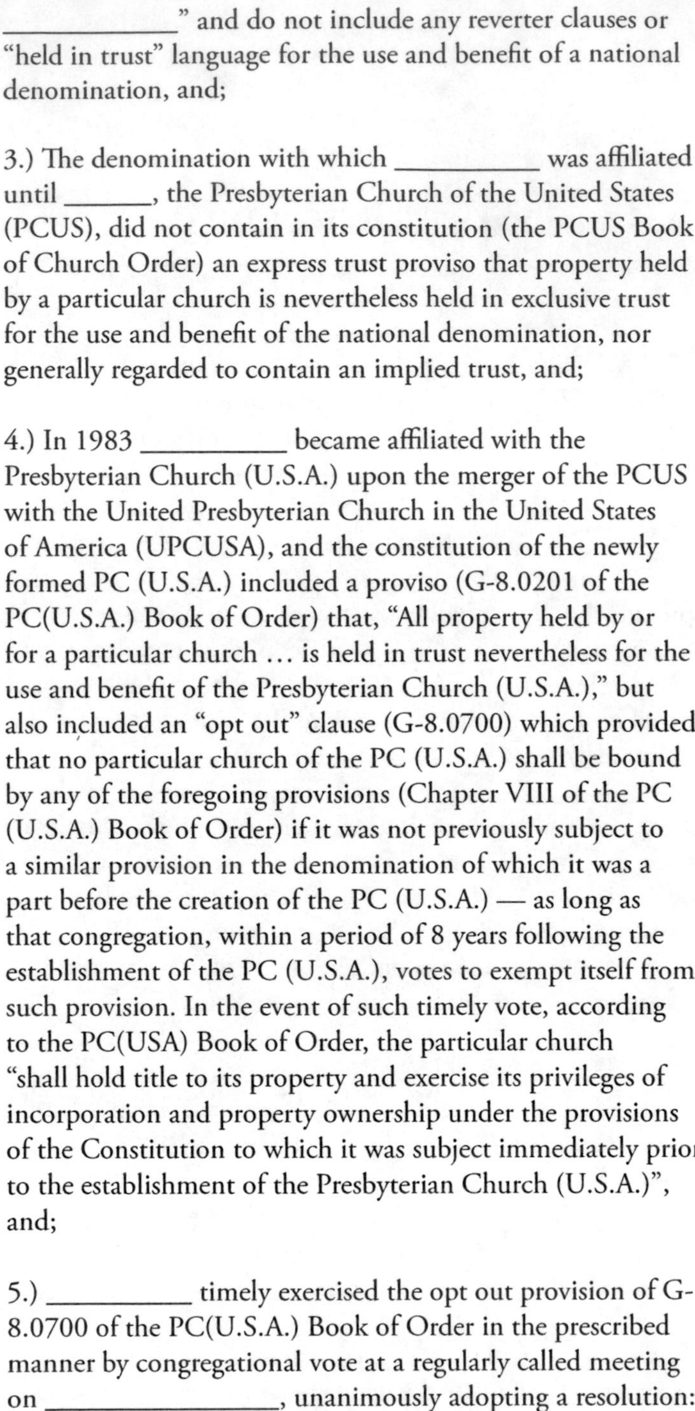

____________" and do not include any reverter clauses or "held in trust" language for the use and benefit of a national denomination, and;

3.) The denomination with which __________ was affiliated until ______, the Presbyterian Church of the United States (PCUS), did not contain in its constitution (the PCUS Book of Church Order) an express trust proviso that property held by a particular church is nevertheless held in exclusive trust for the use and benefit of the national denomination, nor generally regarded to contain an implied trust, and;

4.) In 1983 __________ became affiliated with the Presbyterian Church (U.S.A.) upon the merger of the PCUS with the United Presbyterian Church in the United States of America (UPCUSA), and the constitution of the newly formed PC (U.S.A.) included a proviso (G-8.0201 of the PC(U.S.A.) Book of Order) that, "All property held by or for a particular church ... is held in trust nevertheless for the use and benefit of the Presbyterian Church (U.S.A.)," but also included an "opt out" clause (G-8.0700) which provided that no particular church of the PC (U.S.A.) shall be bound by any of the foregoing provisions (Chapter VIII of the PC (U.S.A.) Book of Order) if it was not previously subject to a similar provision in the denomination of which it was a part before the creation of the PC (U.S.A.) — as long as that congregation, within a period of 8 years following the establishment of the PC (U.S.A.), votes to exempt itself from such provision. In the event of such timely vote, according to the PC(USA) Book of Order, the particular church "shall hold title to its property and exercise its privileges of incorporation and property ownership under the provisions of the Constitution to which it was subject immediately prior to the establishment of the Presbyterian Church (U.S.A.)", and;

5.) __________ timely exercised the opt out provision of G-8.0700 of the PC(U.S.A.) Book of Order in the prescribed manner by congregational vote at a regularly called meeting on ________________, unanimously adopting a resolution:

> "to be exempt from all the provisions of Chapter VIII of said Book of Order the PC (U.S.A.), in order that it may continue to hold title to all of its property and exercise its privileges of incorporation and property ownership, as provided in the Book of Church Order of the Presbyterian Church of the United States that is set forth therein in Chapter 6 prior to the establishment of the Presbyterian Church (U.S.A.)"

, and;

6.) The intent of the congregation by its ________________ __ vote and its understanding of the provisions of Chapter 6 of the PCUS Book of Church Order to which __________ was said to be subject prior to the establishment of the PC (U.S.A.) is indicated in the minutes of that ______________ _____ meeting which state:

> "________________ explained at the time of reunion of our churches all churches were given the option for a period of eight (8) years to have the congregation vote if they wished for our church property to remain in control of the local church or have the property in control of the higher courts of our church as it is outlined in the new Book of Order. He stated that the session was recommending that the congregation vote to retain our property under control of the local church."

, and;

7.) The congregation voted unanimously to approve the above resolution and the minutes were thereafter signed by the senior minister and clerk of session, timely submitted to the __________________________ and, pursuant to G-9.0407 through 9.0409 of the PC(U.S.A.) Book of Church

Order, were accepted without objection by said Presbytery in affirmation that said proceedings were "regular and in accordance with the constitution" and were "prudent and equitable", and;

8.) In the year prior to the formation of the PC (U.S.A.) the PCUS Book of Church Order was reportedly amended to add Section 6-2, relative to particular churches that are incorporated, which provided that the officers of the corporation may be given any or all of specified responsibilities, including holding title to church property for the benefit *of the corporation* and the Presbyterian Church of the United States. At the same time, new Section 6-3 was reportedly added which asserted a trust for the "use and benefit of the Presbyterian Church of the United States" for "all property held by or for a particular church", whether or not incorporated. Notwithstanding the differing interpretations which might be given to these amendments, by the actions recited in paragraphs 1, 2, 5, 6, and 7, above, __________ expressly declined to consent to any provision of the PCUS or PC(U.S.A.) constitutions that purported to impose a trust on property held by __________ in favor of a national denomination, and reaffirmed its understanding and intent that acceptance or validation by __________ of a trust asserted in favor of a national denomination over property held by __________ has not been a requirement for its identification as the __________________________ ________________ or of membership in any predecessor denomination with which it has been identified or affiliated nor is a requirement of its identification or affiliation with the Presbyterian Church (U.S.A.), and;

WHEREAS, the laws of the State of ________________, _______ _________________ Trust Code, R.S. _________, et seq. set forth the requirements generally needed for a valid trust enforceable in __________ ______ and, further, ____________ actions recited herein have precluded creation or acceptance of any trust upon its property under the laws of the State of ________________ by reason of the following nonexclusive list of particulars:

a) An ________________ (nontestamentary) trust must be by authentic act or by act under private signature in the presence of two witnesses, duly acknowledged by the settlor or by affidavit of one of the attesting witnesses (§ ________);

b) It must clearly appear that the creation of a trust is intended (§ _______);

c) A trustee must be either a natural person with capacity to contract or a bank or trust company organized under ______ ______________ law and domiciled in (§ ______________);

d) If _____________ trust includes immovables or other property that title to which must be recorded in order to effect third parties, a trustee shall file the trust instrument for record in each parish in which the property is located (§ ________);

e) Trusts for charitable, benevolent or eleemosynary purposes, whether express or implied, are defined as only those where all or a substantial part of the corpus thereof shall have been contributed by the local beneficiaries, who are those who shall have contributed (or whose predecessor beneficiaries shall have contributed) all or a substantial part of the corpus of the trust and who shall locally, immediately and directly enjoy the benefits of the trust (§ ________),

and none of the foregoing requirements for the establishment of a valid trust enforceable in ________________ in favor of a national denomination have ever been met with respect to any property held by __________, and there are no applicable exceptions under ________________ law which would provide or imply that a trust was created,

THEREFORE, BE IT RESOLVED, that the Board of Trustees of the ______________________________, consistent with __________'s historic position, do faithfully and respectfully make the above recitals, memorialize the facts concerning the history of __________ property, and reaffirm its understanding and intent that all property held by the ______________________________ is held by it in full and complete ownership, and that none of said property is being held in trust for the use and benefit of a national denomination.

THUS DONE AND UNANIMOUSLY PASSED, by the Board of Trustees of the ______________________________, Inc., __________________ this _______ day of ________________, 200__.

WITNESSES:

____________________________	____________________________
Printed Name__________________	____________________, President
____________________________	____________________________
Printed Name__________________	____________________, Secretary
____________________________	____________________________
Printed Name__________________	Printed Name__________________
____________________________	____________________________
Printed Name__________________	Printed Name__________________
____________________________	____________________________
Printed Name__________________	Printed Name__________________

____

______________________, NOTARY PUBLIC

Bar Roll #______________

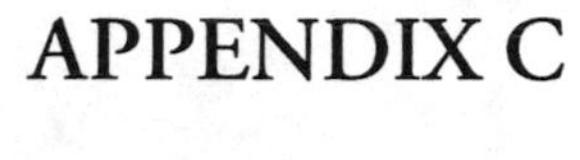

APPENDIX C

CHURCH PROPERTY DISPUTES
A CONSTITUTIONAL PERSPECTIVE[1]

Unfortunately, many of the most contentious conflicts in secular courts arise in the context of schism among members of a single religious body. That schism may be the result of theological disagreement, personality conflict, or secular political division transferred to the religious unit. The religious unit may be a highly structured organization, or a free-standing congregation. Whatever the case, many such conflicts find their way into secular courts under the guise of property disputes, *viz.*, which of two or more competing groups is entitled to the occupancy, use and control of real or personal church property.

At first blush, such conflicts might appear to be the common grist of civil litigation: one party asserts a superior claim or interest in property to that of a competing party. Yet, such is not the case. The First Amendment to the United States Constitution provides, in part, that: *Congress shall make no law respecting an establishment of religion, or prohibiting the free exercise thereof;. ...*[2] Its protections have been applied to the states via the Fourteenth Amendment, which provides, in part: *No State shall make or enforce any law which shall abridge the privileges or immunities of citizens of the United States; nor shall any State deprive any person of life, liberty, or property, without due process of law;. ...*[3]

The initial opinions in this field were based on general legal principles, rather than the specifics of constitutional jurisprudence.Yet, even these general principles were later described in grand terms as:

1 *Church Property Disputes: A Constitutional Perspective* © 2000 by Kenneth E. North (J.D., Duke University School of Law). Originally presented at the Duquesne University School of Law Jubilee International and Ecumenical Canon Law Conference on February 4-5, 2000. Used by permission of the Canon Law Institute, 2727 O Street, N.W., Washington, D.C. 20007; (202) 262-5519/(301) 565-9437; http://www.canonlaw.org.

2 U.S. Constitution; Amendment I, cl.1.

3 U.S. Constitution; Amendment XIV, § 1.

> [radiating] a spirit of freedom for religious organizations, an independence from secular control or manipulation, in short, power to decide for themselves, free from state interference, matters of church government as well as those of faith and doctrine.[4]

Controversies touching this area are varied. For example, if one group asserts that it is entitled to the church property because it has maintained the historic and traditional doctrines of the religious body, whereas the competing group has adopted a heretical belief system, is the secular court to decide as a matter of fact and law which of two competing religious views is "heretical" *vis -a- vis* that religious body? Is such engagement permitted by U.S. Constitutional jurisprudence? If so, is such judicial intervention unbridled, or subject to constitutional parameters, or simply prohibited?

The U.S. Supreme Court has considered these questions and issues on some dozen or so occasions.[5] The result is an anomalous body of Supreme Court jurisprudence wherein there exist two separate, but equally permissible, rules of constitutional jurisprudence. This article considers these cases *seriatim*, and then summarizes the current rules or approaches that may be utilized in dealing with church property disputes. Of course, it should be remembered that there are hundreds of state and federal cases that also have dealt with church property disputes. So, research into this field also requires identifying and understanding the relevant authorities from this larger body of law.

I. Supreme Court Consideration of Church Property Disputes

A. General Common Law

1. Watson v. Jones

The first U.S. Supreme Court foray into the jurisprudence of church property disputes remains the touchstone for such litigation in the Third Millennium. While it may be said that such contemporary referencing is more by way of form than substance, a decision that otherwise could have

4 *Kedroff v. St. Nicholas Cathedral of Russian Orthodox Church in North America*; 344 U.S. 94, 116 (1952).

5 Considered are 11 opinions, one dissent from the denial of a petition for a writ of certiorari, and one single-justice denial of an application for a stay order.

been a historical footnote at best is elevated by subsequent court opinions to penultimate status in this area of constitutional jurisprudence. Our discussion of subsequent opinions will highlight the transformation of this pre-*Erie Co. v. Tompkins*[6] decision based on general common-law principles into one of today's available analytical approaches.[7]

Watson v. Jones[8] tracks the tortuous trek of a post-Civil War division in a Presbyterian Church in Louisville, Kentucky. The underlying cause of the division was a direction from the General Assembly of the Presbyterian Church to the presbyteries, the Board of Missions and to the sessions of the churches that required any person from the Southern states seeking membership, employment as a missionary, or ministers of the church to repent and forsake their sins if any had voluntarily aided the War of the Rebellion, or held the doctrine of a faction of the Presbyterian Church that supported slavery. Members of the Third or Walnut Street Presbyterian Church of Louisville, Kentucky, split on this direction from the General Assembly, resulting in two groups each claiming the right to the use and possession of the church property.[9]

The U.S. Supreme Court determined that the Presbyterian Church in the United States is a voluntary religious organization. It has a written a Confession of Faith, Form of Government, Book of Discipline, and Directory for Worship. Its government is exercised by and through an ascending series of judicatories. The General Assembly, through its hierarchy, recognized the majority faction of the Walnut Street church as the congregation in communion with it. The other faction asserted its claims under Kentucky property and trust laws. The court ruled in favor of the majority faction by deferring to the prior rulings of the Presbyterian Church and its judicatories.[10]

In reaching its decision, the court classified cases concerning the rights to property held by ecclesiastic bodies into three groups:

1. The property is devoted to the teaching, support, or spread of some specific form of religious doctrine or belief by the express language of the deed, will, or other instrument by which the property is held.
2. The property is held by a religious congregation that is strictly

6 304 U.S. 64 (1938).

7 Yet, it should be noted that the continuing vitality of this renowned authority might not withstand a direct, modern-day assault. See *Serbian Eastern Orthodox Diocese for the United States of America and Canada v. Milivojevich*, 426 U.S. 696, 725 (1976) (REHNQUIST Dissent).

8 13 Wall. 679 (1871).

9 Id. at 681-693.

10 Id. at 712.

independent of other ecclesiastic associations, and owes no fealty or obligation to any higher authority.

3. The property is held by a religious congregation or ecclesiastic body that is a subordinate member of a general church organization, which has superior ecclesiastic tribunals with a general and ultimate power of control over the whole membership of that general organization.[11]

The court opined as to the appropriate role for the civil courts in all three classifications. The matter actually before the court, however, concerned the third classification. Thus, the court's view as to the first two classifications is dicta; i.e., not the law of the case or necessarily controlling in future cases. Following are excerpts of the Court's discussion of the three classifications.

> 1. [T]hough the task may be a delicate one and a difficult one, it will be the duty of the court in such cases, when the doctrine to be taught or the form of worship to be used is definitely and clearly laid down, to inquire whether the party accused of violating the [express language of the deed, will, or other instrument by which the property is held] is holding or teaching a different doctrine, or using a form of worship which is so far variant as to defeat the declared objects of the [express language of the deed, will, or other instrument by which the property is held].
>
> 2. In such cases where there is a schism which leads to a separation into distinct and conflicting bodies, the rights of such bodies to the use of the property must be determined by the ordinary principles which govern voluntary associations. *** This ruling admits of no inquiry into the existing religious opinions of those who comprise the legal or regular organization; for, if such was permitted, a very small minority, without any officers of the church among them, might be found to be the only faithful supporters of the religious dogmas of the founders of the church. There being no such trust imposed upon the property when purchased or given, the court will not imply one for the purpose of expelling from its use those who by regular succession and order constitute the church, because they may have changed in some respect their views of religious truth.

11 Id. at 722-723.

> 3. In this class of cases, we think the rule of action which should govern the civil courts, founded in the broad and sound view of the relations of church and state under our system of laws, and supported by the preponderating weight of judicial authority, is that whenever the questions of discipline, or of faith, or ecclesiastic rule, custom, or law have been decided by the highest of these church judicatories to which the matter has been carried, the legal tribunals must accept such decisions as final, and as binding on them, in their application to the case before them. **** In this country, the full and free right to entertain any religious belief, to practice any religious principle, and to teach any religious doctrine which does not violate the laws of morality and property, and which does not infringe personal rights, is conceded to all. The law knows no heresy, and is committed to the support of no dogma, the establishment of no sect. The right to organize voluntary religious associations to assist in the expression and dissemination of any religious doctrine, and to create tribunals for the decision of controverted questions of faith within the association, and for the ecclesiastic government of all the individual members, congregations and officers within the general association, is unquestioned. All who unite themselves to such a body do so with the implied consent to this government, and are bound to submit to it.[12]

From this opinion has emerged what is variously known as the *Watson* rule, or compulsory deference. In essence, secular courts dealing with church property disputes involving hierarchical religious bodies must defer to, and enforce as applicable, decisions by the highest judicatories of such religious bodies as have considered the relevant controversy.

2. Bouldin v. Alexander

The year following the *Watson* decision saw the next excursion into the arena of church property disputes by the U.S. Supreme Court. Surprisingly however, *Bouldin v. Alexander*[13] never mentioned the prior term's opinion in *Watson*. In any event, this controversy revolved around the use and occupancy

12 Id. at 723 – 728.

13 82 U.S. 131 (1872).

of the real property of a congregational Baptist church in the District of Columbia. The founding pastor of this church and a minority of the church membership, after a falling out with the majority of the congregation, ostensibly removed without cause or notice four of the seven trustees who held title to the church property. This minority faction also "excommunicated" the majority membership of the congregation.[14] The court viewed its task succinctly:

> This is not a question of membership of the church, nor of the rights of members as such. It may be conceded that we have no power to revise or question ordinary acts of church discipline, or of excision from membership. We have only to do with rights of property. ... We must take the fact of excommunication as conclusive proof that the persons exscinded are not members. But we may inquire whether the resolution of expulsion was the act of the church, or of persons who were not the church and who consequently had no right to excommunicate others.[15]

The court went on to rule that, in congregational churches, the majority – assuming adherence to organization and doctrines – represents the church. It concluded: "[a]n expulsion of the majority by a minority is a void act."[16] In rendering its decision, the court cited nary a single precedent.

3. Helm v. Zarecor

The first post-*Watson* foray of the U.S. Supreme Court that cited *Watson* is *Helm v. Zarecor,*[17] wherein the court considered a procedural decision dismissing an action for lack of jurisdiction; i.e., complete diversity. At issue was a claim brought by clergy, elders and laymen of the Presbyterian Church in the United States of America individually and on behalf of all members of the Church. Defendants were named individuals alleged to be representing their own interests, as well as those of the membership of Cumberland Presbyterian Church and the Board of Publication of the Cumberland Presbyterian Church. All plaintiffs were citizens of states other than Tennessee. All defendants, including the Board of Publication of the Cumberland

14 Id. at 133-135.
15 Id. at 139-140.
16 Id. at 140.
17 222 U.S. 32 (1911).

Presbyterian Church, a Tennessee corporation, were citizens of Tennessee.

The controversy at issue arose from the merger of two previously independent religious organizations, the Cumberland Presbyterian Church and the Presbyterian Church in the United States of America. The Board of Publication was established before the merger as the publishing arm of the Cumberland Presbyterian Church and owned substantial assets. Organizationally, the officers and managers of the Board of Publication were appointed by the highest judicatory body of the Cumberland Presbyterian Church, its General Assembly. The defendants, alleged to be a minority number of clergy and laity from the Cumberland Presbyterian Church, did not accept the validity of the 1906 merger, whereas the plaintiffs asserted that the union was valid and, consequently, the Board of Publication held its assets in trust for the Presbyterian Church in the United States of America.[18] The post-merger managers of the Board of Publication agreed that it was now an institution of the Presbyterian Church in the United States of America. The defendants, after the merger, reconstituted the Cumberland Presbyterian Church and its General Assembly, declared all positions at the Board of Publication vacant, and elected its own control group of the Board of Publication.[19]

The litigation sought a decree that the Board of Publication held its assets in trust for the Presbyterian Church in the United States of America, and that the members of the board elected by the Presbyterian Church in the United

18 In addition to the U.S. Supreme Court cases discussed in this article, the validity of the 1906 merger between the two churches, and the title to property claimed pursuant to that merger, was the subject of decisions by the highest court in twelve states: Harris v. Cosby, 173 Ala. 81, 55 South. 231; Sanders v. Baggerly, 96 Ark. 117, 131 S.W. 49; Permanent Committee of Missions v. Pacific Synod, 157 Cal. 105, 106 Pac. 395; Mack v. Kime, 129 Ga. 1, 58 S.E. 184, 24 L.R.A.(N.S.) 675; First Presbyterian Church of Lincoln v. First Cumberland Presbyterian Church of Lincoln, 245 Ill. 74, 91 N.E. 761, 19 Ann.Cas. 275; Fussell v. Hail, 233 Ill. 73, 84 N.E. 42; Fancy Prairie Church v. King, 245 Ill. 120, 91 N.E. 776; Pleasant Grove Congregation v. Riley, 248 Ill. 604, 94 N.E. 30; Ramsey v. Hicks, 174 Ind. 428, 91 N.E. 344, 92 N.E. 164, 30 L.R.A.(N.S.) 665; Bentle v. Ulay, 175 Ind. 494, 94 N.E. 759; Wallace v. Hughes, 131 Ky. 445, 115 S.W. 684; Carothers v. Moseley, 99 Miss. 671, 55 South. 881; First Presbyterian Church v. Cumberland Presbyterian Church, 34 Okl. 503, 126 Pac. 197; Brown v. Clark, 102 Tex. 323, 116 S.W. 360, 24 L.R.A.(N. S.) 670; Boyles v. Roberts, 222 Mo. 613, 121 S.W. 805; and Landrith v. Hudgins, 121 Tenn. 556, 120 S.W. 783. The dispute also was considered by three federal district courts: Sharp v. Bonham, 213 Fed. 660; Helm v. Zarecor, 213 Fed. 648 (M.D .Tenn.); and Sherard v. Walton 206 Fed. 562 (W.D. Tenn.). In all cases except Missouri and Tennessee, the complainants were victorious, and the validity of the merger upheld. The Missouri Supreme Court subsequently overruled its decision in Boyles v. Roberts, supra this note, and ruled to affirm the validity of the merger. Hayes v. Manning, 172 S.W. 897 (1914).

19 Id. at 33-35.

States of America constitute the lawful membership of the board.[20]

After denying a variety of preliminary motions by the defendants, the lower court on its own motion dismissed the complaint for lack of complete diversity. In rendering this decision, it held that defendant Board of Publication "was not antagonistic to the complainants, and should be aligned upon the same side of the controversy with the complainants...."[21]

In reversing this ruling, the U.S. Supreme Court stated: "To align the corporation itself with the complainants is virtually to decide the merits in their favor. The Board is simply a title holder,[22] -- an instrumentality, the mastery of which is in dispute."[23]

The court noted that the actual dispute was not limited to membership on the board or the rights of a particular corporation. Rather, "[i]t embraces the fundamental question of the rights of these religious associations, ..., to use and control the corporate agency."[24]

Helm v. Zarecor, as well as the referenced portion of *Watson v. Jones*, appears to teach us that mere corporate formalities will not suffice to resolve underlying religious denominational issues such as schism and its impact on the control of religious property. This teaching, however, is at best called into doubt[25] by the subsequent adoption by the U.S. Supreme Court of

---

20 Id. at 34.

21 Id. at 35.

22 Citing *Watson v. Jones*, 80 U.S. 679, 720 (1871). The reference refers to that portion of the opinion which states, in part:

"One or two propositions which seem to admit of no controversy are proper to be noticed in this connection. 1. Both by the act of the Kentucky legislature creating the trustees of the church a body corporate, and by the acknowledged rules of the Presbyterian Church, the trustees were the mere nominal title-holders and custodians of the church property, and other trustees were, or could be elected by the congregation, to supply their places once in every two years. 2. That in the use of the property for all religious services or ecclesiastical purposes, the trustees were under the control of the church session. 3. That by the constitution of all Presbyterian churches, the session, which is the governing body in each, is composed of the ruling elders and pastor, and in all business of the session the majority of its members govern, the number of elders for each congregation being variable.

"The trustees obviously hold possession for the use of the persons who by the constitution, usages, and laws of the Presbyterian body, are entitled to that use. They are liable to removal by the congregation for whom they hold this trust, and others may be substituted in their places. They [80 U.S. 679, 721] have no personal ownership or right beyond this, and are subject in their official relations to the property to the control of the session of the church."

23 *Helm v. Zarecor*, supra at 38.

24 Id. at 37.

25 Of course, this doubt only applies in those states wherein the neutral-principles of law doctrine is applicable.

the neutral-principles of law approach[26] as permissible in resolving church property disputes.

4. Shepard v. Barkley

The second visit of the merger between the Presbyterian Church of the United States of America and the Cumberland Presbyterian Church to the U.S. Supreme Court was in *Shepard v. Barkley.*[27] That brief Memorandum Opinion affirmed the lower courts' entering decrees in favor of complainant Presbyterian Church of the United States of America. In rendering its decision, the U.S. Supreme Court commented:

> ... the court is of opinion that the doctrines by which the case is controlled have been so affirmatively and conclusively settled by a prior decision of this court as to cause it to be unnecessary as a matter of original consideration to restate them. *Watson v. Jones*, 13 Wall. 679. And the want of any possible reason for removing this case from the control of the doctrines of the *Watson* case is, if needs be, conclusively shown by the many cases referred to by the court below in its opinion, in which the *Watson* case was made controlling and decisive as to controversies not in substance differing from the one here presented.[28]

5. Gonzalez v. Roman Catholic Archbishop of Manila

Gonzalez v. Roman Catholic Archbishop of Manila[29] directly addressed a situation in which the application of secular law probably would have yielded a different result than deference to canon law. At issue was a vacant collative chaplaincy[30] in the Roman Catholic Archdiocese of Manila. The chaplaincy was established in 1820 pursuant to a will, and the requisite ecclesiastical decree provided for its approval. The will provided that the chaplaincy

26 13 Wall. 679 (1871).

27 247 U.S. 1 (1918).

28 Id. at 2.

29 280 U.S. 1 (1929).

30 Such a chaplaincy "is an institution founded by an individual for the purpose of celebrating or causing to be celebrated annually a certain number of masses conforming to the will of the founder.... The ecclesiastical or collative chaplaincy, although also founded by an individual, is one erected into a benefice by the proper spiritual authority, requires a title of ordination, and is thus subject to ecclesiastical control." Id. footnote 1 at 3.

should be held by testatrix's nearest relative. From 1820 until 1910, the chaplaincy was so occupied.[31] In December 1910, however, the chaplaincy was renounced by its then-current holder, who thereafter married and, in 1912, father the petitioner in the instant case. In 1922, this male son of the fifth chaplain was presented to the archbishop for appointment to the vacant collative chaplaincy. The archbishop declined, referencing the then-applicable Code of Canon Law requirement for theological education prior to any such appointment.[32]

Petitioner asserted that his appointment to the chaplaincy was to be governed by the canon law in effect in 1820, not that which became effective when he was presented for the chaplaincy in 1922. On the other hand, respondent archbishop asserted that by virtue of the property of the chaplaincy having been conveyed to the spiritual authorities, the secular courts lacked subject matter jurisdiction. Relying on the authority of *Watson v. Jones*,[33] Mr. Justice Brandeis, affirming the ruling of Supreme Court of the Philippine Islands in favor of the archbishop and writing for a unanimous court, held:

> The fact that the property of the chaplaincy was transferred to the spiritual properties of the archbishopric affects not the jurisdiction of the court, but the terms of the trust. The archbishop's claim in this respect is that by an implied term of the gift, the property, which was to be held by the church, should be administered in such manner and by such persons as may be prescribed by the church from time to time. Among the church's laws, which are thus claimed to be applicable, are those creating tribunals for the determination of ecclesiastical controversies. Because the appointment is a canonical act, it is the function of the church authorities to determine what the essential qualifications of a chaplain are and whether the candidate possesses them. *In the absence of fraud, collusion, or arbitrariness, the decisions of the proper church tribunals on matters purely ecclesiastical, although affecting civil rights, are accepted in litigation before the secular courts as conclusive, because the parties in interest made them so by contract or otherwise.*[34]

31 Id. at 12.

32 Id. at 12-13.

33 13 Wall. 679, 714, 727, 729, 733.

34 280 U.S. 1, 16 (citations omitted, emphasis added).

So we have, consistent with *Watson v. Jones*, two rules thus established. First, secular courts do possess subject matter jurisdiction over church property disputes. Second, such secular courts, absent fraud, collusion, or arbitrariness,[35] must accept the decisions of "proper church tribunals ... as conclusive." It should also be noted that, up to this point in our discussion, none of the opinions has engaged in a constitutional analysis, nor relied on the U.S. Constitution or any of its amendments as the basis for its decision.

B. Constitutional Law Decisions

1. Kedroff v. St. Nicholas Cathedral of Russian Orthodox Church in North America

The dispute in *Kedroff v. St. Nicholas Cathedral of Russian Orthodox Church in North America*[36] began with an ejectment action seeking possession and control of the New York cathedral of the Russian Orthodox Church in North America. The elected head of the American churches affiliated with the Russian Orthodox Church sought the ejectment of the archbishop appointed by "the Supreme Church Authority of the Russian Orthodox Church."[37]

The issue was framed by the U.S. Supreme Court as: "Determination of the right to use and occupy Saint Nicholas depends upon whether the appointment of Benjamin by the Patriarch or the election of the Archbishop for North America by the convention of the American churches validly selects the ruling hierarch for the American churches."[38]

A New York statute[39] provided for the establishment of an administratively autonomous district consisting of those New York churches formerly subject to the administrative control of the patriarch of Moscow. Benjamin, the patriarch's appointee, contended that this New York statute violated the Fourteenth Amendment to the U.S. Constitution and, thus, could not be utilized for resolution of the instant controversy.[40] More precisely, Article 5-C

35 These exceptions to the requirement that secular courts accept the decisions of ecclesiastic tribunals have been subsequently limited. *Serbian Eastern Orthodox Diocese for the United States of America and Canada v. Milivojevich*, 426 U.S. 696, 712 (1976) (eliminating the arbitrariness exception).

36 344 U.S. 94 (1952).

37 Id. at 95-96.

38 Id. at 96-97.

39 Article 5-C, Religious Corporations Law of New York, 50 McKinney's N.Y. Laws § 105 et. seq.

40 344 U.S. 94, 97-98.

was alleged to be proscribed by the First Amendment to the Constitution, which precluded governmental interference with the exercise of religion. The corollary argument was that the Fourteenth Amendment made applicable to the states this First Amendment protection.[41]

For the first time, the court was to resolve an issue involving a church property dispute by directly referencing the Constitution. Preliminarily, the court found that: "From those circumstances,[42] it seems clear that the Russian Orthodox Church was, until the Russian revolution, an hierarchical church with unquestioned paramount jurisdiction in the governing body in Russia over the American Metropolitanate. Nothing indicates that either the Sacred Synod or the succeeding Patriarchs relinquished that authority or recognized the autonomy of the American church."[43]

Having established the hierarchical nature of the Russian Orthodox Church, the court determined that the New York statute[44] transferred control of the New York churches from the hierarchy of the Russian Orthodox Church to the governing judicatories of the Russian Orthodox Church in America. It then held that "[s]uch a law violates the Fourteenth Amendment. It prohibits in this country the free exercise of religion."[45] The court goes on to note that "[h]ere there is a transfer by statute of control over churches. This violates our rule of separation between church and state. That conclusion results from the purpose, meaning and effect of the New York legislation…."[46]

After extensive discussion and reaffirmation of the jurisprudence of *Watson v. Jones*,[47] the court further discussed the constitutional infirmities of New York's Article 5-C. In this elaboration it stated:

"By fiat it displaces one church administrator with another. It passes the control of matters strictly ecclesiastical from one church authority to another. It thus intrudes for the benefit of one segment of a church the power of the state into the forbidden area of religious freedom contrary to the principles of the First Amendment. … New York's Article 5-C directly prohibits the free exercise of an ecclesiastical right, the Church's choice of its hierarchy."[48]

In reversing the Court of Appeals of New York, the U.S. Supreme Court

---

41 Id. at 100.

42 The circumstances referenced are the court's recitation of the relevant history of the Russian Orthodox Church and the American church, 344 U.S. at 100-105.

43 Id. at 105-106. It should be recalled that a hierarchical church structure is one of the three templates utilized by the court in *Watson v. Jones*, supra, for analysis.

44 Article 5-C, supra.

45 344 U.S. at 107.

46 Id. at 110.

47 Id. at 110-117.

48 Id. at 119.

recognized that, as in the case before it, the use and control of property may be dictated by the purely ecclesiastical decisions of hierarchical church judicatories. Clearly, pure property questions are beyond the jurisdiction of such church judicatories. However, "[e]ven in those cases when the property right follows as an incident from the decisions of the church custom or law on ecclesiastical issues, the church rule controls. This under our Constitution necessarily follows in order that there may be free exercise of religion."[49]

In *Kedroff v. St. Nicholas Cathedral of Russian Orthodox Church in North America,*[50] we have *Watson v. Jones* elevated to a position of constitutional jurisprudence and the rules of judicial deference to church judicatories, as well as legislative pre-emption from internal church interference, given constitutional protection via the First and Fourteenth Amendments.[51]

2. Kreshik v. Saint Nicholas Cathedral

While *Kedroff v. St. Nicholas Cathedral of Russian Orthodox Church in North America*[52] clearly established the rule that legislative action that impinges internal church governance is contrary to constitutional proscriptions, it remained for the U.S. Supreme Court in *Kreshik v. Saint Nicholas Cathedral*[53] to extend this rule to judicial action. At issue in this matter was *Kedroff v. St. Nicholas Cathedral of Russian Orthodox Church in North America*[54] after remand and retrial. The New York Court of Appeals in the remanded proceeding again ruled in favor of the New York church, holding that the Russian patriarch was dominated by secular authority and, thus, under New York common law, unable to validly exercise the right to occupy the cathedral. In a *per curiam* opinion again reversing the New York court, the U.S. Supreme Court held that "it is established doctrine that '(i)t is not of moment that the State has here acted solely through its judicial branch, for whether legislative or judicial, it is still the application of state power which we are asked to scrutinize.' N.A.A.C.P. v. State of Alabama, 357 U.S. 449, 463."[55]

So, neither state legislative nor judicial action may interfere with the judicatory decisions of a hierarchical church. For any such state action is contrary to the dictates of the First and Fourteenth Amendments.

49 Id. at 120-121.
50 344 U.S. 94 (1952).
51 Justices Frankfurter, Black and Douglas concurred; Mr. Justice Jackson dissented.
52 344 U.S. 94 (1952).
53 363 U.S. 190 (1960).
54 344 U.S. 94 (1952).
55 Id. at 191.

3. Presbyterian Church in the United States v. Mary Elizabeth Blue Hill Memorial Presbyterian Church

Presbyterian Church in the United States v. Mary Elizabeth Blue Hill Memorial Presbyterian Church[56] involved an action brought by local churches seeking to prohibit the national church from entering local church property.

The controversy arose when two local churches in Savannah, Georgia, voted to withdraw from the hierarchical Presbyterian Church in the United States. The schism was grounded in certain national church action that was viewed by the local churches as contrary to the doctrine and practice in force when the local churches initially affiliated with the national church.[57] After unsuccessful attempts at reconciliation, the national church acknowledged the withdrawal of the local leadership, and moved to assume control of the local church property.[58]

The local churches filed an action in Georgia state court seeking to enjoin the national church from trespassing on the local church property. The litigation was brought under Georgia law, wherein "the right to the property previously used by the local churches was made to turn on a civil court jury decision as to whether the general church abandoned or departed from the tenets of faith and practice it held at the time the local churches affiliated with it."[59] The theory was that Georgia law implied a trust on local church property in favor of the hierarchical church, conditioned upon adherence by that hierarchical body to the "tenets of faith and practice existing at the time

56 393 U.S. 440 (1969).

57 Footnote 1, 393 U.S. 440, 443 recites the specifics of the dispute:

"The opinion of the Supreme Court of Georgia summarizes the claimed violations and departures from petitioner's original tenets of faith and practice as including the following: 'ordaining of women as ministers and ruling elders, making pronouncements and recommendations concerning civil, economic, social and political matters, giving support to the removal of Bible reading and prayers by children in the public schools, adopting certain Sunday School literature and teaching neo-orthodoxy alien to the Confession of Faith and Catechisms, as originally adopted by the general church, and causing all members to remain in the National Council of Churches of Christ and willingly accepting its leadership which advocated named practices, such as the subverting of parental authority, civil disobedience and intermeddling in civil affairs'; also 'that the general church has * * * made pronouncements in matters involving international issues such as the Vietnam conflict and has disseminated publications denying the Holy Trinity and violating the moral and ethical standards of the faith.'" 224 Ga. 61, 62--63, 159 S.E.2d 690, 692 (1968).

58 393 U.S. 440, 443.

59 Id. at 441.

of affiliation by the local churches."[60]

The U.S. Supreme Court reversed the Georgia court's decision in favor of the local churches. In so doing, it held that this so-called departure-from-doctrine element of the Georgia implied trust theory was contrary to the First and Fourteenth Amendments in that "requires the civil court to determine matters at the very core of a religion – the interpretation of particular church doctrines and the importance of those doctrines to the religion. Plainly, the First Amendment forbids civil courts from playing such a role.[61]

However, it also commented:

"Civil courts do not inhibit free exercise of religion merely by opening their doors to disputes involving church property. And there are neutral principles of law, developed for use in all property disputes, which can be applied without 'establishing' churches to which property is awarded. But First Amendment values are plainly jeopardized when church property litigation is made to turn on the resolution by civil courts of controversies over religious doctrine and practice."[62]

Mr. Justice Harlan echoed this comment in his concurrence:

"I do not, however, read the Court's opinion to go further to hold that the Fourteenth Amendment forbids civilian courts from enforcing a deed or will which expressly and clearly lays down conditions limiting a religious organization's use of the property which is granted. If, for example, the donor expressly gives his church some money on the condition that the church never ordain a woman as a minister or elder (see ante, at 442, n. 1) or never amend certain specified articles of the Confession of Faith, he is entitled to his money back if the condition is not fulfilled. In such a case, the church should not be permitted to keep the property simply because church authorities have determined that the doctrinal innovation is justified by the faith's basic principles. Cf. *Watson v. Jones*, 13 Wall. 679, 722--724, (1872)."[63]

Thus, while neutral principles of law may be used by state courts to determine church property disputes, matters relating to the internal belief systems of any such hierarchical religion may not be adjudicated by the secular courts. However, express conditional language in a document of conveyance of property to a church may possibly be enforced by the secular courts.

60 Id. at 443. This implied trust theory was grounded in English law and rejected by *Watson v. Jones*. Id. footnote 2.

61 393 U.S. at 450.

62 Id. at 449.

63 Id. at 452.

4. Maryland and Virginia Eldership of the Churches of God v. Church of God at Sharpsburg

Maryland and Virginia Eldership of the Churches of God v. Church of God at Sharpsburg[64] involved an action by a regional church seeking to prevent local churches from withdrawing their property from the regional church. In a *per curiam* opinion, the U.S. Supreme Court agreed with the regional church that no constitutional question was presented, and ruled that "[s]ince, however, the Maryland court's resolution of the dispute involved no inquiry into religious doctrine, [the regional church's] motion to dismiss is granted, and the appeal is dismissed for want of a substantial federal question."[65]

Yet, the most notable aspect of this case is the concurring opinion by Justice Brennan, in which Justices Douglas and Marshall joined. In it, Justice Brennan proposes an analytical formula within which all church property disputes should reside. His formula consists of three steps, either one or more of which may be adopted by the states for the resolution of church property disputes:[66]

1. Watson v. Jones. States may follow this rule of deferring to, and enforcing the property decisions made by, either (a) a majority of the members of a congregational polity, or (b) the highest judicatory of a hierarchical religious body that has ruled on the dispute. The foregoing is limited by situations in which the express terms of documents of title establish contrary conditions, in which case the express terms control. However, the use of this approach is not appropriate where the resolution of doctrinal or religious policy issues is requisite to ascertaining the appropriate judicatory body.[67]
2. Neutral Principles of Law. The use of generally applicable neutral principles of state law may be used to resolve church property disputes. This "formal title" approach requires secular courts to ascertain ownership by reference to deeds, reverter clauses, general corporate law, and other general principles of state law. The use of

64 Id. at 368.

65 Id. at 368.

66 Id. Mr. Justice Brennan concurring opinion.

67 Id. at 368-370. Footnote 2 of the concurring opinion specifically disapproves that portion of *Watson v. Jones* that permits a court to inquire into doctrinal matters in order to give effect to the express terms of an instrument of title or device, such as a will, trust, or deed. That note suggests that any such express terms are simply unenforceable. Of course, this view is contrary to Justice Harlan's concurrence in *Presbyterian Church in the United States v. Mary Elizabeth Blue Hill Memorial Presbyterian Church*, supra.

this approach is inappropriate when it requires civil courts to resolve doctrinal issues.[68]

3. State Statutes. This third dispute-resolution framework envisions the enactment of special state statutes addressing church property disputes and establishing a resolution mechanism. However, any such mechanism must avoid interference with doctrinal matters or the ecclesiastical polity.[69]

While components of Justice Brennan's framework reside in several of the cases discussed in this article, it never has been accepted as such by a majority of the court.

5. Serbian Eastern Orthodox Diocese for the United States of America and Canada v. Milivojevich

This case, *Serbian Eastern Orthodox Diocese for the United States of America and Canada v. Milivojevich,*[70] presents a classic example of secular court involvement in internal church governance, which is prohibited by the First and Fourteenth Amendments. It also results in the elimination of a long-standing exception to the rule of deference to the decisions of church judicatories, and may have laid the foundation for the ultimate demise of the *Watson* rule.[71]

The controversy related to a reorganization of the North American component of the Serbian Orthodox Church, and the bishop of the North American churches who disagreed with that reorganization. From this humble controversy,[72] the trial, appellate and supreme courts of Illinois engaged in trials, appeals, remands, and the determination of a variety of procedural and substantive issues concerning Serbian Orthodox ecclesiastical and canon law over the course of several years. In essence, the Illinois courts reversed the defrocking of the bishop and reinstated him as diocesan bishop, and determined that the diocesan reorganization was invalid. These were due to arbitrariness and the lack of Serbian Orthodox Church authority as executed, respectively.[73]

With regard to the former, Mr. Justice Brennan, writing for a non-

68 Id. at 370.

69 Id.

70 426 U.S. 696 (1976).

71 Id. at 725 (REHNQUIST Dissent).

72 A detailed recitation of the factual predicate to the U.S. Supreme Court's opinion is set forth at 426 U.S. 698-708.

73 426 U.S. at 708.

unanimous U.S. Supreme Court,[74] identified the prime issue not as one of church property ownership but, rather, a controversy over who is the duly consecrated and acting bishop of the North American churches. As such:

"The fallacy fatal to the judgment of the Illinois Supreme Court is that it rests upon an impermissible rejection of the decisions of the highest ecclesiastical tribunals of this hierarchical church upon the issues in dispute, and impermissibly substitutes its own inquiry into church polity and resolutions based thereon of those disputes."[75]

The opinion went on to narrow the "fraud, collusion, or arbitrariness" exception to the *Watson* rule by eliminating arbitrariness as a basis for secular court review. In so doing, the court said:

"The conclusion of the Illinois Supreme Court that the decisions of the Mother Church were 'arbitrary' was grounded upon an inquiry that persuaded the Illinois Supreme Court that the Mother Church had not followed its own laws and procedures in arriving at those decisions. We have concluded that whether or not there is room for 'marginal civil court review' under the narrow rubrics of 'fraud' or 'collusion' when church tribunals act in bad faith for secular purposes, no 'arbitrariness' exception in the sense of an inquiry whether the decisions of the highest ecclesiastical tribunal of a hierarchical church complied with church laws and regulations is consistent with the constitutional mandate that civil courts are bound to accept the decisions of the highest judicatories of a religious organization of hierarchical polity on matters of discipline, faith, internal organization, or ecclesiastical rule, custom, or law. For civil courts to analyze whether the ecclesiastical actions of a church judicatory are in that sense 'arbitrary' must inherently entail inquiry into the procedures that canon or ecclesiastical law supposedly requires the church judicatory to follow, or else into the substantive criteria by which they are supposedly to decide the ecclesiastical question. But this is

74 Mr. Chief Justice Burger concurred in the judgment. Mr. Justice White filed a concurring opinion in which he assumed that whether the Serbian Orthodox Church is hierarchical, and whether the North American churches are part of that body, are matters within the independent determination of the Illinois courts. 426 U.S. at 725. Mr. Justice Rehnquist, joined by Mr. Justice Stevens, dissented. The dissent divided the line of cases discussed in this article into two branches: the common-law *Watson v. Jones* branch not applicable to the matter at issue, and the First and Fourteenth Amendments branch of *Kedroff v. St. Nicholas Cathedral.* This second branch, according to dissenting Justice Rehnquist, established the rule "that the government may not displace the free religious choices of its citizens by placing its weight behind a particular religious belief, tenet, or sect." [Id. at 733.] Thus, he concludes, the applicable constitutional rule is merely that state courts remain neutral in their analysis and application of internal ecclesiastical and canonical matters of religious bodies. [Id. at 734-735.]

75 426 U.S. at 708.

exactly the inquiry that the First Amendment prohibits; recognition of such an exception would undermine the general rule that religious controversies are not the proper subject of civil court inquiry, and that a civil court must accept the ecclesiastical decisions of church tribunals as it finds them. *Watson* itself requires our conclusion in its rejection of the analogous argument that ecclesiastical decisions of the highest church judicatories need only be accepted if the subject matter of the dispute is within their 'jurisdiction."[76]

Regarding the issue of diocesan structure and organization, the court commented on the lower court decision thusly:

"This conclusion was not, however, explicitly based on the 'fraud, collusion, or arbitrariness' exception. Rather, the Illinois Supreme Court relied on purported 'neutral principles' for resolving property disputes which would 'not in any way entangle this court in the determination of theological or doctrinal matters.' Nevertheless, the Supreme Court of Illinois substituted its interpretation of the Diocesan and Mother Church constitutions for that of the highest ecclesiastical tribunals in which church law vests authority to make that interpretation. This the First and Fourteenth Amendments forbid."[77]

The court concluded its opinion by summarizing the constitutionally permissible action of hierarchical religious bodies, and the concomitant limitations thereby imposed on secular courts.

In short, the First and Fourteenth Amendments permit hierarchical religious organizations to establish their own rules and regulations for internal discipline and government, and to create tribunals for adjudicating disputes over these matters. When this choice is exercised and ecclesiastical tribunals are created to decide disputes over the government and direction of subordinate bodies, the U.S. Constitution requires that civil courts accept their decisions as binding upon them.[78]

The *Watson* rule; i.e., secular court deference to the decisions of religious body judicatories, subject only to the now limited exceptions of fraud and collusion; and the ever-present neutral principles of state law's analytical option remain as constitutionally permissible devices for addressing church property disputes. Must one yield to another? That question is addressed in the next case considered.

76 Id. at 712-713.

77 Id. at 721.

78 Id. at 724-725.

6. Jones v. Wolf

In *Jones v. Wolf*,[79] the U.S. Supreme Court confronted the question of whether a state may forego the *Watson* rule in favor of the application of neutral principles of state law in church property disputes. Writing for a 5-4 majority, Mr. Justice Blackmun succinctly framed the issue:

"This case involves a dispute over the ownership of church property following a schism in a local church affiliated with a hierarchical church organization. The question for decision is whether civil courts, consistent with the First and Fourteenth Amendments to the Constitution, may resolve the dispute on the basis of 'neutral principles of law,' or whether they must defer to the resolution of an authoritative tribunal of the hierarchical church."[80]

In the instant case, the Georgia courts reviewed the deeds, which conveyed title to the local church, as well as the applicable state statutes, organizational charters and constitution of the general church – none of which created an express trust in favor of the general church. The court then ruled that legal title was with the local church and vested in the local congregation. Without further analysis, the Georgia court held that the local congregation was controlled by the majority faction of that local congregation.[81]

The question presented was which faction of the local church is entitled to the use and occupancy of the church property. The general church favored, and ultimately ruled internally, that the minority faction of the local church was entitled to the use and occupancy of the property. The majority of the congregation had split from the general church and asserted its right to the use and occupancy thereof. So, if the *Watson* rule had constitutional preference over the neutral principles of law rule, the Georgia courts would be required to defer to the general church and enforce its decision in favor of the minority faction. However, if either of the two rules were permitted by the U.S. Constitution, then Georgia's selection of the neutral principles of law approach over the *Watson* rule's deference to judicatories of hierarchical churches is permissible, and the majority faction prevails if such a "majority rules" doctrine is part of Georgia's body of neutral state law principles.

The majority opted for the later approach: "We cannot agree, however, that the First Amendment requires the States to adopt a rule of compulsory deference to religious authority in resolving church property disputes, even where no issue of doctrinal controversy is involved."[82]

79 443 U.S. 595 (1979).

80 Id. at 597.

81 Id. at 601.

82 Id. at 605.

In responding to the dissent, the court went on to say:

"This argument assumes that the neutral-principles method would somehow frustrate the free-exercise rights of the members of a religious association. Nothing could be further from the truth. The neutral-principles approach cannot be said to 'inhibit' the free exercise of religion, any more than do other neutral provisions of state law governing the manner in which churches own property, hire employees, or purchase goods. Under the neutral-principles approach, the outcome of a church property dispute is not foreordained. At any time before the dispute erupts, the parties can ensure, if they so desire, that the faction loyal to the hierarchical will retain the church property. They can modify the deeds or the corporate charter to include a right of reversion or trust in favor of the general church. Alternatively, the constitution of the general church can be made to recite an express trust in favor of the denominational church."[83]

The dissent[84] urged a rule of compulsory deference in matters involving schism within an hierarchical church, such that the decision of the judicatory of the religious body would establish which faction was rightfully in control of the local church structure; i.e., governing body. This approach, the dissent argued, is mandated by the First and Fourteenth Amendments to the extent that the application of neutral-principles of law is contrary to these constitutional requirements.[85]

However, as the law now exists, a state may adopt either the *Watson* rule, or the neutral-principles of law approach

7. Synanon Foundation, Inc. v. California

In *Synanon Foundation, Inc. v. California,*[86] Mr. Justice Rehnquist, as circuit justice, denied an application seeking to stay the order of the District Court denying applicants' request for a preliminary injunction to prohibit the attorney general of the state of California from commencing state court proceedings against the applicants.

In rejecting applicants' contention that, as a church, they were entitled to protections and treatment different from those afforded other charitable trusts, Mr. Justice Rehnquist underscored the vitality of *Jones v.* Wolf and stated: "...we held only last Term that state courts might resolve property disputes

83 Id. at 606.

84 Mr. Justice Powell, joined by Mr. Chief Justice Burger, Mr. Justice Stewart and Mr. Justice White.

85 443 U.S. at 610-621.

86 444 U.S. 1307 (1979).

in which hierarchical church organizations were involved in accordance with 'neutral principles' of state law."[87]

8. Little v. First Baptist Church, Crestwood

Little v. First Baptist Church, Crestwood[88] was the denial of a petition for a writ of certiorari from which Justices Marshall and Brennan dissented. At issue was a congregational church that allegedly had voted to terminate its pastor. Certain members of the congregation filed an action seeking to enjoin the former pastor from entering the church premises. The pastor contested the members' authority to speak on behalf of the congregation. The trial court, based solely on the pleadings, appointed a commissioner to hold an election of the congregation, which election confirmed that a majority of the membership had, in fact, voted to terminate the pastor. Justices Marshall and Brennan thought the matter should have been reviewed by the court because, as they read the record, the trial court "imposed its own view of proper procedures on the congregation's decision-making."[89]

Along the way, Mr. Justice Marshall succinctly summarized much of the current state of the law concerning church property disputes:

"Because religious organizations may own property and enter into contracts, it is inevitable that they will become involved in legal disputes. However, where the use of property or the terms of contracts necessitate reference to ecclesiastical principles or authority, courts must exercise extreme care to avoid taking sides on matters of religious belief. This Court set down the basic framework for such situations over 100 years ago, in *Watson*. Although it has undergone some refinements, see, e.g., Jones v. Wolf, 443 U.S. 595 (1979), the Watson approach is simple. A court may apply neutral principles of secular law to the dispute at hand. When that process requires a court to determine the validity of a church decision, the court ordinarily must discern from the relevant canonical law what body is authorized to make a particular decision within the church, and what decision that body has reached. Having done so, the court may not inquire whether the decision was made arbitrarily or whether it conflicts with the ecclesiastical precepts of the organization. *Serbian Eastern Orthodox Diocese v. Milivojevich*, 426 U.S. 696 (1976); *Maryland and Virginia Eldership v. Church of God at Sharpsburg, Inc.*, 396 U.S. 367, 368 (1970) (BRENNAN, J., concurring).[90]

---

87 Id. at 1308.

88 475 U.S. 1148 (1986).

89 Id. at 1148-1149.

90 Id.

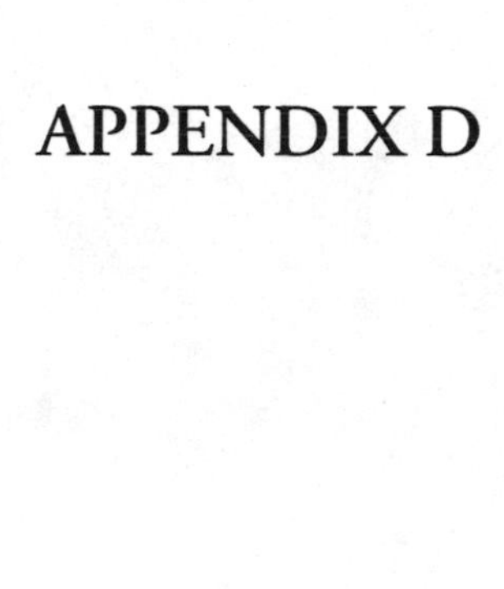

APPENDIX D

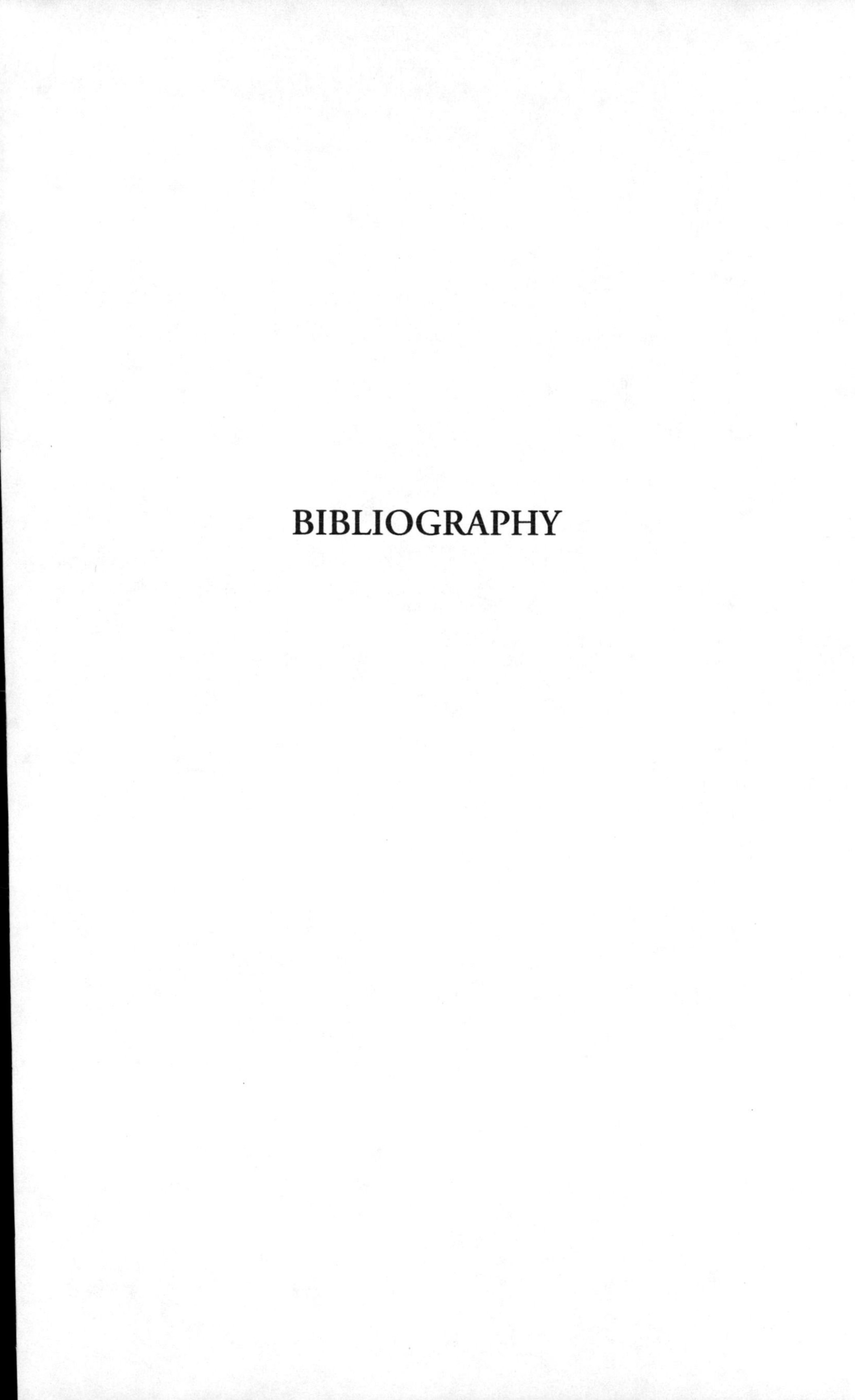

BIBLIOGRAPHY

BIBLIOGRAPHY

George Gleason Bogert et al., *Bogert's Trusts and Trustees* ch. 20, § 399 (Rev. 2d ed., West 2006).

77 C.J.S. *Religious Societies* § 111, Property and Funds; Control, Use, and Disposition; Division, Schism, and Secession (2006).

77 C.J.S. *Religious Societies* § 123, Religious Tribunals and Judicial or Legislative Supervision (2006).

77 C.J.S. *Religious Societies* § 124, Religious Tribunals and Judicial or Legislative Supervision (2006).

45 Fla. Jur. 2d *Religious Societies* § 7, In General (2006).

Ashley Alderman, *Where's The Wall?: Church Property Disputes Within The Civil Courts And The Need For Consistent Application Of The Law*, 39 Ga. L. Rev. 1027 (2005).

William W. Bassett, *Religious Organizations and the Law* vol. 19-2, § 7:32-35 (West 2005).

Christina M. Davitt, *Whose Steeple Is It? Defining The Limits Of The Debtor's Estate In The Religious Bankruptcy Context*, 29 Seton Hall Legis. J. 531 (2005).

Elizabeth Ehrlich, *Taking The Religion Out Of Religious Property Disputes*, 46 B.C. L. Rev. 1069 (2005).

Bruce A. Markell, Roundtable Discussion, *Religious Organizations Filing For Bankruptcy* (San Francisco, CA, Jan. 7, 2005), in 13 Am. Bankr. Inst. L. Rev. 25 (2005).

Marilyn E. Phelan, *Nonprofit Enterprises: Corps., Trusts, and Assoc.* vol. 2, § 16:04 (West 2005).

Catharine Pierce Wells, *Who Owns The Local Church? A Pressing Issue For Dioceses In Bankruptcy*, 29 Seton Hall Legis. J. 375 (2005).

66 Am. Jur. 2d *Religious Societies* § 45, Property and Funds; Judicial Determination and Protection of Property Rights (2005).

66 Am. Jur. 2d *Religious Societies* § 49, Property and Funds; Judicial Determination and Protection of Property Rights (2005).

5 Mich. Civ. Jur. *Constitutional Law* § 232, Personal Liberties; Freedom of Worship, Speech and Press; Religious Liberty (2005).

81 Ohio Jur. 3d *Religious Organizations* § 55, Property and Funds; Judicial Protection and Supervision (2005).

27 S.C. Jur. *Religious Societies* § 28, Property (2005).

19 S.C. Jur. *Constitutional Law* § 47, Freedom of Religion; Establishment Clause (2005).

John L. Soileau & G. Robert Arnold, *Florida Real Property Sales Transactions* ch. 6 (The Florida Bar 2004).

Kathryn Diack, Student Author, *Case Commentaries: Determinations Of A Church's Governmental Structure Will Determine Member's Ability To Settle Disputes With The Organization*, 4 Transactions: Tenn. J. Bus. L. 71 (2002).

Margaret A. Egan, *Annual Survey of Caselaw: Property Law*, 24 U. Ark. Little Rock L. Rev. 1071 (2002).

Frederick Mark Gedicks, *A Two-Track Theory Of The Establishment Clause*, 43 B.C. L. Rev. 1071 (2002).

Sarah M. Montgomery, *Drawing The Line: The Civil Courts' Resolution Of Church Property Disputes, The Established Church And All Saints' Episcopal Church, Waccamaw*, 54 S.C. L. Rev. 203 (2002).

Kenneth E. North, *Church Property Disputes: A Constitutional Perspective.* Originally presented at the Duquesne University School of Law Jubilee International and Ecumenical Canon Law Conference on February 4-5, 2000.

Nicholas P. Cafardi & Jordan Hite, *Rights And Responsibilities Between Dioceses And Religious Communities*, 40 Cath. Law. 59 (2000).

Frederick Mark Gedicks, *Towards A Defensible Free Exercise Doctrine*, 68 Geo. Wash. L. Rev. 925 (2000).

Kimberly Sayers-Fay, Student Author, *Conditional Federal Spending: A Back Door To Enhanced Free Exercise Protection*, 88 Cal. L. Rev. 1281 (2000).

Thomas B. Merritt, *Church Autonomy In The Massachusetts Courts: Parish Of The Advent v. Protestant Episcopal Diocese*, 84 Mass. L. Rev. 23 (1999).

Nathan Clay Belzer, *Deference In The Judicial Resolution Of Intrachurch Disputes: The Lesser Of Two Constitutional Evils*, 11 St. Thomas L. Rev. 109 (1998).

Kent Greenawalt, *Hands Off! Civil Court Involvement in Conflicts Over Religious Property*, 98 Colum. L. Rev. 1843 (1998).

New York State Constitutional Decisions: 1997 Compilation: Establishment Of Religion, 14 Touro L. Rev. 1009 (1998).

John E. Fennelly, *Property Disputes And Religious Schisms: Who Is The Church?*, 9 St. Thomas L. Rev. 319 (1997).

Matthew S. Steffey, *The Establishment Clause And The Lessons Of Context*, 26 Rutgers L.J. 775 (1995).

Michael William Galligan, *Judicial Resolution of Intrachurch Disputes*, 83 Colum. L. Rev. 2007 (1983).

Roger Wm. Bennett, *Church Property Disputes in the Age of "Common-Core Protestantism": a Legislative Facts Rationale for Neutral Principles of Law*, 57 Ind. L.J. 163 (1982).

Roland F. Chase, *Determination Of Property Rights Between Local Church And Parent Church Body: Modern View*, 52 A.L.R.3d 324 (1973).

LIST OF CONTRIBUTORS

RAYMOND J. DAGUE is a New York attorney in a general practice in the firm of Raymond J. Dague, PLLC (www.DagueLaw.com), and has practiced law since 1979. He has been a member for 30 years of St. Andrews in the Valley in Syracuse, N.Y., where he is a lay reader, has served on the vestry, and is currently the parish chancellor. He also is assistant chancellor to the Episcopal Bishop for the Diocese of Albany. His law practice includes representation of numerous churches, both Episcopal and others. He received a B.A. with distinction in political science from the University of Wisconsin-Madison, and a Juris Doctor *cum laude* from the Syracuse University College of Law. He serves on the board of directors of the Christian Legal Society. He and his wife, Pat, reside in Syracuse, N.Y.

PEGGY M. HEDDEN has been an active elder in the Presbyterian Church (USA) for more than 25 years. Born and raised in Natrona Heights, Penn., she received a B.A. in political science from Allegheny College, *magna cum laude*, Phi Beta Kappa, in 1967, and her law degree from the University of Chicago in 1970. Admitted to the Ohio Bar in 1970, she served the Ohio General Assembly as a research attorney for the Ohio Legislative Service Commission for the next six years. From 1976 to the present, she has focused her energies on raising a family and serving Christ in her local congregation, presbytery and denomination. She has served on the board of directors of the Presbyterian Lay Committee since 1995, on the board of the Presbyterian Coalition from 2000-2005, and on the board of the New Wineskins Initiative since January 2005. She and her husband, James Hedden, live in Columbus, Ohio.

ROBERT L. HOWARD received his undergraduate education from Emporia State University and an L.L.B. with "Distinction" from the University of Kansas Law School, where he was a member of the Order of the Coif and an associate editor of *The Law Review.* He was admitted to the Kansas Bar in 1959 and is a member of the Federal Circuit Bar Association, the Bar of the United States Supreme Court, the American Academy of Appellate Lawyers, and is a Fellow in the American College of Trial Lawyers. During more than

40 years of continuous practice in Wichita, Kansas, he specialized in trials and appeals in complex and multi-district litigation with the firm of Foulston & Siefkin LLP, from which he retired as chairman. Howard is a member of the board of directors of the Presbyterian Coalition and the board of directors of the Presbyterian Lay Committee, where he formerly served as chairman. A longtime elder at Eastminster Presbyterian Church in Wichita, he and his wife, Joanne, now reside in Colorado and Florida.

LLOYD J. LUNCEFORD graduated from the University of Toledo *cum laude* and received his Juris Doctorate from the Louisiana State University Law Center. He is a partner in the Baton Rouge firm of Taylor, Porter, Brooks & Phillips, LLP, (www.taylorporter.org) where he has practiced law since 1984. He is a member of the Louisiana State Bar Association, the American Bar Association, the Bar of the United States Supreme Court, the American Inns of Court, and the Christian Legal Society. He is the co-author of *Libel and Privacy Law and Practice in Louisiana,* and has written several articles on topics ranging from professional ethics to church/state relations to document confidentiality. He has served as a guest lecturer at the Louisiana State University Manship School of Journalism and is a frequent speaker in continuing legal education seminars. His practice includes representation of several churches. Formerly a staff member of Campus Crusade for Christ, he has been an active Presbyterian elder for more than 20 years. He is a former director of the Presbyterian Lay Committee and has served as a Presbyterian Coalition task force member. He and his wife, Cynthia, live in Baton Rouge, La.

THOMAS C. ODEN is a Methodist minister, theologian and professor emeritus at Drew University. He received a B. Litt. from the University of Oklahoma, a B.D. from the Perkins School of Theology (Southern Methodist University), and an M.A. and Ph.D. from Yale University. In 1971, he became the Henry Anson Buttz professor of Theology and Ethics at Drew University, where he taught until his retirement. He has been a guest lecturer or visiting professor at Moscow State University, Oxford University, the University of Edinburgh, Duke University, Emory University, Princeton University, and Claremont University. Self-described as an "orthodox, ecumenical evangelical," where orthodoxy "is nothing more or less than the ancient consensual tradition of exegesis," his writings focus on the faith of the universal church, with emphasis on the great Patristic thinkers of the early church. A prolific author, he has published more than 40 books and 80 articles. He serves as general editor of the *Ancient Christian Commentary on Scripture* project, and as a contributing editor to *Christianity Today*.

R. WICKS STEPHENS II has more than 35 years of experience in private practice as a corporate litigator in Los Angeles and is a leading expert in church law. He is the secretary and treasurer for the American Anglican Council, as well as the chancellor and director of development for the Anglican Communion Network in Pittsburgh, Pa. He is a member of the board of trustees for the Trinity Episcopal School for Ministry, is active in the governance of his parish and the Episcopal Diocese of Pittsburgh, and has served on and acted as legal advisor to numerous Christian mission organization boards. He holds degrees from the University of California at Los Angeles (B.S.), Stanford University (LLB), and Fuller Theological Seminary (M.A.).

PARKER T. WILLIAMSON, a longtime leader of the renewal movement within the Presbyterian Church (USA), is editor emeritus and senior correspondent of the Presbyterian Lay Committee. Prior to his present duties, he served for 30 years as an ordained minister in the Presbyterian Church (USA). A graduate of Rhodes College, Union Theological Seminary (Va.) and Yale Divinity School, his books include *Standing Firm: Reclaiming Christian Faith in Times of Controversy; Vanishing Point: Is This The End Of The Line For The World Council Of Churches?* and *Essays from Zimbabwe.*

Printed in the United States
53952LVS00003B/79-96

9 780971 191969